The publisher and the University of California Press Foundation gratefully acknowledge the generous support of the Joan Palevsky Endowment Fund in Literature in Translation.

Greek Poems to the Gods

Greek Poems to the Gods

Hymns from Homer to Proclus

———

Translated by Barry B. Powell

UNIVERSITY OF CALIFORNIA PRESS

University of California Press
Oakland, California

Library of Congress Cataloging-in-Publication Data

Powell, Barry B., translator. | Callimachus. Hymns. English. | Proclus,
   approximately 410–485. Hymns. English.
Title: Greek poems to the gods : hymns from Homer to Proclus / translated
   by Barry B. Powell.
Other titles: Homeric hymns. Selections. English.
Description: Oakland, California : University of California Press, [2020].
Identifiers: LCCN 2020029298 (print) | LCCN 2020029299 (ebook) |
   ISBN 9780520302877 (hardback) | ISBN 9780520972605 (ebook)
Subjects: LCSH: Hymns, Greek (Classical)—Translations into English. |
   Gods, Greek—Poetry—Translations into English. | Epic poetry,
   Greek—History and criticism.
Classification: LCC PA4025.H8 P69 2020 (print) | LCC PA4025.H8 (ebook) |
   DDC 881/.0109382—dc23
LC record available at https://lccn.loc.gov/2020029298
LC ebook record available at https://lccn.loc.gov/2020029299

Manufactured in Malaysia

27   26   25   24   23   22   21
10   9   8   7   6   5   4   3   2   1

CONTENTS

List of Illustrations   *ix*

List of Maps   *xi*

Introduction   *1*

Meter and Performance   *2*

Annotation; the Spelling of Ancient Names and Places; Greek Texts   *4*

The Homeric Hymns   *5*

The Hymns of Callimachus   *8*

The Orphic Hymns   *9*

The Hymns of Proclus   *15*

1. Zeus   *17*

Homeric Hymn 23: To Zeus   *20*

Callimachus Hymn 1: To Zeus   *20*

Orphic Hymn 15: To Zeus   *25*

Orphic Hymn 19: To Zeus the Thunderbolt   *25*

Orphic Hymn 20: To Astrapaios Zeus   *26*

2. Hera   *27*

Homeric Hymn 12: To Hera   *31*

Orphic Hymn 16: To Hera   *31*

3. Poseidon   3?

   Homeric Hymn 22: To Poseidon   32

   Orphic Hymn 17: To Poseidon   33

4. Athena   35

   Homeric Hymn 11: To Athena   36

   Homeric Hymn 28: To Athena   36

   Callimachus Hymn 5: To Athena; On the Baths of Pallas   38

   Orphic Hymn 32: To Athena   45

   Proclus Hymn 7: To Wise Athena   47

5. Demeter, Persephone, and Hades   52

   Homeric Hymn 2: To Demeter   52

   Homeric Hymn 13: To Demeter   75

   Callimachus Hymn 6: To Demeter   75

   Orphic Hymn 40: To Eleusinian Demeter   84

   Orphic Hymn 41: To Mother Antaia   85

   Orphic Hymn 29: To Persephone   86

   Orphic Hymn 18: To Plouton   87

6. Aphrodite   89

   Homeric Hymn 5: To Aphrodite   95

   Homeric Hymn 6: To Aphrodite   107

   Homeric Hymn 10: To Aphrodite   108

   Orphic Hymn 55: To Aphrodite   109

   Proclus Hymn 2: To Aphrodite   111

   Proclus Hymn 5: To the Lycian Aphrodite   112

7. Hephaistos   115

   Homeric Hymn 20: To Hephaistos   115

   Orphic Hymn 66: To Hephaistos   116

8. Apollo and the Muses   117

   Homeric Hymn 3: To Apollo   118

   Homeric Hymn 21: To Apollo   139

   Homeric Hymn 25: To The Muses and Apollo   139

   Callimachus Hymn 2: To Apollo   139

	Callimachus Hymn 4: To Delos	*146*
	Orphic Hymn 34: To Apollo	*165*
	Orphic Hymn 35: To Leto	*166*
	Orphic Hymn 76: To the Muses	*167*
	Proclus Hymn 3: To the Muses	*168*
9.	Artemis	*170*
	Homeric Hymn 9: To Artemis	*171*
	Homeric Hymn 27: To Artemis	*171*
	Callimachus Hymn 3: To Artemis	*173*
	Orphic Hymn 36: To Artemis	*187*
10.	Hermes and Pan	*189*
	Homeric Hymn 4: To Hermes	*191*
	Homeric Hymn 18: To Hermes	*214*
	Orphic Hymn 28: To Hermes	*214*
	Orphic Hymn 57: To Chthonic Hermes	*216*
	Homeric Hymn 19: To Pan	*217*
	Orphic Hymn 11: To Pan	*220*
11.	Dionysos	*222*
	Homeric Hymn 1: To Dionysos	*223*
	Homeric Hymn 7: To Dionysos	*225*
	Homeric Hymn 26: To Dionysos	*228*
	Orphic Hymn 30: To Dionysos	*229*
	Orphic Hymn 45: To Dionysos Bassareus and Triennial	*230*
	Orphic Hymn 46: To Dionysos Liknites	*230*
	Orphic Hymn 47: To Dionysos Perikonios	*231*
	Orphic Hymn 50: To Dionysos Lysios Lenaios	*232*
	Orphic Hymn 52: To Dionysos, God of the Triennial Feasts	*232*
	Orphic Hymn 53: To Dionysos, God of Annual Feasts	*233*
	Orphic Hymn 44: To Semelê	*234*
12.	Ares	*235*
	Homeric Hymn 8: To Ares	*235*
	Orphic Hymn 65: To Ares	*237*

13. Hestia 238

    Homeric Hymn 24: To Hestia 238

    Homeric Hymn 29: To Hestia 239

    Orphic Hymn 84: To Hestia 239

14. Sun, Moon, Earth, Hekatê, and All the Gods 240

    Homeric Hymns 31 and 32: To the Sun and the Moon 241

    Orphic Hymn 8: To the Sun 243

    Orphic Hymn 9: To the Moon 244

    Proclus Hymn 1: To Helios 245

    Homeric Hymn 30: To Earth Mother of All 248

    Orphic Hymn 26: To Earth 248

    Orphic Hymn 1: To Hekatê 249

    *Proclus Hymn 6: To the Mother of the Gods, Hekatê, and
    Janus/Zeus* 249

    Proclus Hymn 4: To All the Gods 250

Bibliography 253

Glossary/Index 257

ILLUSTRATIONS

1. Death of Orpheus *11*
2. "Orphic" gold-leaf tablet *13*
3. Zeus with thunderbolt *18*
4. The wedding of Zeus and Hera *28*
5. Poseidon *33*
6. The birth of Athena *37*
7. Athena *46*
8. The Erechtheion *50*
9. Eleusinian plaque *54*
10. Hades abducting Persephone *56*
11. The ruins of the Telesterion *59*
12. The return of Persephone *73*
13. Woman with *kalathos* *77*
14. Persephone sending forth Triptolemos *79*
15. Ares and Aphrodite *91*
16. Zeus and Aphrodite *98*
17. The Mistress of the Animals *100*
18. Ganymede *105*
19. The birth of Aphrodite *109*
20. Aphrodite on a swan *111*
21. The Roman theatre and monumental Lycian tombs, Xanthos *113*
22. Apollo and Artemis on Delos *123*
23. Temple of Apollo at Delphi *131*
24. The Apollo Belvedere *143*

25. Terrace of the Lions, Delos   *162*
26. Apollo and Artemis   *172*
27. Artemis of Ephesos   *179*
28. A herm from Arcadia   *190*
29. Lyre player   *194*
30. Apollo with lyre   *210*
31. Hermes   *215*
32. Pan   *219*
33. The return of Hephaistos   *225*
34. Dionysos and the pirates   *227*
35. Ares battles Athena   *236*

MAPS

1. The Mediterranean   *xii*
2. The Aegean   *xii*
3. The Peloponnesos   *xiii*

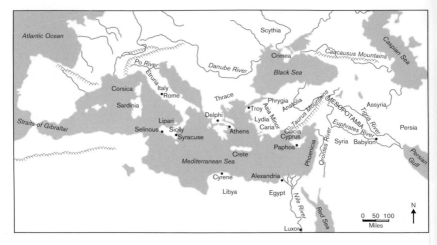

MAP 1. The Mediterranean.

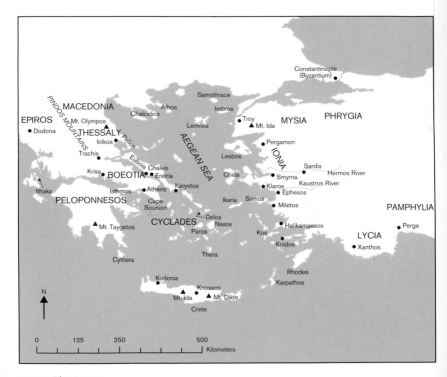

MAP 2. The Aegean.

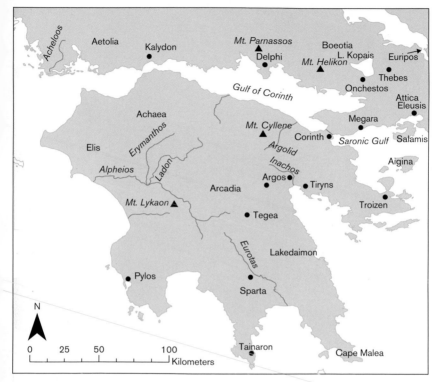

MAP 3. The Peloponnesos.

Introduction

A hymn is a song to a god, originally sung, usually to a lyre. The meaning of *hymn* is unclear and it may have a foreign origin. The word occurs only once in Homer (*Odyssey* 8.429), and Hesiod speaks of winning a prize for a *hymnos* (*Works and Days* 651), but it is unclear what he meant by *hymnos*. Early hymns seem to have been composed in hexameters (see below), but later poems appear in other meters. The standard form was to list the god's names, thus invoking his or her presence, then to continue with some event from the god's career, often the god's birth, and to conclude with a prayer, a reference to the god, or a declaration that the hymnist would now proceed to another song. Hymns to the gods must have been widely circulated in antiquity but, puzzlingly, they are not often referred to by other ancient writers.

A remarkable collection of Greek hymns, by a range of authors, survives in twenty-nine manuscripts, none older than the fifteenth century AD. They are among our most important sources for our knowledge of Greek myth. The collection was evidently made in the early Middle Ages and included, in this order: the anonymous *Orphic Hymns* (c. AD second/third century?); the *Hymns of Proclus,* an important Neoplatonist philosopher of late antiquity (AD 412–485); the anonymous *Homeric Hymns* (eighth/seventh centuries BC–fifth century BC, with one exception), our earliest surviving hymns; and the *Hymns of Callimachus* (c. 310—c. 240 BC), from the Hellenistic Age (323-c. 30 BC); Callimachus was a poet, critic, and scholar at the

Library of ALEXANDRIA (see map 1; place-names that appear in the maps are in small caps), one of the most influential intellectuals of his day. The collection also includes an anonymous *Orphic Argonautica* from the fifth or sixth centuries AD that tells the story of Jason with an emphasis on the role of Orpheus, but it is not a hymn and is not translated here.

One of these manuscripts, discovered in Moscow in 1777 and now in Leiden, is unique in containing a portion of a "Homeric Hymn to Dionysos" and the long "Homeric Hymn to Demeter," poems not included in other versions of the collection. Several papyrus fragments also preserve portions of the *Homeric Hymns.* The manuscripts of the collection are not nearly so well preserved as texts of the *Iliad* and the *Odyssey* and there are many corruptions, some incurable, and occasionally misplaced lines. The collection (missing only the hymns to Dionysos and Demeter) was printed in the *editio princeps* of Homer's *Iliad* and *Odyssey,* published in Florence in 1488 by Demetrios Chalkokondyles, one of the most eminent Greek scholars working in the West, tutor to the sons of Lorenzo de Medici.

This book will contain translations of most of these hymns, arranged not as they are in the collection, but according to each individual deity. In this way the reader can see how Greek poets, during a period of over one thousand years, conceived and celebrated their gods, allowing the reader to form an impression of how notions of each god evolved over nearly a millennium. All the hymns of Callimachus and Proclus are included, together with twenty-eight of the thirty-four *Homeric Hymns,* and thirty-two of the seventy-eight *Orphic Hymns;* hymns to minor gods, such as the *Orphic Hymns* to Justice, Misê, the Seasons, Leukothea, and the like, are omitted. The hymns will be cited in rough chronological order: first the *Homeric Hymns;* then the *Hymns of Callimachus;* then the *Orphic Hymns;* then the *Hymns of Proclus.*

METER AND PERFORMANCE

The hymns are mostly composed in a Greek meter that modern scholars call dactylic hexameter, the same meter used in the *Iliad* and the *Odyssey.* Each line consists of six feet, each of which may be a dactyl (a long and two shorts, ‾◡◡, like the knuckles on a finger, hence the name, which means "finger"), or a spondee (two longs, ——; the name means "libation," being characteristic of poetry that accompanied libations). The last foot is always a spondee. Vergil (70–19 BC) imitates this meter in his Latin *Aeneid:*

> — ∪ ∪/— ∪ ∪/— — /— —/— ∪ ∪/— —
> Arma virumque cano, Troiae qui primus ab oris . . .
> I sing of arms and the man who first from the shores of Troy . . .

as does, in English, Longfellow in his *Evangeline* (1847):

> — ∪ ∪/— ∪ ∪/—∪ ∪/— ∪ ∪/— ∪ ∪ /— —
> This is the forest primeval, the murmuring pines and the hemlocks . . .

This was the meter of Greek oral poets, really an unconscious rhythm. Rhyme is avoided. The oral poet was not conscious of any division of the line into its constituent feet, as indicated above. Such schematization is a result of modern analysis of written texts. Probably, however, the poet "felt" the line as a whole, as a unit. Early inscriptions, based on oral delivery, though very short, seem to divide the text into lines, though the words are run together.

The origin of this complex meter has been the subject of intense speculation because the natural rhythm of spoken Greek is iambic (∪—). Some scholars have thought that dactylic hexameter was adopted from a foreign language; others describe it as a native formation. In fact its origin is not known, but it was already old in antiquity and the oral poet learned it by apprenticeship to a master of the tradition. Dactylic hexameter does not work well in English, and I abandon it entirely in this translation, preferring a rough five-beat iambic line that accurately preserves the meaning of the Greek.

Because the oral poet, always a male entertainer as far as we know, composed in this meter "on the fly" and at a rapid pace he made use of such formulas as "flashing-eyed Athena" or "Artemis of the golden shafts" or "the wine-dark sea." Such preset phrases filled out his line so that he did not have to recreate appropriate metrical locutions every time from scratch. They also provide, in the case of epithets attached to names, a capsule summary of the qualities of the god, person, or thing. We might think of this oral poetry as composed in a special language in which, to a remarkable extent, phrases, rather than words, were the units of expression. Such was the nature of dactylic hexameter in the *Iliad,* the *Odyssey,* and the *Homeric Hymns.* The later, *written* poetry of Callimachus, the *Orphic Hymns,* and Proclus imitated this rhythm, although it had lost its function as an aid to oral performance. So great was the prestige of the Homeric poems.

From the very earliest times the Greek alphabet was used to take down performances of oral poetry, and there is reason to think that this unique technology, alphabetic writing, was invented for the express purpose of recording oral poetry. Once alphabetic written texts came into being, they were memorized by literate aristocrats and reperformed in the symposia ("drinking parties") and perhaps in more public contexts, such as festivals. The *Homeric Hymns* are examples of such compositions. We cannot be sure of when or where they were performed, but we do know that the qualities of this or that god or goddess were celebrated each time. Presumably later hymns composed in writing were also committed to memory and performed at appropriate occasions, but evidence for the circumstances of their performance is entirely lacking.

The great value of these poems is that they give us a profound look into ancient Greek religion and culture, including aspects that may seem alien or troublesome to us. Perhaps the most palpable example of this is the hymns' permissive attitude toward sexual violence. By today's standards, the actions of many gods are violent and reprehensible. The hymns treat as a matter of course the fact that Zeus impregnates his daughter Persephone or has sexual relations with the boy Ganymede. While the hymns themselves do not register these events as coercive, they may look so to modern readers.

ANNOTATION; THE SPELLING OF ANCIENT NAMES AND PLACES; GREEK TEXTS

In the annotation to these translations, I have taken the hymns to each god as a whole so that, for example, when there is a reference to Nysa in the hymns to Dionysos, I explain the first occurrence of Nysa, but not subsequent occurrences.

The spelling of ancient names is always a problem in translations. Dictionaries prefer the Latin forms, for example, Hephaestus or Cronus, but modern taste prefers a direct transliteration, Hephaistos or Kronos. I have chosen a middle way, using the Latin forms if they are familiar—Cyprus not Kupros, Oedipus not Oidipous—but I use the Greek forms otherwise. I do not, however, pretend to consistency, which is in any event impossible. Mostly I render the Greek *upsilon* as *u,* but sometime stick to the more familiar *y,* for example Nysa, but Tituos. The Greek *kappa* is usually rendered *k,* but is sometimes *c.* The Greek *chi* (x) is always *ch.* Pronunciation is according to the Latin convention: if the next-to-last syllable is long, it is accented; if it is short, then the third syllable from the end is stressed. Because it is sometimes hard to know whether the next-to-last syllable is long or short, the Glossary shows the accented syllable in bold with a long mark over the vowel: "Demeter (de-**mē**-ter)." The Glossary includes all important names, but I omit obscure names that appear only once; these are explained in the notes. An ellipsis [. . .] in the text indicates that words are missing; brackets (< >) indicate conjectures. I place a circumflex over final vowels where they should be pronounced, hence Hekatê, except in such common names as Aphrodite. I place a dieresis over a vowel in a vowel cluster, where the vowels are to be pronounced separately: Demophoön. When a place-name first appears in a poem or in the commentary or introduction to it, it is in SMALL CAPS to indicate that the place can be found in one of the maps at the beginning of the text.

For the Greek text, I have used, for the *Homeric Hymns,* M. L. West's *Homeric Hymns, Homeric Apocrypha, Lives of Homer* (Cambridge, MA: Loeb Classical Library, 2003); for Callimachus, I use R. Pfeiffer's *Callimachus,* vol. 2, *Hymni et epigrammata* (Oxford: Oxford University Press, 1953); for the *Orphic Hymns,* I have used A. Bernabé's *Orphicorum et Orphicis similium testimonia et fragmenta,* vol. 2 of *Poetae epici graeci, testimonia et fragmenta* (Munich: De Gruyter, 2004–7); and for the *Hymns of Proclus,* R. M. van Den Berg's *Proclus' Hymns: Essays, Translations, Commentary* (Leiden: Brill, 2001).

THE HOMERIC HYMNS

Evidently it was the custom in early times for *aoidoi,* "oral singers," to preface long poems with an address to a god. We call such long poems "epic," of which the *Iliad* and *Odyssey* are examples, but the Greek word for such a poem was *oimê,* meaning "way, path," a technical term for "the theme of epic song." The address to the god was called a *prooimion,* that is, a "song before the *oimê.*"[1] So in the *Odyssey* (8.499) the oral poet Demodokos begins his song about the Trojan Horse "starting out from the god." Hesiod's *Theogony* begins with a hymn to the Muses and his *Works and Days* with a hymn to Zeus. And Pindar in the opening to a poem (*Nemean* 2.1–6) says:

> Just as the sons of Homer,
> the singers of stitched words,
> often begin with a *prooimion* to Zeus,
> so this man is given a first beginning
> of victory in the sacred games
> in the much-hymned grove of Nemean Zeus.

Pindar means that the athlete's victory in the Nemean games is the predictor of future victory in other games, even as a *prooimion*—a poem in Homeric meter—precedes a longer song.

The *Homeric Hymns* are a collection of thirty-three such *prooimia,* probably put together before the first century BC by some Alexandrian scholar whose identity remains unknown. One hymn, "Hymn 8: To Ares," is of late composition, probably by the Neoplatonist philosopher Proclus (AD 412–85), whose other hymns I here translate also. Ancient authors rarely referred to the *Homeric Hymns,* for some reason. Thucydides (c. 460–c. 400 BC) is the earliest writer to refer to one, the "Hymn 3: To Apollo," calling it a *prooimion* (3.104.4). He quotes eighteen lines from the poem. A third-century BC scholar, Antigonos of Karystos (on Euboia), quotes one line from "Hymn 4: To Hermes." The Epicurean philosopher and poet Philodemus (c. 110–c. 35 BC) refers to a single word in "Hymn 2: To Demeter," and the Greek historian Diodorus of Sicily (first-century BC), quotes lines 1–9 of "Hymn 1: To Dionysos." Diodorus refers to the *Homeric Hymns* three times, calling them the "Hymns of Homer," evidently referring to the very collection that has come down to us.

Later references are equally scarce. In the second century AD the travel-writer and geographer Pausanias (c. 100–c. 180) refers twice to "Hymn 2: To Demeter" and once to "Hymn 3: To Apollo." The late second-century AD grammarian and rhetorician Athenaeus quotes

---

1 The word *prooimion* first appears in Pindar *Nemean* 2.3; *oimê* appears in the *Odyssey* three times: 8.47, 8.481, and 22.347.

from "Hymn 3: To Apollo"; he is the first to call into question Homer's authorship. His contemporary, the famous orator Aelius Aristides (c. 117–c. 180 AD)—over fifty of his orations survive—also quotes from "Hymn 3: To Apollo." Otherwise these poems are ignored, although recent scholarship on the Latin poets suggests that the *Homeric Hymns* were studied and imitated in ROME, but not named. Thucydides attributes "Hymn 3: To Apollo" to Homer, but the Alexandrian scholars seem to have decided that Homer did not write any of them, which may explain the general silence about these poems.

Modern scholars agree with the Alexandrians that the poet of the *Iliad* and the *Odyssey* did not compose the *Homeric Hymns*. Their attribution to Homer derives from a pious attachment to a tradition of poetic composition of which Homer was the most prominent exemplar. The *Homeric Hymns* are anonymous compositions from widely various dates, from the eighth or seventh century BC to the fifth century BC and possibly later. "Hymn 31" and "Hymn 32," to the Sun and the Moon respectively, are probably Alexandrian (from the third to first centuries BC) and the anomalous "Hymn 8: To Ares" (perhaps by Proclus) seems to be from the fifth century AD. These anonymous poets lived in various parts of Greece, to judge by geographical references in the poems, which sometimes allow us to speculate about the occasions on which they were performed. For example, "Hymn 2: To Demeter" may have been performed at a festival in ELEUSIS, where the goddess of the fertility of grain reigned. "Hymn 3: To Apollo" contains a description of a festival on DELOS, where it must have been performed.

The original purpose of the *Homeric Hymns* as prefaces to longer poems can be confirmed by internal evidence. Thirty-one of the thirty-three *Homeric Hymns* mention a god in the first line, indicating their function as invocations of the god's power. Places where the god is powerful are often mentioned as part of the god's attributes. Most end with an invocation to a god, some ask for a benediction, then state that the singer will proceed to another topic: "I will remember you and another song."

There is an enormous difference in the length of the *Homeric Hymns*. Four are long, running to hundreds of lines: the hymns to Aphrodite, Apollo, Demeter, and Hermes. Two (to Dionysus and Pan) are of intermediate length, but the rest are short, not more than twenty-two lines. The long hymns, which come first in the collection, celebrate the god's birth or other notable exploit, whereas the short hymns focus on the god's sphere of influence and activity. Many consider Hesiod's *Theogony* as a kind of "Hymn to Zeus," similar to the long hymns that narrate the birth and exploits of a god, in this case expanded to Zeus's family history and to cosmogony. Probably the long hymns, like Hesiod's *Theogony*, were never intended as preludes, although they include the common formulas, but always existed as independent compositions. This would make sense, but we have no real information about the performance of any of these poems.

THE HYMNS OF CALLIMACHUS

Callimachus (c. 310–c. 240 BC) was born in CYRENÊ, the Greek colony in Libya, five hundred miles west of ALEXANDRIA, founded from the island of THERA, north of CRETE, around 630 BC. He was productive and famous as a poet, literary critic, and scholar in the Museion ("temple of the Muses") at Alexandria during the third century BC, when Egypt was ruled by the Macedonian pharaohs Ptolemy II Philadelphus ("brother-loving," 283–46 BC) and Ptolemy III Euergetes ("benefactor," 246–22 BC). Callimachus was of the highest birth, claiming to be descended from the colony's founder, Battos of Thera, who died c. 600 BC. He seems to have been educated in ATHENS, then moved to Alexandria to work in the Ptolemy's newly founded Museion.

Callimachus was famous for his remark that "a big book is a big evil" *(mega biblion, mega kakon)*, which scholars have taken to mean that he opposed long poems like Homer's (or he may have been referring to the size of the papyrus roll!). He had no way of knowing that Homer's poems—and the *Homeric Hymns*—were composed orally and taken down by dictation, quite unlike his own learned verse, which was composed in writing. In any event, a feud was rumored between Callimachus and Apollonius of RHODES, author of the long *Argonautica,* an epic poem about Jason that in form and length imitates Homer.

Callimachus made a bibliographic survey of the enormous contents of the Alexandrian Library, by far the largest in the world, in an exhaustive and original prose work that occupied 120 papyrus rolls, called the *Pinakes,* "Lists," the first known catalog of a library's holdings. He organized titles by genre, including biographies of each author, and cited their works by first lines. In all, Callimachus was said to have been the author of eight hundred "books," that is, rolls of papyrus, on all kinds of topics.

Callimachus wrote in a learned and obscure style. There are eighty-six neologisms, words of his own creation, found only in his hymns, and another ninety-six words that are used later but first appear in Callimachus, evidently influenced by his usage. Though most of his works have been lost, he was the most productive of all the Greek Hellenistic poets. He had a profound influence on the Roman poets Catullus, Ovid, and Propertius, who studied him closely and whose works do survive. Only Homer is quoted more than Callimachus in later writers. Six of his hymns (translated here) and sixty-four "epigrams" (brief poems on various topics) survive complete. From commentators and fragments we know that, in addition, he wrote iambic poems (especially the "Ibis," a mocking poem imitated by Ovid); a thousand-line poem on Theseus' meeting with the Bull of Marathon (called "Hekalê," after an old woman who helped Theseus); poems praising the Ptolemies; and victory odes. His most famous work was the *Aitia,* "Causes," a six-thousand-line composition in four books that survives only in fragments. The *Aitia* was a collection of poems that celebrated the foundation of cities, little-known cults and religious practices, and odd local customs. In it the poet imagines that he was carried in a dream from LIBYA to MOUNT HELIKON in BOEOTIA, where he converses with the Muses. The poems of the *Aitia* are formulaic, first asking a question such as "Why on the island of PAROS, do worshippers of the Graces use neither flutes nor crowns?"

Callimachus certainly knew the *Homeric Hymns,* although not necessarily in the collection that has come down to us, and he sometimes quotes them. Yet his poems are unlikely to have been performed as memorized texts in public, as no doubt were the *Homeric Hymns*, but were probably read aloud to small groups of highly educated intellectuals and possessors of political power, who could understand and delight in his refined and learned references.

THE ORPHIC HYMNS

There is no reference to the *Orphic Hymns* in antiquity. They are first mentioned in a commentary to Hesiod's *Theogony* in a manuscript dated to the twelfth century AD, but there is no information about where or when they were composed. They are, however, included in the fifteenth-century collection of hymns referred to above. They created a stir among Italian intellectuals when published because they were thought to be genuine poems by the famous Orpheus, founder of the mysterious religion called Orphism, on which Plato was supposed to have based much of his philosophy. However, modern scholars do not think there ever was a "religion" called Orphism, but merely "Orphic poems," poems ascribed to Orpheus, whose name gave them the authority of great antiquity and prestige. Of these there were many, but most are lost. As for Orpheus, there is doubt that he ever existed or that he wrote any of the poems ascribed to him.

Orpheus is a figure of myth, curiously unrelated to the genealogies elaborated in the poetry of Homer and Hesiod. He has no connection with the Mycenaean world (c. 1600–1100 BC). He was said to have come from THRACE, his father a certain Oiagros, about whom nothing is known. Several stories were persistently attached to him in classical literature. His music was so powerful that birds and animals stopped to listen, rivers halted in their course, and even rocks and trees gathered around him. He was a member of the Argonautic expedition, which he saved from the Sirens by his exquisite singing. He descended into Hades to recover his wife Eurydikê (yur-**id**-i-kē), enchanted its denizens, and persuaded them to release her, but lost her again when he turned back to see if she was behind him as they neared the upper world. He was killed by Thracian women, or followers of Bacchus, who cut off his head, which continued to sing.

These stories have much in common with reports of shamans, who have an intimate relationship with nature, can pass into the other world, do things there, and return, and many scholars see in Orpheus a shamanistic figure who entered Greek myth from Thrace independently of Mycenaean saga. Shamanism was vigorous in Thrace and in lands still further north. As a figure who had journeyed to the other world, Orpheus was logically said to be the author of poems that revealed the truth about the nature and destiny of the soul and the reality and power of the gods. He knew secrets, especially about the life of Dionysos, that he imparted to his followers. The poems ascribed to him, some classical and some post-classical, survive in fragments scattered in the works of many authors, both Greek and Latin.

FIGURE 1. The death of Orpheus at the hands of Thracian women, by Hermonax. Orpheus raises his lyre to defend himself while a Thracian woman stabs him with a spear. Two other women stand on either side. Athenian red-figure vase, c. 470 BC. Musée du Louvre, Paris. Photograph by Marie-Lan Nguyen / Creative Commons.

The Orphic poets offer a cosmogony (a story about the origin of the universe) and an anthropogony (a story about the origin of humanity). The early poems are mostly lost but, based on later and varied sources, we can say the following:

The first principle, the origin of all things was Chronos, "Time." Chronos begot Aither, "Upper Air"; Chaos, "Chasm"; and Erebos, "Darkness." Then Chronos formed an egg within Aither, from which sprang the bisexual Phanes, the "One Who Shines," also called Protogonos, the "First Begotten," the actual creator of the world. On his daughter Nux, "Night," Phanes/Protogonos begot Ouranos, "Sky," and Gaia, "Earth," at which point the story picks up from that told in Hesiod's *Theogony*: from Ouranos and Gaia came Kronos and Rhea; from Kronos and Rhea came Zeus and the other Olympians. The contradiction between two primal creators—Protogonos/Phanes and Zeus—

was gotten around by having Zeus swallow Protogonos/Phanes, after which everything was created anew.

Zeus then had intercourse with his sister Demeter, who conceived Persephone. Taking the form of a serpent, Zeus had intercourse with Persephone, who bore Dionysos (sometimes called Zagreus, though Zagreus was probably a separate god). When Dionysos was a little child, the malevolent Titans lured him with sparkling toys, tore him to bits (Orpheus too was torn in pieces), and ate him, so angering Zeus that he destroyed the Titans with a thunderbolt. However, Athena saved the heart of Dionysos and carried it to Zeus, who placed it in the womb of Semelê, a Theban princess, so that Dionysos was born again. From the ashes of the Titans, humans spontaneously generated themselves. Human flesh is therefore of a corrupt, Titanic nature, but humans contain within themselves, from the consumed Dionysos, a spark of the divine. Thus Plato said that the Orphics declared the body *(soma)* to be a tomb *(sêma)*. This notion stands in strong contradiction to the Homeric version wherein a person is the body, and the soul, that is, the "breath" *(psychê)*, is a pale shadow of the person.

Prominent among the features of the lives of those who followed Orphic teaching was an abstention from killing animals and eating flesh, perhaps because of their belief in the transmigration of souls. This set Orphic ritual against standard Greek religious practice, which always involved the killing and eating of sacrificial animals. The followers of Orphic teachings believed that a person would experience a happy afterlife once the soul was freed from the fetters of the body, provided that person had pursued purification in this life and had been initiated into the mysteries. Otherwise one would lie in the mire of the underworld, eternally denied the chance for transmigration and eventual release from the chain of rebirth.

Thirty-nine gold leaf tablets have been found in graves in Italy, Crete, and other places, dated from c. 350 BC to c. AD 200, that seem to attest to Orphic belief. Some give only the name of the dead person (all of them men), but others give instructions about what the dead man should say in the other world: that he was a child of Earth and Sky, thirsty, and longing for a drink from the Lake of Memory. Though the gold leaves are not explicitly Orphic, they are taken to reflect similar thought.

In 1962, in Thessaloniki in northern Greece, near the town of Derveni, what one scholar has called "the most important textual discovery

FIGURE 2. "Orphic" gold-leaf tablet found in THESSALY in a bronze funeral urn, fourth century BC. The inscription reads:

ΔΙΨΑΙΑΥΟΣΕΓΟΚΑΠΟΛΛΜΑΙ
ΑΛΛΑΠΙΕΜΟΥΚΡΑΝΑΣΑΙΕΙΡΟΩ
ΕΜΙΔΕΞΙΑΛΕΥΚΗΚΥΠΑΡΙΣΣΟΣ
ΤΙΣΔΕΣΙΠΩΔΕΣΙΓΑΣΥΙΟΣΕΙΜΙ
ΚΑΙΟΥΡΑΝΟΥΑΣΤΕΡΟΕΝΤΟΣ
ΑΥΤΑΡΕΜΟΙΓΕΝΟΣΟΥΡΑΝΙΟΝ

I burn with thirst and I perish,
but give me to drink from the ever-flowing spring.
On my right is a white cypress.
"Who are you? From where are you?"
I am the son of Earth
and starry Sky
but my race is from the sky.

J. P. Getty Museum, Malibu, CA. Photograph © Remi Mathis / Creative Commons.

of the twentieth century" was found.[2] The papyrus roll, from sometime in the second half of the fourth century BC, had been placed on a funeral pyre. It was thoroughly burned and so preserved in Greece's moist climate. It is the oldest surviving papyrus in Europe. The bottom half of the roll was lost, but the upper portion has been reconstructed. The text is an idiosyncratic prose allegory interpreting a hexametrical poem on the

2. R. Janko, "The Derveni Papyrus: An Interim Text," *Zeitschrift für Papyrologie und Epigraphik* 141 (2002): 1.

creation of the world written "by Orpheus," from which it quotes lines. The author, who seems to belong to the philosophical school of Anaxagoras at Athens (c. 510–c. 428 BC), attempts to show that Orpheus' poem does not mean what it seems to, but that the poem is an allegory.

The poem that the papyrus's author is interpreting follows the usual Orphic narrative. Nux, "Night," gives birth to Ouranos, "Sky," the first king. Then Kronos becomes king, succeeded by Zeus. Zeus rapes his mother, Rhea, who becomes pregnant with Demeter. There the story is lost—how Zeus slept with Demeter, who gave birth to Persephone, who gave birth to Dionysos. The papyrus's author uses far-fetched etymologies to argue that the poem he is analyzing really is an allegory describing the creation of the world according to Anaxagorean principles. In the beginning, Zeus swallowed Protogonos, but Zeus is really Mind and Air, and is in all things. The unique Derveni papyrus is proof of the early dating of Orphic poems, special texts that were preserved and studied by initiates into the Orphic mysteries, who were privy to Orphic teachings about the nature and destiny of humans.

The collection of *Orphic Hymns,* as preserved in the manuscripts, is hard to date, but it is late, perhaps from the second or third centuries AD. A single author may have written them. He may have lived in ASIA MINOR, perhaps PERGAMON, to judge from various minor deities referred to—Misê, Hipta, Melinoê—who are otherwise found in inscriptions only in Asia Minor. The author, or authors, depended on earlier hymns for form and content, evidently influenced by the philosophical school of Stoicism. Hence there are poems to such various personified natural forces as Aither ("Upper Air"), Physis ("Nature"), Boreas ("North Wind"), Zephyros ("West Wind"), and Notos ("South Wind"). The prominence of the element of fire in the hymns may also reflect Stoic influence. On the other hand, the philosophical sources are very mixed, reflecting the syncretism that characterized philosophy in the Hellenistic and Imperial Roman ages. Elements of traditional Orphic theogony, anthropogony, and eschatology appear in the hymns, but they are not prominent. The prominence of Dionysos, to whom seven hymns are dedicated, accords with the hymns' Orphic background because the resurrection of Dionysos is the pattern for the Orphic's own hope for a renewed life.

Unlike in the *Homeric Hymns,* there is no plot or action in the *Orphic Hymns.* Rather, through the piling up of epithets and names they hope to invoke the god's presence. The hymns seem to have been commissioned, and used, by a group of followers who through prayer, libation, and secret ceremonies called on various gods so that through their presence they could receive the blessings of health, wealth, and a happy, purified life. But we can only speculate about the actual rituals that accompanied the singing of the hymns.

THE HYMNS OF PROCLUS

Proclus (AD 412–85), born in CONSTANTINOPLE, was the last of the great classical Greek philosophers. He established the full outlines of what today is called Neoplatonic philosophy, so critical to medieval and European Renaissance philosophical schools. His family was prominent in Byzantine society. He trained in Aristotelian philosophy and mathematics in Alexandria, became a prominent lawyer, then in AD 431 traveled to Athens to study at the famous Academy founded by Plato in 387 BC. Eventually he became head of the Academy, living in a house, recently discovered, near the theater of Dionysos. He was initiated in various mystery cults and was a devotee of the goddess Athena. He died at age seventy-three and was buried in Athens.

Most of Proclus' writings are commentaries on the dialogues of Plato in which Proclus presents his own philosophical theories as interpretations of the master, whom Proclus considers to have been divinely inspired. "Neoplatonism" is a modern term to describe the writers, beginning with Plotinus (c. AD 203–70), who elaborated on Plato's thought, though such thinkers did not see themselves as "New Platonists": they were simply interpreters of Plato. Proclus also wrote two systematic expositions of Plato's theories *(Theological Doctrine* and *Concerning the Theology of Plato)* in addition to several minor works.

In his essays, Proclus explains how all things began in the One ("*to hen*" in Greek) and then descended into the material world. The universe consists of distinct components arranged hierarchically, yet such components are aspects of a single continuous emanation from the One, an eternal, changeless, timeless, and original source, utterly without qualities. This One, the true reality that lies beyond thought, can be known by the human soul in spite of the variegated reality that the senses present to us, because the human soul, which lies beyond thought, shares in the reality of the One. Various levels of intermediate reality separate us from the One, including Nous ("Mind" or "Intellect"), also called the Demiurge ("subordinate creator"). Subordinate to Nous, are a group of *henads,* "Unities," which are like the One itself: each stands at the head of a chain of causation to which it imparts a particular character. The *henads* are none other than the Greek gods. Thus the *henad* Helios is the cause of all sunny things and Aphrodite is the cause of all things pertaining to love.

Within Nous live the Forms (*eidea,* whence our word "idea"), the eternal unchanging models for all things that exist in the changing world of perishable matter. The soul (*psychê*) is itself a Form, a product of Nous, but it does not grasp the unity of the world. Instead, in trying to grasp the One, it produces its own unfoldings of the Forms, the material world, by which it is bedazzled and distracted with passions that overwhelm reason. The soul forgets its own nature. But philosophy can liberate the soul from its subjection to matter and bodily passions, remind it of its origin in Nous and the One, and prepare it to ascend to higher levels. The gods (the *henads*) extend through their series of causations down to the material world and can draw the soul back to the realm of Intellect and, ultimately, even unification with the preintellectual unity of the One. Thus philosophy, a form of intellectual activity, is, ironically, a means of its own overcoming, pointing the soul beyond itself.

It is these realities that Proclus hoped to invoke in his hymns. Through the hymn, the individual human soul can rise to the level of a higher reality, not yet the One, but closer to it than is the material world presented by the senses. Through poetry about the gods, the *henads,* the soul can be liberated from subjection to bodily passions and can ascend to higher levels.

Proclus' influence on later European philosophy and culture, mostly through intermediaries, is incalculable. He deeply influenced Boethius' *Consolation of Philosophy* (c. AD 524), the writings of Saint Thomas Aquinas (c. 1224–74), and the thinking of the Italian scholar and Catholic priest Marsilio Ficino (1433–99), the most influential humanist philosopher of the Italian Renaissance, who was in communication with every major thinker and writer of his day. Proclus inspired Ralph Waldo Emerson (1803–82); in more recent years the novelist Philip K. Dick (1928–82) has claimed adherence to Neoplatonic principles, and a crater on the moon is named after Proclus.

1

Zeus

Zeus is the only Olympian for whose name there is a transparent Indo-European etymology. The name has the same root as the Sanskrit Dyaus Pitar, "Father Sky"; the Roman Juppiter; the Germanic Tiu, hence "Tuesday"; and the Latin *deus,* "god," and *dies,* "day." He is, then, the god of the bright sky, the "shiner." He was identified with Near Eastern weather gods, who preside over rain and storms, and he belongs to this type. He is mentioned in the economic tabulations that survive from the Mycenaean Age (c. 1600–1100 BC), written in a pre-alphabetic syllabic script called Linear B. He may have been the highest god even at this time.

In Homer Zeus is the father of gods and humans, presiding over MOUNT OLYMPOS like a warlord in his palace. He is the "cloud-gatherer," the "thunderer on high," the "hurler of thunderbolts." His emblem is the eagle, king of the birds. In Greek religion, he was worshipped on mountain tops: on MOUNT LYKAON in ARCADIA, on Mount Hymettos near ATHENS, and on MOUNT IDA in CRETE. He was associated with the highest mountain in Greece, Mount Olympos, though many other mountains bore this name (Olympos seems to be a pre-Greek word meaning "mountain"). The weather could be controlled through him, sometimes assisted by human sacrifice, as apparently took place on Mount Lykaon. His power is manifest in the irresistible thunderbolt by which he strikes down humans and gods. If a person were hit by a thunderbolt, that was the doing of Zeus Kataibatês, "Zeus the Descender," and an altar was built at the site.

FIGURE 3. Zeus with his thunderbolt and his kingly scepter. He is bearded and wears a wreath of ivy leaves. Athenian red-figure vase, c. 470 BC. Museo del Prado, Madrid. Photograph © Rowanwindwhistler / Creative Commons.

In myth, as in Hesiod's *Theogony*, a main source about Zeus's family history and exploits as well as the configuration of power on which his reign relies, it is made clear that Zeus did not always rule. Before him, crooked-counsel Kronos was king of the gods. Kronos swallowed all his children, but Zeus's mother Rhea saved the infant and concealed him in a cave on Crete. There he grew to manhood and defeated his father and his father's allies, the Titans, by the invincible power of his thunderbolt.

Zeus is repeatedly threatened by women who are predicted to bear children greater than himself, even as he was greater than his own father, Kronos. One such woman was Metis, "Mind." His response was to swallow her when she was pregnant so that "mind" became part of Zeus's own nature. The child was Athena, who burst from Zeus's head when she came to term, wholly Zeus's child and obedient to him alone. Another threat came from the sea-nymph Thetis, to whom Zeus was attracted. Warned of the danger, he refrained from intercourse with her and instead compelled Thetis to marry a mortal, Peleus, who became the father of Achilles, the greatest warrior that ever lived. Other threats to his rule came from the monster Typhoeus, the child of Earth (Gaia) and Tartaros, shown in art as a beast with snakes for feet. Zeus destroyed him with his thunderbolts and imprisoned the carcass beneath Mount Etna in SICILY, where it continues to smolder even to this day. The giants, too, opposed his reign, but with the help of the other Olympians he defeated them and sent them into the underworld.

Parallel to Zeus's power in combat is his sexual potency. Zeus had sexual relations with many goddesses and mortal women—ancient commentators counted 115 consorts! He took many guises in these affairs, appearing to Europa as a bull; as a golden shower of rain to Danaë; as a swan to Leda. His mortal children are always exceptional in strength and skill: Herakles, Helen, Minos. He is transcendent in homosexual love too: he abducted the Trojan prince Ganymede in the form of an eagle. Zeus is the only god to beget other gods. Apollo, Artemis, Hermes, Persephone, Dionysos, and Athena are all his children.

Zeus was the source of all sovereignty in the city, in the family, in all of society. He was the source of justice. He was the supreme god and, in Stoic thought, the divine fire that pervades everything, gives form to everything, and makes the world.

Hymns to Zeus are, however, rare in surviving Greek literature. The two translated here are the most prominent, but the Homeric "Hymn

23: To Zeus," likely from c. 600 BC, is only four lines long. Callima-
chus' "Hymn to Zeus" may have been performed at a festival to Zeus
in Alexandria in the third century BC, but, as usual, there is no defi-
nite information.

HOMERIC HYMN 23: TO ZEUS

*Zeus, the son of Kronos, is in league with Themis, the goddess of order in
the world.*

I will sing of Zeus, best and greatest of the gods, far-seeing,
king of all, fulfiller of what happens, who whispers wise words
to Themis° as she sits by his side.
                              Be kind, O far-seeing
son of Kronos—most honored and greatest of all!

CALLIMACHUS HYMN 1: TO ZEUS

Zeus, born and nurtured on CRETE, *is the sponsor and legitimizer of all
kingly power. He is the power behind the great Ptolemy, king of* EGYPT.

At the libations of Zeus would anything be better than to sing
of the god himself—ever great, ever the king, the destroyer
of the Titans, the minister of Justice for the children of Sky?
But how shall we sing of him, as the Diktaian or the Lykaian?°
5   My heart is in doubt, for your birth is much contested. O Zeus,
some say you were born on the mountains of Ida, others say that
you—O Zeus!—were born in Arcadia.° Which, O father, is lying?

3. *Themis:* "Law," that which is established by custom. Usually a wife of Zeus, here
she is also an adviser. Zeus is the god of law and justice.

4. *Diktaian or Lykaian:* That is, in his role as the god of MOUNT DIKTÊ in Crete, or
of MOUNT LYKAON on the mainland, in ARCADIA. Both mountains had famous cults to
Zeus. Mount Diktê is confused and identified with MOUNT IDA on Crete. In origin
Mount Diktê was probably a separate mountain in eastern Crete (Mount Lasithi today),
where there was also a cave dedicated to the cult of Zeus.

6–7. *on the mountains of Ida . . . in Arcadia:* There were two Mount Idas in the Greek
tradition, one southeast of TROY, where Hera seduced Zeus in the *Iliad,* and one in
central Crete, where there was a cave in which the infant Zeus was hidden. Arcadia is in
the central PELOPONNESOS.

"Cretans, always liars!"° Yes, for the Cretans made a tomb
10   for you, O king, though you did not die, but you are forever!°
      Rhea bore you in Parrhasia,° where the mountain was covered
      all around with thick bushes. Afterwards, that place was sacred.
      Nothing needing Eileithyia° comes close, no crawling thing nor
         woman,
      but the Apidaneans° call it the primordial birthing-bed of Rhea.
15   When your mother had set you aside from her great womb,
      right away she sought out a flow of water by which she might
      cleanse herself from the pollution of birth, by which she might
      wash your flesh. But the mighty LADON did not yet flow,
      nor ERYMANTHOS, the whitest of rivers, and the whole of Arcadia
20   was still without rain, but soon it was to be called *very* well
      watered. At the time that Rhea loosened her sash,° the waters
      of Iaon supported many oaks above, and the Black River
      carried many wagons, and above the Karnion, though now it
         is wet,
      many serpents cast their lairs, and a man, parched with thirst,
25   was accustomed to walk above the Krathis and the Metopê
      with its many pebbles, but the abundant waters lay beneath his
         feet.°
         Utterly at a loss, Queen Rhea spoke: "Dear Earth,

---

9. *Cretans, always liars:* This alludes to a famous quip attributed to the legendary
sage Epimenides of Crete (c. sixth century BC). It is a paradox because Epimenides was
a Cretan, hence his statement that all Cretans are liars must be a lie, if it is true!

9–10. *Yes, for the Cretans . . . forever:* That is, because Cretans are liars, one cannot
believe their claim that Zeus was born in Crete, especially because they also had a place
said to be Zeus's tomb. The Cretan Zeus seems to have been a pre-Greek dying god
consort of the Great Mother Goddess, identified by the Greeks with their own sky god.
As a dying god, he had his own tomb.

11. *Parrhasia:* The region in Arcadia where Mount Lykaon was.

13. *Eileithyia* (ē-lē-**thui**-a): The goddess of childbirth; no pregnant creature dares
approach this spot.

14. *Apidaneans:* The early inhabitants of Arcadia.

21. *loosened her sash:* That is, gave birth.

26. *abundant waters lay beneath his feet:* The prior lines are images of the desiccated
Arcadian landscape before the birth of Zeus, when the course of all these minor Arca-
dian streams ran beneath the ground. Such refined and obscure geographical details are
characteristic of Callimachus' learned verse.

you too gave birth! Your birth pangs are easy to bear!"°
She spoke and the goddess, lifting high her great arm,

30   struck the mountain with her scepter. It was split wide
for Rhea and a great torrent poured forth. There she washed
your flesh, O king, and wrapped you in swaddling clothes.
Then she gave you to Nedê to take to a hiding place in Crete
so that she might raise you in secret. She was the eldest

35   of the nymphs who at that time accompanied Rhea as midwives
in their earliest generation, after Styx and Philyra.° Nor was
the goddess thankless, but named the flood "Nedê."° Somewhere
near the city of the Kaukones (which is called Lepreion) this great
stream mixes with the waters of Nereus, the most ancient water

40   that the descendants of the bear of Lykaon—his daughter—drink.°
When the nymph, O Father Zeus, carried you to Knossos,
    leaving Thenai
    —Thenai was near KNOSSOS—there, divine one, your umbilical
    cord
    fell away, and that is why the Kudonians° call that plain
    "Umbiliko."

28. *easy to bear:* That is, it is easy for Earth to give birth to water because she was the mother of many primordial gods.

36. *Styx and Philyra:* Styx is usually said to be the oldest daughter of Ocean, but the name is also given to a stream in Arcadia. Philyra was the mother of the Centaur Chiron, fathered by Zeus.

37. *Nedê:* That is, for the nymph Nedê's service, a stream that flowed from Mount Lykaon to the sea was named for her.

38–40. *the Kaukones . . . drink:* The Kaukones were descended from Kaukon, a son of Lykaon, a legendary king after whom Mount Lykaon was named (according to a famous story, Lykaon cooked his son and served him to Zeus to test Zeus's omniscience; immediately he was turned into a wolf). Lepreion was near to where the Nedê enters the sea. Nereus (**nē**-rūs) was a prophetic sea god, the Old Man of the Sea. A daughter of Lykaon was Kallisto, with whom Zeus fell in love. She was turned into a bear and placed in the sky as Ursa Major (the Great Bear, or Big Dipper). Her son by Zeus was Arkas, ancestor of the Arkadians. He too became a constellation, Ursa Minor (the Little Bear, or Little Dipper).

43. *Kudonians:* That is, the Cretans in general. Strictly speaking, the Kudonians were the inhabitants of ancient KUDONIA in northwest Crete, modern Chania.

O Zeus, the female companions of the Korubantes° took you
45   into their arms. The ash-nymphs of Mount Diktê and Adrasteia°
lay you in a golden cradle, and you suckled from the rich
breast of the goat Amaltheia, and you ate sweet honeycomb;
for of a sudden there appeared the work of the Panakrian bees
in the mountains of Ida, which they call Panakra.° Vigorously
50   the Kouretes danced the war dance around you, banging
with their weapons so that the sound of the shield would reach
the ears of Kronos, and not your childish cries.

You grew

handsomely, handsomely you were nourished, O heavenly
Zeus! Growing up swiftly, down soon appeared on your cheeks.
55   When you were still a child, all things that you devised were
already fulfilled. Thus your siblings, though born before,
did not begrudge that you held the sky as your allotted home.
The poets of old are not always truthful: They say that for the
children
of Kronos a lot divided the house into three portions. But who
60   would cast lots for Olympos and Hades, unless he were quite mad?
It seems that one casts lots for things that are equal, but these
things
are very unlike.° I would lie, telling such things as would persuade
the listener. Lots did not make you king of the gods, but the works
of your hands, your strength and power, which you have set by
your throne.

---

44. *Korubantes:* The Korubantes (of unknown etymology) were originally the armed followers of Cybelê, the Great Mother Goddess of PHRYGIA, who celebrated her with dance and drumming. Here they are the attendants of Zeus. Usually they are called Kouretes ("youths," ku-**rē**-tēz), who danced outside Zeus's cave on Crete, banging their spears against their shields so his infant cries could not be heard.

45. *The ash-nymphs of Mount Diktê and Adrasteia:* The ash-nymphs sprang from the blood of the castrated Sky (Ouranos), here said to live on Mount Diktê. Adrasteia ("invincible") was the sister of Amaltheia ("tender goddess"), Zeus's foster-mother, who took the form of a goat and suckled him.

49. *Panakra:* Otherwise unknown.

61–62. *but these things are very unlike:* Such early poets as Homer claimed that the Olympians cast lots for their domains (*Il.* 15.187–93), but Callimachus follows Hesiod (*Th.* 881–85), who thought that Zeus was exalted by divine consensus.

65   And you made the most excellent of birds° the announcer
of your omens (may you show favorable ones to my friends!).
You chose what is best among lusty men: Not those skilled in ships,
nor the shield-wielding man, nor the singer, but you at once
gave such qualities° to others of the lesser blessed ones, other
     spheres
70 for others to look after. You chose the rulers of cities themselves,
under whose authority are the farmers, the strength of the spear,
of the oar—all things!
                    What is not beneath the power of the ruler?
For example, we say that bronze-workers are under Hephaistos,
warriors under Ares, hunters under tunic-clad Artemis, and those
75 knowing the pathways of song under Phoibos;° but "kings
belong to Zeus,"° for nothing is more godly than Zeus's kings.
Thus you chose them for your allotment. You gave them cities
to rule, and you yourself took your place in the highest parts
80 of the cities, on the lookout for who rules by crooked judgments
and who rules by straight—the opposite. You gave them the flow
of wealth and abundant prosperity—to all, but not evenly.
You can tell this from the example of our own king: He surpasses
by far all the rest. By nightfall he accomplishes that which
85 he conceives in the morning; by nightfall, the greatest tasks
and the least—as soon as he thinks of them! Others accomplish
some things in a year, other things not; you yourself entirely
prevent the achievement of other men, thwarting their desire.°
     Fare mightily well, O greatest son of Kronos! Giver
90 of good things, deliverer from pain! Who could sing of your deeds?
There has never been such a one, there will never be.

65. *the most excellent of birds:* The eagle.

69. *such qualities:* That is, skill in seafaring, war, and poetry-making.

75. *Phoibos:* Apollo, god of song.

75–76. *"kings belong to Zeus":* Callimachus quotes from Hesiod's *Theogony,* line 96. This passage is undoubtedly in praise of whichever Ptolemy was in power when this poem was written.

86–88. *Others accomplish . . . thwarting their desire:* That is, common men take a whole year to get something done, and other men, who have ill designs, you prevent from acting altogether, or even from having the desire to act.

Farewell, father, farewell again! Grant excellence and wealth.
Wealth without excellence knows not how to increase a man,
nor excellence without wealth. So grant excellence, and wealth!

ORPHIC HYMN 15: TO ZEUS

The initiate prays to the father of the gods, creator of all, for health, peace, and wealth.

O Zeus, most honored—Zeus, who lives forever!
We offer you this testimony that shall redeem us, this prayer.
O Zeus, by your will have all things been made clear—
earth, goddess and mother, the towering crags of the mountains,
5   and the sea, and all that the sky encompasses. O Zeus,
son of Kronos, scepter-wielding, descending in thunder
and lightning, powerful of spirit, father of all,
beginning and end of everything!
                         Earth-shaker,
increaser, all-shaker, purifier, striker with lightning,
10 thunderer, big boomer, Zeus the sower! Listen
to me, you who have many forms! Grant me stainless
health and divine peace, wealth, and blameless fame!

ORPHIC HYMN 19: TO ZEUS THE THUNDERBOLT

A prayer to Zeus, master of thunder.

O Father Zeus, you who drive on the sublime and fiery
cosmos, flashing with your ethereal lightning you shake
the highest seat of the blessed gods with your divine
thunder. You set on fire the clouds of rain with your
5   blazing flash of light. You hurl furious storms,
sheets of rain, tornados, mighty bolts of lightning
boiling with fire, terrible, shivery, wrecking the spirit,
roaring, all aflame! You cast your winged, savage
weapon, hiding in clouds, shivering the heart, making
10 the hair stand on end, unforeseen, booming, a holy
invincible weapon spinning with an endless whistling,

all-devouring in its rush, unbroken, glowering, irresistible,
a penetrating weapon from the sky swooping down
in a fiery hurricane! It frightens the earth and the radiant
15   sky, and wild animals cringe when the booming reaches
their ears. Faces gleam in the brilliant light as the thunder
crashes in the hollows of the air. You tear the robe
that cloaks heaven, you hurl the blazing bolt!
    But, O blessed one, cast your mighty spirit
20   on the waves of the sea and the peaks of the mountains.
We all know of your power. In return for this libation
give all things that are pleasing to the heart—a bountiful
life, and health that is queen to all, and a divine
peace that nourishes youths, splendidly honored,
25   and a life blooming forever with happy thoughts.

ORPHIC HYMN 20: TO ASTRAPAIOS ZEUS

Astrapaios means "of lightning" and refers to the fire that accompanies Zeus's thunderbolt. Here Zeus is invoked as giving a sweet end to life.

I call upon great, holy, resounding, famous,
ethereal Zeus, whose fiery glare shines running
and blazing through the air! Your brilliance flashes through
the clouds with a deafening clap. O terrible, wrathful,
5   holy, invincible god! Lightning Zeus! Begetter of all!
Greatest king—bless my life and bring to it a sweet end!

2

Hera

Hera, the daughter of Kronos and Rhea, is the goddess of weddings and marriage; to Aphrodite belongs seduction and carnal pleasure. She is wife and sister to Zeus, and in myth always holds a position of power and influence. She is, however, an unpleasant wife who constantly complains about his illicit affairs, treats his mistresses cruelly, and persecutes his illegitimate offspring, especially Herakles. In a famous comic scene in the *Iliad* she succeeds, with the help of a love charm that Aphrodite has given her, in seducing her own husband. Zeus, helpless with lust, wishing to sleep with her, flatters Hera by listing all the women by whom he has betrayed her!

> Hera quickly advanced
> to Gargaros, the highest peak of lofty IDA.° Zeus
> the cloud-gatherer saw her. He saw her and lust overran
> 290 his wise heart, just as when first they lay together
> in love, going to the couch without the knowledge
> of their parents. He stood before her and spoke, addressing her:
> "Hera, with what desire have you come here from Olympos?
> Your horses are not at hand, nor your chariot for you to mount."
> 295   With crafty mind the revered Hera answered:
> "I have come to visit the limits of the much-nourishing earth,

288. *IDA:* Not the Mount Ida on CRETE, but a mountain of the same name near TROY.

FIGURE 4. The wedding of Zeus and Hera, a metope (a square sculpture on a frieze) from the temple to Hera at SELINOUS, at the southwestern tip of SICILY, c. 540 BC. Selinous ("parsley") was the westernmost of the Greek cities in Sicily, destroyed by the Carthaginians in 409 BC. A half-naked Zeus, sitting on a rock, clasps the hand of Hera. One of Hera's breasts is exposed as she removes her head-covering in a traditional gesture of sexual submission. Museo Archeologico, Palermo, Sicily. Photo by Giovanni Dall'Orto.

and Ocean, the origin of the gods, and Mother Tethys,°
who nourished and reared me in their home. I am going
to pay them a visit, and I hope to resolve this endless
300 quarreling of theirs. For a long time they have held aloof
from the marriage bed and from lovemaking, because anger has
taken their hearts. My horses stand at the foot of Ida

297. *Ocean, the origin of the gods, and Mother Tethys:* Ocean is a Titan, and the river that flows around the world. Tethys (**tē**-this) is a watery goddess, the consort of Ocean.

with its many fountains. They will carry me over the solid
land and the watery sea. But now it is on your
305 account that I have come down here from Olympos, so that
you will not become angry with me afterwards, if I go
without saying anything to the house of deep-flowing Ocean."
  Zeus the cloud-gatherer then answered her: "Hera,
you can always go there later, but for now let the two
310 of us take delight, going to bed and making love.
For never yet has the desire for goddess or mortal woman
so poured itself about me and overmastered my heart
in my breast—no, not when I lusted after the wife of Ixion,
who bore Peirithoös, a counselor equal to the gods.
315 Nor when I desired Danaë of the delicate ankles—
the daughter of Akrisios, who bore Perseus, preeminent above
all men. Nor when I longed for the far-famed daughter
of Phoinix, who bore Minos and godlike Rhadamanthus. Not even
when I fell in love with Semelê, nor Alkmenê in Thebes,
320 who gave birth to strong-minded Herakles as her son; and Semelê
bore Dionysos, a joy to mortals. Nor when I loved Queen Demeter,
who has beautiful tresses. Not even when I loved famous Leto—
nor even yourself!—as now I long for you and sweetest desire
possesses me."°
  The revered Hera answered him with crafty
325 words: "Most dread son of Kronos, what words you've spoken!

313–24. *the wife of Ixion . . . desire possesses me:* Ixion was himself a notorious rapist
who lusted after Hera, then ejaculated his semen into a cloud that had her form and so
begot the Centaurs, who raped the women at Peirithoös' wedding. Zeus came to Ixion's
wife as a stallion and begot Peirithoös ("very swift"); later Peirithoös tried to marry
Persephone but was entrapped in the lower world. Zeus came to Danaë as a shower of
gold that fell into her prison chamber. The daughter of Phoinix is Europa, whom Zeus
carried to Crete from PHOENICIA (named after Phoinix) in the form of a bull and there
possessed her. Minos became king of CRETE and Rhadamanthos a judge in the under-
world. Zeus appeared to Semelê while pregnant in the form in which he appeared to
Hera—a thunderbolt!—and burned her to a crisp. Dionysos was brought to term by
being sewn into Zeus's thigh. Zeus appeared to the princess Alkmenê disguised as her
husband, but her husband, Amphitryon, impregnated her on the same night so that she
gave birth to one son fathered by Zeus, Herakles, and another son fathered by her hus-
band. Zeus begot Persephone on Demeter. Hera drove Leto all over the earth before she
gave birth to Apollo and Artemis on the Aegean island of DELOS.

If you want to make love on the peaks of Ida, where everything
is out in open, how would it be if some one of the gods
whose race is forever should peep at us as we sleep and then
go tell all the gods? Then I could not rise up from the bed
330 and go to your house—it would be too shameful! But if you want
and it is your desire, there is always your chamber, which your dear
son Hephaistos made for you, and fitted with strong doors to the
    doorposts.
Let us go and lie down there, since the couch is your pleasure."
    The cloud-gatherer Zeus then answered her: "Hera,have no fear
335 that the gods or men will see! I will wrap a cloud about us,
a golden cloud. Not even Helios° could see through it,
he whose sight is the keenest for seeing things."

                                              He spoke
and the son of Kronos clasped his wife in his arms. Beneath them
the shining earth made the luxuriant grass to grow,
340 and lotus covered with dew, and crocus, and thick
and tender hyacinth that bore them up from the ground.
The two lay there and were covered in a cloud—beautiful,
    golden!—
from which fell drops of dew. And so the father slept peacefully
on the peak of Gargaros, overcome by sleep and love.
345 Thus he held his wife in his arms.

Oddly, though she was the sponsor and protector of marriage, and
though her union with Zeus is the archetype for all marriage, Hera has
only one important child, Ares, whom Zeus describes as the most
hated of his children. She can, however, give birth parthenogenetically
and in some stories produced Typhoeus, the monster who threatens
Zeus's reign. She also conceives Hephaistos without intercourse, whom
she hurls from Olympos, disgusted by his lameness. She is sometimes
said to have given birth to Eileithyia, the birth-goddess, but she is
never herself invoked as a mother or shown as a mother with child.
The collection has few hymns to Hera: only a short Homeric hymn,
and an Orphic hymn.

336. *Helios:* The sun-god Helios sees all things.

HOMERIC HYMN 12: TO HERA

Hera is the equal to Zeus in honor.

> I sing of Hera of the golden throne, whom Rhea bore,
> queen of the deathless ones, of exceptional beauty,
> the sister and wife of loud-thundering Zeus—glorious!
> whom all the blessed ones in tall Olympos revere
> 5. and honor, like Zeus who delights in the thunder.

ORPHIC HYMN 16: TO HERA

Hera is the sponsor of fertility, associated with the rains and with air (Plato interprets her name as meaning "air").

> Seated in dark valleys, shaped like air—Hera
> queen of all!—blessed bedmate of Zeus,
> you send gentle soul-nourishing breezes to mortals.
> Mother of rains, nurse of winds, you give birth
> 5. to all that is. Apart from you I do not know
> of any life at all. You are part of everything,
> mixed in with the holy air. You alone have power
> over all things, you rule over all things. You are shaken
> with the flow of the whistling winds.
>   But, O blessed
> 10. goddess of many names, queen of all, may you come
> with kindness on your lovely blessed face.

3

Poseidon

Poseidon is the son of the Titans Kronos and Rhea and brother to Zeus and Hades. The first part of his name means "husband" *(potis)* but the second part has not been explained. He was important in the Mycenaean Age (c. 1600–1100 BC) and is mentioned in the prealphabetic syllabic Linear B tablets. According to the usual story, after Zeus won his war against the Titans the three brothers—Zeus, Poseidon, Hades—divided up the world by lot, Zeus taking the sky, Poseidon the waters, and Hades the underworld. He is also the ruler of earthquakes, called "Shaker of the Earth" and "Holder of the Earth," the force that makes the land move. His association with horses is a prominent feature, but we cannot say why. Perhaps the sound of a herd of horses galloping across the plain was reminiscent of the sound of an earthquake. He is the father of the winged horse Pegasos, which sprang from Medusa's neck when Perseus beheaded her, and in the *Odyssey* he is father of the Cyclops Polyphemos and famously the punisher of Odysseus. In the form of a stallion, Poseidon had intercourse with Demeter and conceived the wonder-horse Arion.

HOMERIC HYMN 22: TO POSEIDON

The hymnist praises Poseidon as lord of horses and the sea and asks for his protection.

> I begin to sing of Poseidon, the great god, mover
> of the earth and the barren sea, god of the deep,

FIGURE 5. Poseidon. The naked and bearded sea-god, holding his trident, rides in a chariot across the waves, pulled by fish-tailed sea-horses. Roman mosaic, c. third century AD. Sousse Archaeological Museum, Tunisia. Photograph © Touzrimounir / Creative Commons.

who presides over Helikon and broad Aigai.° The gods
gave you two functions, O Earth-shaker, to be a tamer
5   of horses and a savior of ships.
                        Hail, O Poseidon,
holder of earth! Dark-haired one! Be kind of heart,
O blessed one, and help those who travel at sea.

ORPHIC HYMN 17: TO POSEIDON

Poseidon is praised as lord of the sea, horses, and earthquakes.

Hear O Poseidon, holder of the earth, dark-haired,
lord of horses, holding a trident made of bronze
in your hands, you live in the depths of the full-bosomed
sea—lord of the waters, sea-resounding, loud-thundering

3. *Helikon and broad Aigai:* Towns called Helikê and Aigai on the GULF OF CORINTH were sacred to Poseidon.

5   earth-shaker, abounding with waves, graceful one,
     driving on your four-horsed chariot, rushing
     on the sea, splashing through the rippling brine!
         You who won a third part of the world, the deep
     swirling of the sea, delighting in its waves and its monsters,
10   spirit of the deep! May you save the foundations
     of the earth and the swift seafaring of ships,
     bringing peace, health, and wealth without blame.

4

Athena

Athena is one of the great gods of the Greek pantheon. She had a strange origin. Zeus's first wife was Metis, "mind," but when she became pregnant he was warned that her child would be greater than the father. Zeus's grandfather, Sky (Ouranos), had faced the same problem. Sky therefore pushed his children by his wife Earth (Gaia) into a cranny—that is, back into her womb—as they were born. But his son Kronos escaped and castrated his own father to become king of the gods. Kronos attempted to foil the same prophecy given to Sky by swallowing his own children, but the infant Zeus escaped, grew up in a cave on Crete, and overthrew Kronos. To stop this pattern of succession, one generation overthrowing the preceding, Zeus did not wait for Metis to give birth: he swallowed her while she was still pregnant. Then he had a ferocious headache. The craftsman god Hephaistos struck his head with a mallet and out sprang Athena, fully armed and giving the war cry (sometimes it is Hermes or Prometheus who assists the birth). Hence Athena was Zeus's child alone and, instead of overthrowing him, was a loyal defender of his interests.

The fully armed Athena was a war goddess, but, unlike Ares, who gloried in the blood and guts of battle, she was concerned with war tactics and strategy. She is a virgin goddess, uninterested in love-making, but the protector of many heroes, especially Herakles, Perseus, Diomedes, and Odysseus. She is the supervisor of every kind of craft, especially weaving for women and carpentry for men. She is the protector of cities, hence of civilization and its arts. Athens, to which she gave the olive, was

named after her (or she was named after the city, but she is also Panhel-
lenic and her name appears in the prealphabetic Linear B tablets). The
Athenians built there one of the world's most famous buildings, the Par-
thenon, "temple of the virgins," in her honor on their Acropolis. The Par-
thenon's pediments had sculptures with scenes of her birth and of her
contest with Poseidon over who would be suzerain of the city.

HOMERIC HYMN 11: TO ATHENA

*This hymn, unusually, conjoins Athena with the war-god Ares; in Near
Eastern myth, war is the province of great female deities.*

> I begin by singing of Pallas Athena, the city's guardian
> —dread one!—who with Ares loves the deeds of war,
> and the sacking of cities, and the war cry, and battles,
> and she protects the people when they go out to war
> 5   and return.
> > Hail, goddess! Give us fortune and happiness!

HOMERIC HYMN 28: TO ATHENA

Athena is born from the head of Zeus.

> I begin to sing of Pallas Athena, splendid god,
> flashing-eyed, wise, with a truculent heart, chaste,
> virgin, guardian of cities, audacious, Tritogeneia,°
> to whom wise Zeus himself gave birth from his majestic
> 5   head, wearing golden shining armor, and all the deathless
> ones were amazed when they saw her.
> > She sprang quickly
> from the deathless head of Zeus who carries
> the aegis,° shaking her keen spear, and great Olympos
> reeled terribly at the power of the flashing-eyed goddess.
> 10   The earth moaned mightily round about, and all

---

3. *Tritogeneia* (tri-to-ghen-ē-a): An ancient epithet of Athena, of unknown origin,
although it was sometimes connected with a Lake Triton either in Boeotia or in Libya
and so meaning "she born near Lake Triton."

7–8. *carries the aegis*: The aegis is a sort of mantle with a fringe of serpents (see figure
7). Both Zeus and Athena wear this device, which inspires terror in anyone who sees it.

FIGURE 6. The birth of Athena: she springs fully armed from the head of Zeus with shield, spear, and war helmet in the presence of gods and goddesses. A bearded Zeus sits on his throne with a lightning bolt in his left hand and a scepter in his right. Poseidon, on the right, is recognizable by his trident. Hephaistos, on the left, holds his right hand up in astonishment; in his left hand he holds his double-edged axe, with which he struck Zeus's head. In the far left (only partly visible) is Dionysos with a wreath of ivy. The three goddesses, two on either side of Zeus and a third at the far right, are not identified, but probably represent Aphrodite, Hera, and Artemis. An unidentified youth, or the carving of a youth, squats at the side of Zeus's throne. Athenian black-figure ceramic tripod, c. 570 BC. Musée du Louvre, Paris. Photograph by Bibi Saint-Pol / Creative Commons.

the sea was stirred, tossed with purple waves, and foam
suddenly poured forth. The glorious son of Hyperion°
stopped his swift-footed horses for a long time, until
the maiden, Pallas Athena, had taken the divine armor
15   from her deathless shoulders. Wise Zeus rejoiced!
        So hail to you, O daughter of Zeus who carries
the aegis! I will remember you and another song too.

12. *son of Hyperion*: Helios.

CALLIMACHUS HYMN 5: TO ATHENA;
ON THE BATHS OF PALLAS

This hymn is written in the Doric dialect, instead of the usual Ionian, and in elegiac couplets, in which every other line is a truncated hexameter made up of the two first halves of a hexameter (that is, ⁻∪∪/⁻∪∪ /—). The Greek has many unfamiliar words. The scene is ARGOS *in Greece. A narrator speaks to a group of girls who are preparing to welcome a statue of Athena that is being drawn in a chariot and is coming near. The statue is the Palladion, an ancient cult statue that the Argive hero Diomedes captured from* TROY, *thereby enabling the capture of the city. They will carry the statue to the river* INACHOS *and there bathe it. They will also bathe the shield of Diomedes, giving the poet a chance to describe Athena's own bathing customs. The nymph Chariklo was Athena's favorite, the mother of the Theban prophet Teiresias, and the poet tells the story of how Chariklo and Athena were bathing when Teiresias inadvertently saw the goddess naked and was blinded as punishment. However, Teiresias was compensated for his blindness by a long life and the gift of prophecy. The myth is a warning to men to avert their eyes from the ritual bathing of the Palladion.*

> For all of you women who will bathe Pallas—come out!°
>   Come out! Just now I heard the neighing
> of her sacred mares.° The goddess is ready to come.
>   Be quick, you blond-haired Pelasgian women!°
> 5 Athena never washed her powerful arms before chasing
>   the dust from her mares' flanks, not even
> when she returned from battling the Earth-born ones,°
>   who lived without justice. Her equipment was

----

1. *come out:* That is, from their houses to join the procession. The narrator, presumably female, speaks to the women who will bathe the statue of Athena, here called by her common epithet Pallas (of unknown etymology).

3. *sacred mares:* The mares draw the chariot that holds the statue.

4. *Pelasgian women:* That is, the women of Argos, a town supposedly founded by one Pelasgos, who gave his name to the primordial pre-Greek inhabitants of Greece. So the action is set in the city of Argos.

7. *Earth-born ones:* The gods defeated the Giants, children of Earth, in a terrible battle in which Athena was a participant.

wholly bespattered with gore, but the very first thing she did
10   was to free the necks of her steeds from
their cars and wash away the sweat and filth with streams
        from Ocean. Then she cleaned the clotted
foam from their bit-eating mouths.°

                                    So come, Achaean women!
But don't bring myrrh or perfume-jars,
15   you bath-pourers (I hear the sound of axles twisting
        in the hubs°)—no, not myrrh for Pallas,
nor perfume jars (for Athena does not like mixed ointments°),
        and do not bring her a mirror. Her looks are ever fair!
Not even when the Phrygian judged the contest
20   on IDA, did the great goddess look into
the gold-bronze mirror, nor into the transparent eddies
        of Simoeis.° Hera didn't either—but Aphrodite,
repeatedly taking up the shining bronze, twice adjusted the same
        lock of hair. No, after twice running
25   sixty double-courses along the EUROTAS, just like
        the Lakedaimonian stars, she took
a simple oil and skillfully rubbed herself down
        —the product of her own planting, ladies!—
and a healthy blush came over her, like a fresh rose,
30   or the color of a pomegranate seed on
its surface.° So bring now only some manly olive oil

12–13. *then she cleaned . . . bit-eating mouths:* The implication is that the horses carrying the Palladion will be washed before the statue itself is.

15–16. *I hear the sound of axles twisting in the hubs:* That is, the chariot is coming near.

17. *Athena does not like mixed ointments:* Like male athletes, Athena prefers to anoint herself with pure olive oil, unmixed with scents.

19–22. *Not even when the Phrygian . . . Simoeis:* The Phrygian is Paris, who judged the beauty of the three goddesses Hera, Aphrodite, and Athena on Mount Ida. "Gold-copper" is *oreichalchos,* literally "mountain bronze," an unknown ancient alloy. The Simoeis is a river that flows across the Trojan plain, whose clear waters are here compared to a mirror.

24–31. *After twice running . . . its surface:* Athena lost the contest in the Judgment of Paris, but she is a fit athlete, like the Spartans Kastor and Polydeukes (Castor and Pollux), "Lakedaimonian stars" because they were transformed into the constellation Gemini, worshipped in ALEXANDRIA. To prove her competence, Athena has run sixty *diauloi* ("double course"), a standard race course in which the athlete ran from a starting post to a terminus, then back. This give her a healthy glow so that she does not require

with which Kastor and Herakles, too,
anointed themselves. And bring a comb, made of solid
gold, that she might comb out her hair,
35   once she has cleansed her shining locks.
                                        Come forth,
Athena! A crew dear to your heart
is at hand, virgin daughters of the Argive line.
O Athena, the shield of Diomedes
is being carried, a custom that Eumedes taught the Argives
40   in the days of old, a priest most beloved
of you.° He, recognizing that the people were preparing
death for him, fled, taking your holy
image, to Mount Kreion—yes, and he settled on Mount
Kreion. And he placed you, O goddess
45   on the rugged rocks that now have the name of Pallatides.°
Come forth, O Athena, sacker of cities!
Wearer of a golden helmet! Who delights in the cacophony
of steeds and shield!
                        Today, water-carriers,
do not dip your pitchers. Today, O Argives,
50   drink from the springs and not the river
Inachos. Today, you slave women, carry your water
vessels either to the spring of Phusadeia
or Amumonê, the daughter of Danaos.° For Inachos,
mixing his waters with gold and flowers,

---

cosmetics. The Eurotas is the river that runs past SPARTA, hometown of Kastor and
Polydeukes. Olive oil is the special gift of Athena to the city of Athens.

38–41. *The shield of Diomedes . . . of you:* The Trojan hero Diomedes was from
ARGOS, and apparently his shield was kept there as a revered memento. Nothing else is
known about Eumedes.

43–45. *Mount Kreion . . . the name of Pallatides:* The image of Athena is the Pallad-
ion. Mount Kreion is unidentified, as are the Pallatides, evidently named for Pallas.

53. *Danaos:* Danaos was the twin brother of Aigyptos, a king of Egypt. Danaos had
fifty daughters, the Danaïds, and Aigyptos had fifty sons. Aigyptos ordered his sons to
marry the Danaïds, but Danaos fled to Argos, to which he was connected because of his
descent from Io, daughter of the river Inachos, a priestess of Hera at Argos. Zeus had
loved Io, but Hera turned her into a cow that wandered to EGYPT, where she resumed
human form and founded a dynasty. When Danaos arrived at Argos, the city was ruled

55   will arrive from the nourishing mountains bringing beautiful
      bath-water for Athena. But you, O Pelasgian,
   be careful that all unwitting you do not see the queen,
      for whoever sees Pallas, the savior of cities,
   when she is naked will see this city of Argos
60   for the very last time.°
                  Lady Athena,
   do come forth while I say something to these women.
      The tale is not my own, but I got it
   from others.°
           Girls, once upon a time in Thebes,
      Athena loved one nymph above all
65   the others, the mother of Teiresias,° and they were
      never apart. When Athena would drive
   her horses off to ancient Thespiai [*several words are corrupt*]
      or to Haliartos, crossing the tilled
   fields of the Boeotians—or to Koroneia, where her fragrant
70   grove and altars stood on the banks
   of the Kouralios river°—the goddess would often place her
      on her chariot. The whisperings of the nymphs

---

by Pelasgos, but Danaos claimed the kingship because of his descent. Aigyptos then arrived with his fifty sons to claim their brides, but Danaos told his daughters to kill their husbands on their wedding night. Forty-nine did, but one, Hypermnestra, did not, because her husband honored her wish to remain virgin. Hypermnestra then began a dynasty of Argive rulers. Two of the daughters were named Phusadeia ("abundant") and Amumonê ("blameless"). The location of the spring of Phusadeia is unknown, but Amumonê was a major Argive source of water.

56–60. *you, O Pelasgian . . . last time:* "Pelasgian" here means "any Argive male": males are forbidden to view the rites. Callimachus warns males against espying the statue when it is undressed to be bathed in the Inachos river, then tells the story of Teiresias to illustrate his point.

62–63. *The tale is not my own . . . from others:* That is, the story Callimachus is about to tell is not common property, as was the story about the Judgment of Paris, but was received from an arcane source, probably a (lost) historian of the city of Argos.

65. *mother of Teiresias:* Chariklo, whom Callimachus will soon mention.

67–71. *ancient Thespiai . . . Kouralios river:* The towns of Thespiai, Haliartos, and Koroneia, and the Kouralios river, are on the northern and eastern slopes of MOUNT HELIKON in BOEOTIA. There were cults to Athena in all three town.

and ordering of their dances were never sweet when
 Chariklo was not leading them.
75 But many tears awaited her, although she was the heartfelt
 companion to Athena.
        One day the two
of them, having loosed the pins of their robes, bathed
 in the beautiful flowing waters of the Spring
of the Horse on HELIKON.° The peace of midday had fallen
80 on the mountain. Both were bathing,
the midday hours had come, and great peace held that
 mountain. Teiresias alone, with his hounds,
his beard just then ripening, came to the holy spot.
 Unspeakably thirsty, he went up to the gushing
85 spring—poor thing! He did not want to, but he saw
 what must not be seen!°
       In a rage,
Athena nonetheless spoke to him: "What ill fortune
 has led you down this harsh path,
O son of Eueres,° who will never recover sight
90 in your eyes?"
      So she spoke, and night fell
on the boy's eyes. He stood there speechless,
 his knees were in pain, and his voice had
no sound. But the nymph shouted out: "Goddess, what
95 have you done to my boy? Is this
the sort of friendship you can expect from goddesses?
 You have taken away sight from
my son's eyes. Child, you are accursed! You have
 seen the breast and thighs of Athena,
100 but you will never again see the light of the sun.
 I am wretched! O mountain,

73–74. *Spring of the Horse on* HELIKON: The Spring of the Horse (Hippocrene) is mentioned by Hesiod in the opening lines of his *Theogony* (1–8). It was sacred to the Muses, formed by Pegasos striking the ground with his hooves. The water was supposed to bring forth poetic inspiration.

86. *what must not be seen:* That is, he saw Athena naked.

89. *Eueres:* The father of Teiresias, by Chariklo. Nothing else is known of him.

O Helikon, where I may never come again!
    You have taken a great price
    for a little loss—a few gazelle and deer, but you have
105   taken the light from my son."
Then the mother took up her beloved son in both
    her arms and, bewailing the sad lament
    of nightingales, she led him away.
                                    But the goddess
    took pity on her companion and Athena
110 spoke the following words: "Bright lady,
    take back all that you have said
    in anger. It is not I who made your son blind.
    It is no sweet thing for Athena
    to take away the sight of children. It is the laws of Kronos°
115   that have stated thus: 'Whoever gazes on
    an immortal where that god has not chosen, he sees
    at a great price.' Bright lady, the deed
    is not reversible in the future, for the threads
    of the Fates have woven it so when you
120 first gave birth to him. Now take the payment
    that is owed to you, O son of Eueres.
    How many burnt offerings will the daughter of Kadmos
    make in later times, how many
    will Aristaios make, praying that their only son,
125   the youthful Aktaion, will only be blind?°
    And he will hunt with great Artemis, but neither
    their running together in the mountains,
    nor their shared skill in archery, will save him when,
    though he did not mean to, he saw

---

114. *Kronos:* Kronos was the just lawgiver who ruled over the Golden Age (see for example, Plato, *Laws* 713a–14a).

124–25. *praying that . . . will only be blind:* Aktaion's parents would wish this because, instead of just being blinded for seeing a goddess naked, Aktaion will be torn apart by his own hounds. The daughter of Kadmos of THEBES, Aktaion's mother, is Aristonoê. His father, Aristaios, is the son of the nymph Cyrenê and Apollo (see Callimachus' *Hymn to Apollo*). Aktaion sees Artemis naked while she is bathing and she curses him with this terrible punishment.

130 the lovely bath of the goddess. His bitches will devour
        their former master. His mother
    will explore through all the brush, gathering the bones
        of her son. *You* she will declare to be
    most happy and blessed, because you received your son
135   from the mountains—though blind.
        O my companion, do not lament! For to your son
        —on your account, from me—many
    gifts shall remain, because I shall make him a prophet,
        the subject of song for men of the future.
140 He will be greater by far than all the others. He will
        understand the flight of birds, which
    are of good omen, which fly without meaning, and which
        fly with ill omen. He will give many
    prophecies to the Boeotians, and many to Kadmos
145   and, later, many to the Labdakids.°
        And I will give him a great staff, which will guide his feet
        where he wishes to go, and I will give
    him a long limit to his life, and he alone, when he dies,
        will go among the dead as a sentient
150 being, honored by the great Leader of the Peoples.°
        Thus she spoke and nodded her assent.

    145. *Labdakids:* "The sons of Labdakos," that is, the Thebans. Labdakos was the
grandson of Kadmos and the grandfather of Oedipus.
    148–50. *he alone, when he dies . . . Leader of the Peoples:* When Odysseus descends to
the underworld, he sees that Teiresias alone retains his cognitive functions and pro-
phetic powers in that place (*Odyssey* 10.494–95). "Leader of the People" (Agesilaos) is
Hades, also called "He Who Receives Many" (Poludegmon) and other euphemisms.
Teiresias lived for seven generations in Thebes, starting out as an advisor to Kadmos. In
another traditional adventure he changed his sex. Teiresias came on two copulating
snakes, hit them with his staff, and was transformed into a woman. As a woman, Teire-
sias married and had children. After seven years "she" again came on a pair of copulat-
ing snakes, struck them again, and was turned back into a man. In a separate account of
the origin of his blindness and longevity, he was drawn into an argument between Hera
and Zeus about who had the most pleasure in sex. Hera said that, of course, the man
did, but Zeus said that the woman had more pleasure. Teiresias, having experienced
both, said: "Of ten parts, a man enjoys one part only." For saying this Hera struck him
blind, and Zeus, in recompense, gave him the gift of prophecy and a long life. Teiresias
appears as a venerable Theban prophet in several Greek tragedies. He died after drink-
ing water from a tainted spring.

What Pallas nodded to, came to pass, because Zeus gave
    this to Athena, alone of his daughters,
that she should possess all things that belong to her father.°
155   O pourers of the bath, no mother bore
    the goddess, but she came from Zeus's head. The head
      of Zeus does not nod assent to falsehoods,
    <and neither does>° his daughter.
                              Athena is really
    coming now!° Receive the god,
160 O girls, it is your task! With fair speech, with prayers,
    with joyous cries! Hail, O goddess!
Have a care for Inachian Argos!° Hail, when you drive
    forth your mares, and when you drive
them back again, and save the estate of the Danaäns!°

ORPHIC HYMN 32: TO ATHENA

The hymnist prays for the benefaction of Athena, slayer of the Giants.

Pallas,° only begotten one, reverend child of Zeus,
blessed shining goddess who raises the din of war,
strong in spirit, warlike, celebrated, great of name,
dweller in caves, who traverses the rocky hilltops
5   and shadowy mountains—you delight in the valleys!
You delight in arms, stinging the souls of men
with madness!
               O athletic maid, with a shivery heart!

---

154. *all things that belong to her father:* Whatever Zeus nodded to, came to pass.

158. *<and neither does>:* Words are missing here, but this must be the meaning.

159. *coming now:* The statue arrives on the cart.

162. *Inachian Argos:* Inachos is both the river in which the statue will be washed and the founder of the line that led to Danaos.

164. *Danaäns:* The descendants of Danaos, the Argives.

1. *Pallas:* The common epithet is of unknown etymology, though it was often explained as deriving from *pallô,* "to brandish" or "shake." In Orphic literature it was said to refer to Athena as the one who saved the heart of Dionysos while it was still "shaking," that is, beating.

FIGURE 7. Athena, by the Brygos Painter. The goddess holds a helmet and a spear. She wears the aegis, "the goat-skin fetish," a shawl with a fringe of serpents and a central blazon of the Gorgon's head. An owl, her emblem, flies to the left. Athenian red-figure oil-jar, c. 490 BC. Metropolitan Museum of Art, New York. Photograph © Marie-Lan Nguyen / Creative Commons.

Killer of Gorgo,° you flee the marriage bed,
rich mother of the arts.° Impetuous, you bring frenzy
10   to the wicked and wisdom to the good. You are male,
and you are female, clever begetter of war.
Changeable in shape, she-dragon, lover of inspired
frenzy, splendidly honored, destroyer of the Phlegraian
Giants,° driver of horses, Tritogeneia° looser
15   from evils, victory-bringing spirit, flashing-eyed, inventor
of the arts, queen who are sought with many prayers
during the day and the night into the wee hours—
hear me as I pray! Give me the wealth of peace!
And riches, and health amidst happy seasons.

PROCLUS HYMN 7: TO WISE ATHENA

*Because Athena was born from the head of Zeus, she is the goddess of
wisdom. Armed with shield and spear, she is the protector of cities and so
received the Acropolis in Athens as her place of devotion. She does not
apply her cleverness to war alone, but also to the ability to do things of all
kinds: she is goddess of handicrafts. She presides over Athens where Hep-
haistos attacked her, spilling semen on her thigh. She wiped off the fluid
and threw it to the ground, whence sprang up the Athenians. The Parthe-
non and older temples on the Acropolis honored her, as did the annual
festival of the Panathenaia. As goddess of wisdom, she presides over the
philosophical search for truth, the quest to obtain knowledge of Nous
rather than the false knowledge of the material world, with its passions
and temptations.*

8. *Killer of Gorgo:* In the battle between the gods and the giants Athena killed the
giant Gorgo and stripped him of his breastplate bordered with snakes, the origin of the
aegis that Zeus and Athena carry. She also killed giants named Pallas (some think she
derived her epithet from this giant) and Enkelados.

9. *mother of the arts:* Athena was not only a goddess of war, but sponsored every
kind of craftsmanship, including the building of the Trojan Horse and the ship *Argo*.

13–14. *Phlegraian Giants:* The battle between the gods and the Giants was localized
in Phlegra, an ancient name for the westernmost of the three peninsulas that constitute
CHALCIDICE in THRACE.

Hear me, child of Zeus who carries the aegis,
sprung from the fatherly fountain and the summit of series,°
with a male's spirit, shield-bearing, most powerful, from a mighty
father—Pallas, Tritogeneia, lance-brandisher, golden-helmeted°—
5   hear me! Receive this song with a kind spirit, my lady.
Do not let my word pass in vain to the winds, you who
opened the gates of wisdom walked through by the gods,
who once conquered the tribes of earth-born Giants
who fought against the gods°—you who fled the desire

2. *series:* The Greek word is *seira*—cord, chain, series—a technical term in Neoplatonism that depends on an allegorical interpretation of the golden "chain" (*Iliad* 8.19), where Zeus boasts that if he suspended a golden *seira* from heaven with all the gods tugging at the lower end and Zeus at the upper end, they could still not drag Zeus down to the earth. A Neoplatonic *seira* is a group of entities that depends on a cause, hence shares in a quality characteristic of that group. Zeus is the Demiurge, the creator subordinate to the One, who contains in himself all causes, which emanate from him: he is thus "the summit of series." The first phase of these emanations are the leader-gods, the *henads* (see the Introduction), including Athena, who stand at the head of the series of entities, all of which share in its distinctive characteristics.

4. *lance-brandisher, golden-helmeted:* Complex explanations are given for these epithets in Neoplatonic thinking, and are summed up in Proclus' commentary to Plato's *Timaeus:* "[Athena] is a war-lover because she upholds the oppositions in the universe and because she is an unconquered and ruthless god. Therefore, she keeps Dionysos pure, battles down the Giants along with her father Zeus, moves the aegis all by herself without orders from Zeus, and casts her spear, 'by means of which she overcomes the ranks of heroes, against whom the daughter of a mighty father is angry'" (see *Iliad* 8.390, *Odyssey* 1.100).

8–9. *Giants who fought against the gods:* According to a Neoplatonic allegorical interpretation, the Giants stood for the material world and the gods for the Platonic Forms *(eidea)* that are the basis of the material world and that emanate from the Demiurge. Athena is a "lover of wisdom" because she is the thought of the Demiurge. She is a lover of war because a war is going on between the material world, represented by the Giants, and the eternal immaterial Forms, represented by the gods, which constantly threaten to mingle with the material world. Athena does not allow the Forms to be contaminated by matter. The war between the Olympians (the intelligible world, the world perceived by the intellect) and the Giants (the material world) takes place not only in the universe as a whole, but also in the human soul, which is attracted to the material side of existence (the realm of the Giants) and forgetful of its spiritual side (the Olympian realm). Athena, then, goddess of wisdom, inspires us to flee the material realm and seek the divine world.

10   of the lustful Hephaistos and preserved the unconquerable
      girdle of your virginity;° who spared the heart of Lord Bacchus,
      not yet chopped up at the hands of the Titans in the halls
      of the upper air, when once upon a time they divided
      up his body. And you brought it to his father so that,
15   through the unspoken words of his begetter,° a new Dionysos
      might arise from Semelê and grow all around the cosmos.°
      Your axe, by slashing away at the roots the heads of all-seeing
      Hekatê's animals of passion, has put becoming to sleep.°
      You have loved the holy strength of the virtues that awaken
20   mankind;° you have interjected our whole life with all kinds
      of skills, thrusting into our souls the craftsmanship that leads
      to knowledge of Mind;° you have received the Acropolis of Athens,

9–11. *who fled the desire . . . virginity:* Hephaistos was overcome with desire for Athena
and chased her across the Acropolis. She fought him off, but his semen fell on her thigh.
Athena, in disgust, wiped it away with a scrap of wool *(erion)* and flung it to the earth
(chthôn): hence Erichthonios, future king of Athens, sprang up from the earth. Athena
placed the infant Erichthonios in a box and gave the box to the three daughters of Kekrops,
then the king of ATHENS, and warned them never to look inside. They did anyway and were
terrified by what they saw: a snake wrapped around the infant or a child that was half-
human and half-serpent. The daughters of Kekrops went insane and committed suicide by
throwing themselves off the Acropolis. Athena's preservation of her virginity stands, in the
Neoplatonist interpretation, for her remaining undefiled by contact with matter.

15. *his begetter:* That is, Zeus.

15–16. *a new Dionysos . . . around the cosmos:* These verses refer to the Orphic myth
of Dionysos. The Titans enticed the young Dionysos with a mirror and other gewgaws
attractive to a child. They then cut him into pieces and boiled the pieces in a pot, but
Athena rescued the still beating heart and carried it to Zeus, who served it in a soup to
Semelê, a Theban princess. She became pregnant and gave birth to Dionysos. In the
Neoplatonist interpretation, the Titans represent the material world and the dismem-
bered Dionysos its manifold objects, united however by the heart of Dionysos, which
represents Nous or intellect, whose emanations "grow all around the cosmos."

17–18. *Your axe . . . to sleep:* Athena is never portrayed with an axe (her weapon is
always a spear) and the myth of her slaying the animals of Hekatê is otherwise unknown.
Hekatê, ordinarily goddess of witchcraft and the dark arts, must here represent the
temptations of the material world. Athena slays Hekatê's animals because through Ath-
ena's power the products of the harmful material world are overcome.

19–20. *the virtues that awaken mankind:* According to Socrates, virtue is knowledge;
Athena makes knowledge of the eternal Forms possible.

21–22. *craftsmanship that leads to knowledge of Mind:* Handicrafts used in everyday
life are an expression of divine creative activity at the level of Nous (Mind).

FIGURE 8. The Erechtheion in Athens. Built entirely of marble on the Acropolis between 421 and 406 BC, it was designed by Phidias, the architect of the Parthenon, and is named after the Greek hero Erechtheus. In this complex building was kept the Palladion, the magical statue of Athena. The marks of Poseidon's trident were visible through an opening in the north porch (left of picture). A replanting of Athena's sacred olive tree by Sophia of Prussia, granddaughter of Queen Victoria, is visible in the forefront. On the south side (right of picture) is the famous Porch of the Maidens *(karyatids)*. The building enclosed the graves of Kekrops and Erechtheus (an early king, confused with Erichthonios) and the daughters of Kekrops. Photo by M. M / Creative Commons.

    on its high-crested hill, as a symbol, O lady, of your being
    at the top of your great series; you, who loved the land
25   that nourishes men, the mother of books, who resisted
    with power the holy lust of your father's brother, you gave
    the city to have your name and your fine mind—there,
    at the topmost edge of the mountain you made an olive
    tree bloom as a clear symbol of battle for those who came

28–32. *an olive tree bloom . . . much-resounding waves:* Athena and Poseidon were rivals for control of Athens. The contest took place on the Acropolis. Poseidon struck the rock with his trident and produced a salt spring, but Athena, who brought forth an olive tree, was proclaimed the victor. In fact the olive was the foundation of the Athenian economy. Angry at losing, Poseidon sent a monstrous flood over the Attic plain. The depression made by Poseidon's trident lay beneath the northern hall of the Erechtheion, visible through a hole in the masonry.

30 after, when at the direction of Poseidon a huge wave
    rolled up from the sea and came on the children of Kekrops,
    lashing everything with its much-resounding waves.°
        Hear me, from whose face shines forth a holy light!
    Give me a happy harbor as I wander over the earth!
35 Give to my soul a holy light from your sacred myths
    —and give me wisdom and love! Breathe into my love
    a strength so great and of such a nature that it draws
    me back from the earthly bosom into the realm of your
    father on Olympos. And if some grievous fault in my life
40 overcomes me—for I know I am beset from every side
    by unholy acts, thoughtlessly committed—well, be gracious!
        You are a goddess with mild counsels, a savior of
            mortals.
    Do not let me become prey and spoil for shivery
    punishments, face down on the ground, because I say
45 that I belong to you. Give a firm and painless health
    to my limbs. Drive away the herds of bitter flesh-melting
    sickness, yes, I beg you, O queen, and stop with your
    immortal hand every wretchedness of black pain. Give
    me calm winds as I journey through life, children, a wife,
50 happiness, lovely joy, the power to persuade, conversation
    with friends, a clever spirit, strength against my enemies,
    prominence among the people.
                            Hear, hear, O queen!
    I come to you with earnest supplication, out of pressing
    necessity. And you—lend me a gentle ear!

5

Demeter, Persephone, and Hades

Demeter and her daughter Persephone were conjoined in cult and myth and called simply the Two Goddesses. Demeter was the goddess of the growth of wheat and was widely adored in Greece. Her name should mean "wheat-mother," or "earth-mother," but the *De-* portion of the name cannot be explained in this way and remains a mystery. Similarly, the name Persephone is opaque. While it is common in literature, usually in cult contexts she is called simply Korê, "young girl" or "maiden." In many accounts she is conjoined with her husband Hades as queen of the dead and was in many cults recognized as such. In the pairing of Demeter and Persephone/Korê, Greek religion recognizes the complementarity of life and death: You can't have one without the other.

HOMERIC HYMN 2: TO DEMETER

"Homeric Hymn 2: To Demeter" tells the foundation story of the famous cult at ELEUSIS, where initiates were promised a happier afterlife than those uninitiated in the mysteries. The hymn tells how Zeus approved the marriage of his brother Hades, lord of the underworld, to Persephone, here called Korê. Hades snatched her up in his chariot as she played in the Nisaean field (an unknown location) as she was about to pluck a flower with a hundred blooms. Still today we are familiar with the image of the loss of virginity as the "plucking" of a maidenhead. Her mother, Demeter, did not know where she was, but Hekatê, a powerful

goddess, heard Korê cry out. Demeter and Hekatê went to Helios, who sees all, and learned what had happened.

Demeter wandered about, looking for Korê, and came to Eleusis, a town about thirteen miles west of Athens, disguised as an old lady. She sat by a well. Princesses from the palace saw the disguised Demeter and hired her as a nurse to the young prince of the house, Demophoön. She entered the palace, where she sat silently on a chair covered by a fleece. Demeter drank a beverage, called kykeon, *made from barley. Every night she placed Demophoön in the fire to burn away his mortal parts but the child's mother, Metaneira, surprised them one night and cried out in horror. Demeter threw the child to the ground and revealed her true identity, ending the child's purification. She commanded that a temple be built in her honor.*

Then Demeter continued her wandering, bringing barrenness to the world. Henceforth people would starve and the gods be deprived of sacrifice. To appease the angry goddess, Zeus ordered that Korê be released from the underworld. Mother and daughter were joyfully reunited, but Korê could not be wholly restored because she had eaten a pomegranate seed that Hades gave her in the underworld, a blood-red fruit associated with death. Therefore Korê would spend two-thirds of the year in the upper world and a third below in the house of Hades.

Various details of the myth foreshadow practices in the Eleusinian cult, although they do not reveal what actually happened inside the mysteries: To divulge the ritual was punishable by death, and in one thousand years of the cult's vitality the secret rites were never revealed, although the Eleusinian Mysteries were the most famous of the religious rites of ancient Greece. From various sources, including the "Homeric Hymn to Demeter," however, we can reconstruct some external details of the rite.

Initiations were held every year. The cult seems to have originated in the Mycenaean period (c. 1600–c. 1100 BC), perhaps as an agrarian ritual designed to foster the fecundity of the wheat crop, but nothing certain is known about its origins. The name Eleusis is pre-Greek, probably related to Elysium, the blissful afterworld, and perhaps also to the name of the birth-goddess Eileithyia. The story of the hymn reflects the ritual, which in some way reenacted Hades' abduction of Demeter's daughter, Demeter's search for her child, and Persephone's return to the upper world and her mother, bringing back fertility to the earth according to the seasonal pattern. By extension, by participating in the rite one would

FIGURE 9. The Eleusinian Mysteries. This plaque, from c. 370 BC, found at Eleusis, is a principal source for what little information we have about the Mysteries. The figures are placed on two levels. In the upper right Demeter sits on a chest. Persephone stands before her holding a torch. Beneath her is Iakchos with a torch: Iakchos is the personification of the ritual cry *Iakchê!,* made during the Eleusinian procession from Athens to Eleusis. He greets the initiates, both men and women, who arrive at the sanctuary. Below, in the center, is an *omphalos* ("navel") with a garland on top and two *bachoi,* branches that initiates swung on the ground as they walked along the Sacred Way from Athens to Eleusis. These objects seem to symbolize the hidden rituals of the cult. The identity of the woman sitting to the right of the *omphalos,* pouring out a libation *(kykeon?)* is not clear; perhaps she is a priestess. The plaque represents the night festival when a flute player, on the lower left (the flute he holds is not visible), accompanies the procession. All the participants are crowned and hold flowering branches and staffs. The women have *kernoi* on their heads, round vessels containing cups for offerings. The figure in the center of the triangle above the scene has been interpreted as the Moon (?), with adorants. The inscription at the bottom says, "Niinnion dedicated this." Red-figure plaque. National Archaeological Museum, Athens. Photograph © Marsyas / Creative Commons.

experience a renewal of one's personal life, a foretaste of personal salvation. A person initiated into the cult's truths would not have to fear death—he or she would not hope for immortality, but be sure of a happy fate in the underworld. The cult was popular during the classical period and, later, under Roman domination. The Roman emperor Theodosius I closed the sanctuary at Eleusis in AD 392.

The mysteries were controlled by two families, the Eumolpidai, "good singers," and the Kerykês, "heralds." The only requirements for initiation into the mysteries were freedom from blood guilt—that is, murderers were not allowed—and an ability to speak Greek. Initiation was open to men and women, and even to slaves. Everyone swore a vow of secrecy.

The mysteries were divided into two parts, the "Lesser" and the "Greater." The Lesser Mysteries were held in early spring. Participants sacrificed a piglet to Demeter and Persephone/Korê and ritually purified themselves in a river in ATHENS. *Having completed the Lesser Mysteries, participants were* mystai *("initiates") and eligible for the Greater Mysteries, which took place in late summer and lasted for ten days.*

The first act in the Greater Mysteries was the bringing of sacred objects from Eleusis to the Eleusinion, a temple at the base of the Acropolis of Athens. The Eleusinian priests opened the rites with a sacrifice. The mystai *washed themselves in the sea. A festival was celebrated and a feast held that lasted all night. A procession to Eleusis began at the Athenian cemetery just outside the walls of the city. The people walked along a road called the "Sacred Way," swinging branches. At one spot, where they crossed a bridge, the procession was met by masked celebrants who shouted obscenities at the passersby, in* aischrologia, *"dirty talking," evidently in commemoration of Iambê who, in the hymn, had made Demeter smile. The procession also shouted the ritual cry "Iakchê, O Iakchê!"*

When they reached Eleusis, the participants celebrated an all-night vigil in memory of Demeter's search for Persephone. They drank the kykeon. *On the next day, the initiates entered a great columned hall called the Telesterion (see figure 10) in the center of which stood the Anaktoron ("palace"), a small, oblong room off-center in the Telesterion with a door on one of the long sides. Only the hierophant, the "revealer of sacred things," could enter the Anaktoron. Sacred objects were stored there. There was a sacred chest (kistê) and a lidded basket (kalathos) but what these contained is unknown.*

FIGURE 10. Hades abducting Persephone/Korê. The lord of death holds the reins of his horses with his right hand while with his left he carries off the half-naked Persephone, his hand cupping her breast. She stretches out her arms helplessly. The plundered tomb in which this painting was found may have belonged to a queen of the Macedonian royal family. In a nearby tomb was found the intact burial of what many think to be the bones of Philip II, the father of Alexander the Great, one of the most sensational archaeological finds of the twentieth century. Fresco wall painting in the small royal tomb at Vergina, Macedonia, c. 350–200 BC.

The rites inside the Telesterion had three elements: the dromena *("things done"), evidently a dramatic reenactment of the Demeter/Persephone myth; the* deiknumena *("things shown"), when sacred objects— perhaps among them a grain of wheat—were displayed from the* kistê *and the* kalathos; *and the* legomena *("things said"), which accompanied the things shown. Nothing more is known about these rites.*

Then there was another all-night feast. A bull was killed and there was much dancing and general merriment. These superficial features do not, however, reveal what actually happened in the initiation ceremony, which is still a "mystery."

This hymn may have been performed at Eleusis, perhaps at the games that were held there three out of four years. By the fourth century BC, Orpheus was alleged to be the founder of the Eleusinian rite, and a papyrus survives, allegedly by Orpheus, that quotes passages from this hymn, a sort of official explanation of the cult. But the hymn is much older than that. It never mentions Athens, so most scholars date the hymn before the adoption of the rite by the Athenian politician Peisistratus in the sixth century BC (he died c. 528 BC). But there is no certainty.

> I sing first of Demeter of the sweet tresses, blessed goddess—
> I sing of her and her slender-ankled daughter, whom Hades
> snatched away; for deep-thundering wide-sounding Zeus
> granted it as she played with the deep-bosomed daughters
> 5 of Ocean,° apart from Demeter of the golden sword,°
> of glorious fruit, while she plucked flowers in the soft meadow
> —roses and crocus and beautiful violets and iris and hyacinth
> and narcissus° that Earth sent up as a trap for the girl,
> with eyes like blossoms, fulfilling the will of Zeus
> 10 and pleasing the Receiver of Many°—an amazing, radiant
> flower, awesome for all to see, for the deathless gods

3–5. *Zeus granted it . . . daughters of Ocean:* As the father of Persephone, Zeus's consent is required for her marriage. The daughters of Ocean are nymphs of the sea, the Oceanids, who often care for the young.

5. *golden sword:* Why Demeter should carry a golden sword has never been explained.

8. *narcissus:* A kind of daffodil.

10. *Receiver of Many:* A euphemism for Hades.

and for mortal humans. From its root grew one hundred
blooms, and its scent was most sweet, and all the broad sky
above and all the earth laughed and the salty swell of the sea.

15   She was amazed and reached out both her hands
to pluck the lovely delight. But the wide-wayed earth
opened up in the plain of Nysa,° and the Lord Receiver of Many
leaped out at her with his deathless horses, the son
of Kronos who has many names. He seized her all-unwilling

20   in his golden car and carried her away, lamenting.
She gave a shrill cry, calling out to her father, the son
of Kronos, the highest and best. But no one of the deathless
ones, nor of mortal humans, heard her cry, not the olive
trees bright with fruit, except the daughter of Persaios,°

25   tender in her mind, heard the girl from her cave, Hekatê°
with her bright headband, and Lord Helios, the glorious
son of Hyperion,° as the daughter called out to her father,
the son of Kronos. But he was sitting aloof, apart
from the gods in his temple where many pray, receiving

30   beautiful offerings from mortal humans.

And so the girl's
uncle, the son of Kronos who has many names—the Ruler
of Many, the Receiver of Many—carried her away all
unwilling on his deathless horses at the prompting of Zeus.

So long as the goddess looked on the earth and the starry sky,

35   and the violent fish-filled sea and the rays of the sun, and she still
hoped to see her dear mother and the tribes of the gods
who live forever, for so long hope calmed her great heart,
in spite of her anguish. And the peaks of the mountains echoed
and the depths of the sea at her deathless cry.

Her revered

---

17. *Nysa:* A mythical place, often associated with Dionysos.

24. *Persaios:* An obscure Titan.

25. *Hekatê:* Etymology unknown. She is a great goddess with an ambivalent relationship to the Olympians, often considered protective in cult contexts and, later, seen as goddess of witchcraft and the crossroads (see hymns to Hekatê, chapter 14).

27. *Hyperion:* "He who goes over," a Titan sun-god.

FIGURE 11. Old photo of the ruins of the Telesterion, the great hall of initiation at Eleusis. The Telesterion was a forest of enclosed columns surrounded by steps on which the initiates stood, visible here. Beyond the temple, at the top of the picture, is the sea and the island of SALAMIS. The Maiden's Well was located to the left of the picture, outside the great temple. From R. S. Hichens and J. V. Guérin, *The Near East; Dalmatia, Greece and Constantinople* (London, Hodder and Stoughton, 1913).

40   mother heard her, and right away a sharp pain seized
      her heart, and she tore her veil from off her immortal locks
      with her dear hands. She cast a dark cloak about both
      her shoulders and rushed as a bird over dry land and sea,
      seeking her daughter. But no one of the gods, nor of mortal men,
45   nor of the birds, was willing to tell her the truth.
          Then for nine days revered Deo° wandered over the earth
      holding blazing torches in her hands,° and in her grief
      she did not taste ambrosia or sweet nectar,° nor did she bathe
      her flesh with water. But when the tenth brilliant dawn had come,
50   Hekatê met her, holding a torch in her hands, and she spoke
      and addressed her with the news:
                              "Lady Demeter, bringer of seasons,
      giver of splendid things, who of the heavenly gods or of mortal
      men has snatched Persephone and given anguish to your
      dear heart? I heard her cry, but I did not see with my eyes
55   who it was. Swiftly I tell you all the truth."
                                          So spoke Hekatê.
      But Demeter spoke no word in reply, the daughter of well-tressed
      Rhea, but right away she rushed off with Hekatê, carrying
      blazing torches in her hands.
                              They came to Helios,
      the watchman of gods and men, and they stood before
60   his chariot, and the divine goddess asked:
                                          "O Helios,
      do show me respect, as a god to a goddess, if ever
      in word or deed I have pleased your heart and your spirit.
      The daughter whom I bore, my sweet child, famed for her beauty
      —I heard her loud cry through the unresting air, as if
65   she was seized, but I did not see her with my eyes. But you
      look down over all the earth and the sea from the shining air
      with your rays—tell me then, truly, of my child, if perhaps

---

46. *Deo:* Another name for Demeter, probably a shortened form.

47. *holding blazing torches in her hands:* Celebrants of the Eleusinian Mysteries carried torches too in a nighttime procession (see figure 9).

48. *ambrosia or sweet nectar:* Ambrosia is the food of the gods and nectar is their drink.

you saw who of gods or mortal men took her away
from me by force, all unwilling, and made off with her."
70   So she spoke, and the son of Hyperion answered her
in this way: "O daughter of well-tressed Rhea, Queen Demeter,
you shall know, for I greatly respect you and I take pity
on you grieving for your slim-ankled child. Nor is one
of the gods responsible, except for Zeus the cloud-gatherer
75 who gave her to Hades to be called the blooming wife
of his own brother. He snatched her and carried her away
in his chariot, loudly crying, down to his realm of mist
and darkness.
           "But goddess, cease from your great lament.
Nor is there a need for you constantly to feel vast
80 and vain anger. For Hades, the Ruler of Many, is not
an unseemly husband among the deathless ones. He is your own
brother and of the same stock. In the division at the beginning
he received one third part as his realm, and was made lord
of those among whom he dwells."
                So speaking, he called out
85 to his horses, and at his shout quickly they bore his swift chariot,
like long-winged birds. But anguish more bitter and savage
came into the heart of Demeter. Enraged at the son
of Kronos, the cloud-gatherer, she avoided the assembly
of the gods and tall Olympos. She went into the cities of men
90 and their rich fields, disguising her appearance for a long time.
No one of men nor of deep-bosomed women recognized
her when they saw her, until she came to the house
of wise Keleos, who at that time was the lord of Eleusis,
whose scent was fragrant.
             Grieving in her heart, she sat close
95 to the road, near the Maiden's Well, from where the women
of the city drew their water. She sat in the shade where a thick
olive grew in the likeness of an old woman full of years,
past child-bearing, who lacks the gift of children and of garland-loving
Aphrodite, like the nurses of the children of justice-dealing kings,
100 or like their housekeepers through their echoing halls.
      The daughters of Keleos, son of Eleusis, saw her when they

came out to fetch water, easy to draw, that they might carry
it in bronze jars to the house of their dear father. There were four
of them, like goddesses, in the flower of youth—Kallidikê
105 and Kleisidikê and lovely Demo and Kallithoê,° who was
the eldest of all of them. They did not recognize her,
for gods are not easily discerned by mortals. They stood
near her and spoke winged words:
                                        "Who are you? Where
do you come from, old woman, of folk born long ago?
110 Why have you come far from the city, and do not
go near the houses where women of just your age stalk
through the shadowy halls, and others who are younger?
For they would welcome you both in word and deed."
       So they spoke, and the revered goddess answered them
115 in this way: "My dear children, whoever you are of blooming
women—greetings. I will tell you, for it is not improper to tell
the truth to you who have asked. My name is Doso.°
My revered mother gave me this name. I have come from CRETE
over the broad back of the sea, not willingly but unwillingly,
120 forced by violence. Pirates carried me off. And then they
put in with their swift ship at Thorikos,° where the women
disembarked on the shore in a group and the men too.
They prepared a meal near the ship's stern, but I had no desire
for delicious food, and in secret I set out across the darkened land,
125 fleeing my arrogant masters, that they might not transport
me unsold and profit from selling me for a good price.
       "And so I have come wandering here, and I do not know
what land I have come to and who these people are.
But I pray to all who have houses on Olympos, that they
135 give you wedded husbands and the birth of children,
as parents desire. Only take pity on me, maidens,
<and tell me>° clearly, dear children, so that I may know:

104–5. *Kallidikê and Kleisidikê and lovely Demo and Kallithoê:* "Beautiful Justice,"
"Famous Justice," "People," and "Beautiful Swift" are names probably invented by the poet.
     117. *Doso:* "I will give" in Greek, an appropriate name for a goddess of bounty.
     121. *Thorikos:* On the northeast coast of Attica, a natural landing place for boats from
Crete. A small temple to Demeter/Persephone has been found there.

To the house of what man or woman I may go to work
for them, cheerfully, at whatever tasks are suitable for a woman
140 my age? I might well nurse a newborn child, holding him
in my arms, or care for a house, and make up my master's
bed in a cranny of the well-made chamber, and teach
women their work."
                                   So spoke the goddess. And right away
the unwed maiden Kallidikê answered, the most beautiful
145 of the daughters of Keleos:
                                   "Mother, we humans have no choice
but to bear by necessity what the gods give us, though
we grieve. For they are far stronger. And now I will clearly
set before you these things, and name who among men
holds the power of office here and looks after the people
150 and guards the battlements of the city with their sagacity
and their righteous judgments. Wise Triptolemos and Diokles
and Poluxeinos and blameless Eumolpos and Dolichos
and our own noble father°—all these have wives who manage
the house. Not one of them, once they had seen you,
155 would show you disrespect and turn you away from the house,
but they would take you in. For you are like unto a god.
    "Now stay here, if you want, so that we can go to the house
of our father, and tell our deep bosomed Mother Metaneira
all of this, thoroughly, in the hope she might urge you to come
160 to our house and not seek out the houses of others. She has
a darling son, late-born, who is being nursed in her well-built

---

137. <*and tell me*>: There is something wrong with the text here.

151–53. *Wise Triptolemos . . . noble father:* In this hymn Triptolemos (perhaps "thrice-plowed") is just a leader of Eleusis, but in later Athenian propaganda he became a culture-hero who traveled throughout the world teaching the benefits of agriculture, whose secrets Demeter had divulged to him (see figure 14). Diokles ("famous because of Zeus") is a hero associated with the city of MEGARA. Poluxeinos ("entertaining many guests") is a shadowy figure. Eumolpos ("good singer") gives his name to the Eumolpidai, the family of priests who controlled the Eleusinian cult during the classical period; he initiated Herakles before his descent into the underworld. Little is known about Dolichos ("long race"). The father's name, Keleos, may mean something like "ship commander."

hall, a child for which she prayed long, who is most welcome.
If you could raise him up until he reaches the full measure
of youth, then any woman who saw you would easily be filled
165 with envy, so great are the gifts our mother would give you
for raising him."

So she spoke, and the goddess bowed her head
in assent. And the girls, filling their shining vases with water,
carried them off, exulting. Quickly they came to the great house
of their father, and straightaway they told their mother what
170 they had seen and what they had heard. She ordered them to go
as quickly as possible to summon the woman, to hire her on
at a magnanimous wage. Even as when, in spring, young deer
and cattle leap about in a meadow once they have had their
fill of forage, even so they darted, holding up the folds of their
175 lovely garments, down the rutted wagon path, their hair
streaming about their shoulders, like crocus flowers.

They found
the noble goddess near the road where they had only recently
left her. Then they led her to the house of their dear father.
She walked behind, grieving in her heart, her head covered
180 by a veil, and her dark cloak swirled around the slender feet
of the goddess.

Swiftly they came to the house of god-reared
Keleos. They went through the portico, where their lady
mother sat beside the pillar of the well-built roof, holding
her child at her breast, tender and young. The girls ran up
185 to her, but the goddess stepped on the threshold and her head
struck the rafters. The doorway was filled by a divine radiance.
Awe and reverence and pale fear took hold of Metaneira,
and she got up from her couch and urged her to take
a seat. But Demeter—the bringer of seasons, the giver
190 of wonderful gifts—did not wish to be seated on the shining
couch. She waited in silence, her beautiful eyes cast down,
until wise and careful Iambê° set out a jointed seat and cast
over it a silver fleece. Sitting there she held her veil

192. *Iambê:* She gave her name to the iambic poetic rhythm, a short and a long
($\cup-$), used in cult songs at Eleusis, which may have been obscene in content.

before her face with her hands. She sat for a long time
195 on the chair, silent, grieving. She greeted no one by word
or gesture, but she sat without smiling, not eating or drinking
anything, pining for her deep-bosomed daughter until
Iambê, who knew many things, made many jests and jokes
for her, and turned her aside to smile and laugh and to have
200 a beneficent heart—and in aftertimes Iambê oftentimes
pleased the holy lady with her moods.°
                                        Then Metaneira
filled a cup of sweet wine and offered it to Demeter.
She refused it, saying that it was not right for her to drink
red wine. She urged Metaneira to mix barley and water
205 with delicate mint and to give her that to drink.
So Metaneira made the *kykeon*° and gave it to the goddess
as she had asked. And the exalted Lady Deo received
it for the sake of the rite . . .°
                                        Well-girdled Metaneira
began to speak with these words: "Greetings, O woman,
210 for I do not think that you are born of lower-class parents,
but that your parents are well born. For in your eyes there's
a modesty and charm, as if from kings who deal out justice.
But we mortals must of necessity endure what the gods grant,
though we suffer. Their yoke lies upon our necks.
215 But now, since you have come here, you shall have
what I can provide. Be a nurse to this child that the gods
have given me late in my life, unhoped for, but in answer
to many a prayer. If you would raise him and he would
come to the full measure of youth, any one of womankind
220 who saw you would envy you: I would reward you greatly
for his upbringing."
                                        Demeter of the lovely crown answered her:

---

201. *with her moods:* Other sources report that Iambê raised her skirt to expose
herself, thus cheering Demeter, or that she danced to an iambic meter.

206. *kykeon:* "Stir-up," so named because it was necessary to stir up the mixture to
get the barley grains up from the bottom. *Kykeon* was the special drink given to initiates
in the Eleusinian Mysteries. The drink seems to have had no intoxicating properties.

208. *for the sake of the rite:* Initiates to the mysteries did drink *kykeon*. But one or
more lines are missing here, so the meaning is obscure.

"And to you, O woman, many greetings. May the gods grant
you good things. I will gladly take on your child, as you ask,
and I will raise him, and never, I think, will he be harmed
225 by the thoughtlessness of his nurse, nor by any witchcraft,
nor by any rootcutter, because I know a remedy far stronger
against the woodcutter, and a fine protection against
harmful witchcraft."°

Having so spoken, she took the child
in her fragrant bosom and her deathless hands, and her mother
230 rejoiced in her heart. And so she nourished in the palace
the glorious son of wise Keleos to whom Metaneira had given
birth,
Demophoön.° He grew like a divine being, though not eating food,
nor sucking milk from a mother's breast. By day lovely-crowned
Demeter anointed him with ambrosia as if he were the child
235 of a god, sweetly breathing down upon him as she held him
in her bosom. And at night she hid him like a brand in the strength
of the fire, concealing this from his dear parents. He was
a great marvel to them, the way he blossomed—he seemed
face to face with the gods! And she would have made him
240 ageless and deathless, if well-girdled Metaneira had not
thoughtlessly kept watch one night from her fragrant chamber
and seen him. She cried out and struck her two hips, in fear
for her son and thoroughly maddened in her heart. And
lamenting,
she spoke winged words: "Demophoön my child, this stranger
245 woman buries you in the blazing fire, and she places
agony and bitter pain in my heart!"

So she spoke, lamenting.
The shining goddess heard her. In anger at Metaneira
the lovely-crowned Demeter snatched up with her deathless
hands the dear child, whom Metaneira had borne unhoped

226–28. *nor by any rootcutter . . . witchcraft:* The rootcutter and woodcutter would
be harmful magicians gathering dangerous herbs in the forest.

232. *Demophoön:* "Light of the people." His name is never found in inscriptions at
Eleusis. His role seems to have been taken over by Triptolemos (figure 14), who in Athe-
nian myth brought agriculture to humankind.

250   for in the palace, and laid him down away from her on the ground,
       removing him from the fire in her heart's great anger. At the same
       time she spoke to well-girdled Metaneira:
                                          "You humans
       are unknowing and unable to foresee the good or bad fortune
       that comes upon you! And you are another one who in your folly
255   have done irreparable harm. May the cruel waters of the Styx,
       on which the gods swear their oaths,° be my witness:
       I would have made your darling child deathless and ageless
       throughout all his days, and I would have granted him
          imperishable
       honor. But as it is, there is no way that he might escape
260   death and his fate. Yes, there will be everlasting honor
       for him, because he came onto my lap, and he slept in my arms.
       In due season, as the years roll around, the Eleusinian youth
       will wage war and dread strife for him against one another
       for all their days.°
                            "I am the honored Demeter, who makes
265   the greatest blessing and joy for the deathless ones and for
       mortals. But come, may the whole city build a great temple
       and an altar beneath it under the sheer wall of the city,
       above Kallichoron where the hill juts out.° I will myself
       teach you my rites so that, in future time, you might perform
270   them with reverence, and so appease my mind."°
                                                So speaking
       the goddess changed her size and her appearance, putting

       255–56. *the Styx, on which the gods swear their oaths:* An oath sworn by a god on the
       waters of the underworld river Styx ("hateful") was inviolable.

       263–64. *wage war and dread strife . . . all their days:* A reference to a ritual mock bat-
       tle, involving rock-throwing, in honor of Demophoön held annually at Eleusis, called
       the Balletus, "throwing."

       268. *Kallichoron where the hill juts out:* Kallichoron, "the fountain of goodly dances,"
       is probably the same as the Maiden's Well mentioned earlier.

       270. *and so appease my mind:* Commentators have been puzzled by the incident
       with Demophoön, which seems to have nothing to do with Demeter's grief and mourn-
       ing for her daughter. But even as Hades has snatched away Persephone, Demeter threat-
       ens, in revenge against the dispensation of Zeus, to cheat Hades of his ordinary due by
       making a child immortal. However, the plan is thwarted by Metaneira's curiosity.

aside old age. Around her beauty wafted, and a lovely
scent came from her fragrant robes, and a light
shone afar from the deathless flesh of the goddess,
275 and golden locks fell onto her shoulders. The sturdy
house was filled with a brilliance as if from lightning,
and she went outside the palace.

                              Immediately Metaneira's knees
were loosened. For a long time she remained speechless.
She did not remember to take up her darling child from the floor,
280 but his sisters heard his pitiful crying and sprang down
from their well-made beds. One of them took up the child
in her hands and placed him in her bosom, another
stirred up the fire, while a third rushed on gentle feet
to raise up her mother from the fragrant chamber. They
285 gathered around him and washed him while he struggled,
and they embraced him with love. But he was not to be com-
    forted:
Rougher nurses and handmaids held him now.

   All night long they sought to appease the illustrious goddess,
quaking with fear. When dawn appeared, they told everything
290 exactly to wide-ruling Keleos, what the goddess had com-
    manded,
Demeter of the lovely crown. He gathered his far-flung people
to an assembly and commanded them to build a rich temple
and an altar where the hillside jutted out. Quickly they obeyed,
listening to him as he spoke, and they built it just as he ordered.
295 And the temple grew by divine dispensation.

                                        When they
had finished the temple and ceased from their labors, each man
went to his house. But Demeter sat there, apart from all
the blessed gods and stayed, wasting away from desire
for her deep-bosomed daughter. And she made a grievous
300 and cruel year for humans upon the nourishing earth. Seeds
would not sprout from the ground, for Demeter of the lovely
    crown
hid them away, and oxen drew in vain many curved plows through
the fields, and much white barley grain fell useless on the earth.
And she would have destroyed the whole race of humans from

305 bitter starvation, and deprived those who inhabit the houses
of Olympos of the glorious honor of gifts and sacrifice,
if Zeus had not taken notice and considered in his heart.
    First of all he sent down Iris° with her golden wings to call
on fair-tressed Demeter, who has so beautiful an appearance.
310 So he commanded, and she obeyed Zeus the dark-clouded,
the son of Kronos, and swiftly she sailed on her feet
through the space between. She came to the city of fragrant
Eleusis and she found dark-robed Demeter in the temple.
And she spoke to her winged words:
                              "Demeter, Father Zeus,
315 wise in everlasting things, calls you to come among the tribes
of those who live forever. So come, and let not the word
from Zeus be unfulfilled."
                        So Iris spoke, imploring.
But Demeter's heart was not persuaded. The father
then sent all the blessed gods who live forever, one
320 after the other. And so they went in turn, each begging
her to return, and they offered her many very beautiful gifts,
and whatever privileges she wanted to choose among
the deathless ones. But no one was able to bend her will,
so angry was she in her heart. Stubbornly she rejected
325 their words. She said she would never return to sweet-smelling
Olympos, nor permit the earth to yield its fruit, before
she saw with her own eyes her fair-faced daughter.
    Now when far-seeing Zeus, the deep-thunderer, heard this,
he sent the Killer of Argos, who carries a golden staff,°
330 into the underworld, that he might persuade Hades with
gentle words to send up chaste Persephone from the misty
gloom into the light to join the gods, so that her mother
might see her with her own eyes and abandon her anger.
Hermes did not disobey, but leaving the seat of Olympos

---

308. *Iris:* A daughter of Ocean. She was a personification of the rainbow and the
gods' messenger in the *Iliad.*

329. *Killer of Argos, who carries a golden staff.* Hermes is Argeïphontes, "Killer of
Argos," because he killed the many-eyed monster Argos. The golden staff is the
caduceus, a rod intertwined with copulating snakes.

335 he quickly sped down beneath the recesses of earth. He found
      its king inside his house, seated on a bed with his modest wife,
      greatly against her will because of her desire for her mother . . .
      [*this line in unintelligible*]
           . . . Standing near him, the powerful Killer of Argos said:
340 "O Hades with the dark hair, king of those who have perished,
      Father Zeus has ordered me to lead illustrious Persephone
      out from the underworld to them so that her mother can see
      her with her own eyes and let go her anger and harsh
      resentment against the gods. For she has contemplated a great
345 deed, to destroy the feeble tribes of humans who live
      on the earth by hiding the seed beneath the ground and ruining
      the tribute owed to the gods. She is extremely angry, nor will
      she have anything to do with the gods, but sits far off
      in her fragrant temple, dwelling in the rocky town of Eleusis."
350   So he spoke, and Hades, king of those beneath the earth,
      smiled with his brows, but he did not disobey the commands
      of King Zeus. Hastily he gave orders to wise Persephone:
      "Go, Persephone, to your dark-robed mother's side,
      having a kind feeling in your heart and your breast, and do not
355 be angry too much, far beyond the others. I will not be
      an unfit husband for you among the deathless ones,
      being a brother to Father Zeus. So long as you are here
      you will rule over all that lives and creeps along,
      and you will have the greatest honors among the deathless ones.
360 There will be punishment for all their days for those
      who act unjustly, for those who do not appease your anger
      with sacrifices, acting in a holy fashion and making the proper
           gifts."
           So he spoke. And wise Persephone rejoiced. She promptly
      leapt up, filled with delight. But secretly he gave her the honey-
           sweet
      seed of a pomegranate to eat, looking about him so that she might
365 not remain for all her days up above with reverend dark-robed
      Demeter. Then Hades, the Ruler of Many, harnessed his deathless
      horses at the front beneath a golden chariot. She mounted
      the chariot. By her side the powerful Killer of Argos
      took up the reins and the whip in his hands and he drove

370 out of the palace. The horses flew forward willingly
and swiftly they accomplished their long journey. Not sea,
not the water of rivers, not the grassy valleys, not mountain
peaks checked the onrush of the deathless horses, but they passed
over them, cutting the deep air.

                                        Hermes brought them
375 to a standstill where Demeter of the lovely crown waited
in front of her fragrant temple. When she saw them, she rushed
forward, like a maenad° across the mountain dusky with forest.
Persephone on her side, <when she saw>° her mother's
<beautiful eyes>, leaped down <from the chariot> and ran up
380 <and fell on her neck with an embrace>.

                                        <But even while she held
her dear child in her arms, Demeter's mind suddenly suspected
some trick, and she was very afraid>, and stop<ped her fondling
and quickly asked>:

                    "My child, surely you <did not eat any> food
<while you were in the underworld?> Tell me, <and conceal
     nothing,
385 so that we both may know>. If you have not, then you may come
back from loathsome Hades and be with me and <the other
     deathless
ones> and your father, the dark-<clouded son of Kronos>,
and be honor<ed by all the deathless> ones. But if you have eaten
something, you must go back <again beneath the hidden places
390 of the earth> and dwell a third part of the seasons <in a year>,
and spend two parts with me and the <other deathless ones>.
And when the earth blooms with sweet-smelling flowers of every
kind in the spring, then you will arise again from the misty gloom,
a great wonder to the gods and to mortal humans. <Now tell me
395 how he snatched you beneath the misty gloom>° and with what

---

377. *maenad:* A female ecstatic worshipper of Dionysos, famous for running wildly
through the woods.

378–95. *<when she saw>* . . .: The manuscript is torn here. The lacunae were repaired
in the sixteenth century by an unknown hand. The supplements are conjectural but
accepted by most editors.

394–95. *Now tell me . . . misty gloom:* This line has been restored by various editors.

trick the mighty Receiver of Many deceived you?"

And beautiful
Persephone answered: "I will tell you truthfully exactly
what happened. When luck-bringing Hermes came, the swift
messenger, from my father, the son of Kronos, and the other
dwellers
400 in Olympos, urging me to come out from the underworld
so that you might see me with your own eyes and give up
your anger and bitter wrath at the deathless ones, right away
I sprang up from joy. But secretly he put in my mouth
the seed of a pomegranate, a sweet morsel, and he forced
405 me to taste it against my will. I will tell you, too,
how through the shrewd plan of the son of Kronos,
my father, he snatched me up and carried me beneath
the hidden places of the earth—I will tell you everything,
just as you ask.

"All of us were playing in a lovely meadow—
410 Leukippê, and Phaino and Elektrê and Ianthê and Melitê
and Iachê and Rhodeia and Kallirhoê and Melobosis and Tuchê
and Okurhoê, as pretty as a flower, and Chruseis and Ianeira
and Akastê and Admetê and Rhodopê and Plouto and lovely
Kalypso and Styx and Ouraniê and charming Galaxaurê°
415 and Pallas,° who stirs up battles, and Artemis who delights
in arrows—we were playing and picking lovely flowers
in our hands—gentle crocus mixed with iris and hyacinth
and the blooms of rose and lilies, a wonder to see,
and the narcissus that the wide earth sends up like a crocus.
420 This I plucked in my joy. Then the earth split open beneath
and there the mighty Receiver of Many sprang forth.
In his golden chariot he carried me beneath the earth,
though I was greatly unwilling. I cried out with a shrill voice.
All this is true, though it grieves me to tell you."

410–14. *Leukippê . . . and charming Galaxaurê:* This is a fairly standard catalogue of
Oceanids.

415. *Pallas:* That is, Athena. Many have thought the addition of Athena and Artemis
to the catalogue of Oceanids odd, but this is what the manuscript gives.

FIGURE 12. The return of Persephone. On the far left, Korê rises to the upper world through a rocky outcrop, assisted by Hermes, the guide of souls, who stands beside her with his caduceus, wearing a traveler's hat. Hekatê holds out two torches and, on the far right, Demeter, holding a scepter, awaits her daughter's return. Athenian red-figure wine-mixing bowl, c. 440 BC. Metropolitan Museum of Art, New York.

425   Thus then with like mind all the day did they greatly
     warm one another's heart and spirit with close embrace.
     Their hearts ceased from grief. They gave and received joy
     from one another. Hekatê, brightly crowned, came up close
     to them. Often did she embrace the holy daughter of Demeter
430 and from that time the goddess was her minister and attendant.
       And all-seeing deep-thundering Zeus sent a messenger to them,
     Rhea with the lovely hair, to bring dark-robed Demeter
     to join the tribes of gods. He promised to give her
     the privileges she might choose among the deathless gods.
435 He agreed that his daughter should go down for a third of the
      circling
     year beneath the murky gloom, but that for two parts she should
     live with her mother and the other deathless ones.
                                So he spoke.
     The goddess did not disobey the message of Zeus. Swiftly
     she rushed down from the peaks of Olympos. She came

440 to Rharion,° once a life-bearing plow-land to be milked, but
    then not life-bearing: it lay idle, bereft of every leaf, all white
    barley hidden through the designs of beautiful-ankled Demeter.
    But soon, when spring came, it was about to wave with slender
    ears of grain, and on the ground its rich furrows to be heavy
445 with wheat, while some were bound in sheaves. There first
    Rhea came to earth from the barren air. They saw each other
        gladly,
    and they rejoiced in their hearts. Rhea of the shining crown
    spoke to Demeter:
                    "Come, my child. The deep-thundering
    far-seeing Zeus summons you to come to the tribes of gods,
450 and he has promised to give you whatever privileges you desire
    among the deathless gods. He has agreed that his daughter
    should go down for a third of the circling year beneath the murky
    gloom, but that for two parts she should live with her mother
    and the other deathless ones. He has declared that it shall
455 be so, and he has bowed his head in assent. But come,
    my child, do obey. Be not too relentless in your anger
    against the dark-clouded son of Kronos. Quickly
    increase the growth of life-giving fruits for humankind."
    So she spoke, and lovely-crowned Demeter did not
460 disobey her. Quickly she sent up fruit from the rich
    plowlands. And all the wide earth grew heavy with leaves
    and flowers. Then she went to the justice-giving kings
    Triptolemos and horse-goading Diokles and powerful
    Eumolpos and Keleos, leader of the people, and showed
465 them the performance of the sacred rites. She taught
    the beautiful mysteries to Triptolemos, Poluxeinos
    and Diokles too—the solemn mysteries, which one may
    never transgress nor ask about nor broadcast, for the mighty
    awe of the gods holds back the voice. Blessed is he
470 among humans upon the earth who has seen them,
    but he who has not been initiated into the sacred rites,

---

440. *Rharion:* A plain near Eleusis. Prizes of grain from this field are recorded in
inscriptions from Eleusis.

who has no share of them, never has a similar lot
when he is dead and has gone beneath the misty gloom.
    When the divine goddess had taught them all, she went
475 to Olympos and the assembly of the other gods. And there
they dwell with Zeus who delights in the thunder, reverend
and august. Most blessed is he among humans who dwell
on the earth whom they enthusiastically love. Quickly they send
Ploutos° as a guest to their great house, he who gives wealth
480 to humans who die.
                But come, lady, who possesses
the fragrant land of Eleusis, and Paros washed by waves,
and rocky Antron°—giver of wondrous gifts, bringer
of seasons, Queen Deo—you and your daughter, most beautiful
Persephone, be gracious and give heart-filling sustenance
485 in return for my song. I will remember you and another song too.

HOMERIC HYMN 13: TO DEMETER

A prayer for protection.

I begin to sing of Demeter of the fair tresses, the blessed
goddess, of herself and her daughter, most beautiful Persephone!
Hail goddess! Keep this city safe! Give a beginning to my song!

CALLIMACHUS HYMN 6: TO DEMETER

*This hymn, written in the Doric dialect rather than the Ionic familiar from
Homer and Hesiod, is set in the approaching evening when celebrants in the
cult of Demeter, who have been fasting, return to her temple. A chariot
containing a large sacred basket (the* kalathos *familiar from Eleusinian
cult), drawn by four white horses, accompanies the celebrants. The female
narrator advises the celebrants not to look into the basket. The narrator*

---

479. *Ploutos:* "Wealth," usually said to be a son of Demeter and a certain Iasion, is a
god of agricultural prosperity.
    481–82. *Paros . . . and rocky Antron:* PAROS was an important center for the cult of
Demeter. This is the only mention of Antron, a town in THESSALY opposite EUBOIA, in
connection with Demeter.

reviews the familiar story of Persephone's rape and Demeter's wandering in search of her, then tells the story of Erusichthon, a king of THESSALY. *Erusichthon is cutting down trees in a grove of Demeter to make way for a banqueting hall when Demeter herself appears to him, disguised as a priestess. She warns him to desist, but he arrogantly refuses. As punishment she causes him to be beset with a relentless and never-satisfied hunger. Erusichthon consumes all the house's stores, and all their cattle and even the horses. At last he is seen wasting away at a crossroads, begging for crusts. The poem returns to the festival of Demeter and ends with a prayer for prosperity.*

The embedded tale of Erusichthon is similar to stories in fourth-century comedy, where the excesses of consumption, especially by kings and the aristocracy, are parodied. Demeter is a goddess of plenty and agricultural wealth; when Erusichthon abuses these benefits, he commits a kind of sacrilege and is suitably punished. The poem is an amusing criticism of aristocratic excess.

> As the basket° comes back, give the ritual cry, O women:
> "O Demeter, mighty greetings! Great-nourisher! Provider
> of abundant wheat!" Those not initiated, you will watch
> the basket as it returns, sitting on the ground—not from
> 5   the roof, nor from up above, whether a child or a woman
> or one who has let down her hair°—not even when
> we spit from our mouths parched from fasting.°
>
>   Hesperos°
> has looked out from the clouds—when will the basket come?—

1. *the basket:* The *kalathos,* a large basket with a flaring top often used in wool making (figure 13), was also important in the cult to Demeter/Persephone at Eleusis, where it contained (unknown) sacred objects.

3–6. *Those not initiated . . . who has let down her hair:* The uninitiated are allowed to sit on the ground and watch the basket but those on the flat rooftops, or in upper chambers, must look away as the basket passes (or else they could see inside). The women who have let down their hair are evidently unmarried women who wore their hair unbound, but the context is unclear.

7. *we spit from our mouths parched from fasting:* Fasting is part of the ritual behavior of the celebrants, in accordance with the story that Demeter fasted when searching for her daughter. Spitting is an apotropaic act but not permitted when the basket is passing.

8. *Hesperos:* Hesperos is the evening star, the planet Venus, which rises as the sun sets, indicating that evening is near, the usual time for abandoning one's fast.

FIGURE 13. A woman with a *kalathos*. She appears to be juggling objects of some kind, perhaps stored in the basket. Athenian red-figure vase, c. 410 BC. Museo provinciale Sigismondo Castromediano, Lecce, Italy. Photograph © Sailko / Creative Commons.

Hesperos, who alone persuaded Demeter to drink° when she
  pursued
10 the unknown footsteps of her daughter who had been snatched
  away.
    Lady, how could your feet carry you to where the sun sets?
  To where the Black Men live?° To where the Golden Apples grow?°
  You did not drink, nor eat, during all that time, nor did you bathe.
  Three times you crossed the swirling silver eddies of ACHELOÖS,°
15 as many times you passed over each of the ever-flowing rivers,
  and three times you sat down on the ground before the well
  of Kallichoron, parched and thirsty, and you ate nothing,
  nor bathed.
    But do not—do not!—speak things that bring a tear
  to Deo. Better to speak of how she gave pleasant laws
20 to cities; better to tell of how she first cut stalks and holy sheaves
  of wheat and placed them before cattle to eat, when Triptolemos
  was taught the excellent art;° better (so that one may avoid
  transgression!) to see . . .°
                Not yet did they live in KNIDOS,
  but they dwelled in Dotion° and to you yourself the Pelasgians°

---

9. *Hesperos, who alone persuaded Demeter to drink:* In the "Homeric Hymn to Demeter" it is Metaneira, queen of Eleusis, who persuades Demeter to drink (line 206).

12. *where the Black Men live:* That is, the Ethiopians, in the far south.

12. *Golden Apples:* The apples that Heracles had to gather, here probably imagined as in the far North, in the land of the Hyperboreans, though usually the apples are in the far West, overseen by the Hesperides, the "nymphs of the west." So Demeter travels west (to the setting sun), south (to the Ethiopians), and north (to the Hyperboreans)—that is, everywhere.

14. *Acheloös:* The largest river in Greece, in AETOLIA.

22. *the excellent art:* See figure 14.

23. *to see . . . :* The manuscript is torn here, but the missing line must prepare for the warning tale of the sinful Erusichthon about to come.

24. *they dwelled in Dotion:* Triopas, the father of Erusichthon, had migrated to THESSALY, expelled the earlier population of Pelasgians, and settled on the Thessalian plain of Dotion through which the Peneios River flows, "holy" because it was an ancient center of the worship of Demeter. Later Triopas settled in Knidos, after the sacrilege of Erusichthon that Callimachus is about to describe. Knidos is located at the end of a peninsula on the southern Ionian coast, south of KOS.

24. *Pelasgians:* The pre-Greek inhabitants of the Aegean area (etymology unknown).

FIGURE 14. Persephone/Korê sends out Triptolemos to teach the growing of agriculture to the world. The Eleusinian prince, holding a scepter in his left hand, sits in a winged dragon-chariot while Korê, who holds a torch in her left hand, pours a libation into a dish held by Triptolemos. Athenian wine-cup, c. 460 BC. Musée du Louvre, Paris. Photo by Marie-Lan Nguyen / Creative Commons.

25   made a beautiful grove, abundant with trees. An arrow
      could scarcely have penetrated it. There were pines
      in it, and great elms, and pear trees, and beautiful
      sweet-apples, and water bubbled up looking like amber
      from the irrigation ditches, and the goddess was mad
30   for the place, as much as for Eleusis, as much as she was
      for Triopas or for Enna.°

    30–31. *as much as for Eleusis . . . or for Enna:* Eleusis is the sanctuary near Athens. "Triopas" here must not refer to the man, the father of Erusichthon, mentioned later

But when the good spirit came
to hate the offspring of Triopas, then a worse plan
took hold of Erusichthon.° He rushed out with twenty
companions, all in the prime of life, all men with the strength
35   of giants able to lift up an entire city. He armed them with
both double-axes and with hatchets. Devoid of shame,
they ran into the grove of Demeter. There was a certain
poplar, a great tree reaching to the sky near which
the nymphs danced at noontime. When first struck
40   the tree cried out a mournful song to the others.
Demeter sensed that her sacred forest was in pain.
In anger she spoke: "Who is cutting my beautiful trees?"
Immediately she took on the likeness of Nikippê,°
whom the city has made priestess of the people.
45   She held a wreath in her hand and a poppy, and against
her shoulder a large key.° She spoke gently to the wicked
and shameless man: "My child, who are cutting trees
dedicated to the gods—child, do cease!—child, much prayed
for by your parents, stop! . . . and dismiss your attendants
50   so that Lady Demeter does not grow angry because
you are plundering her sanctuary!"
But he, glaring at her
more balefully than a lioness who has just given birth
stares at a hunter in the Tmarian Mountains°—they say
that her stare is then most baneful—"Get lost!" he said.
55   "Or I will sink this great ax in your flesh! These will make
my house water-tight, in which I will everlastingly host
abundant luscious banquets for my companions!"

(line 81), but to the sanctuary to Demeter in Knidos founded by Triopas after he left
Dotion in Thessaly; Callimachus is compressing time. Enna is a plain in central Sicily
often said to be where Hades abducted Persephone.

31–33. *But when the good spirit . . . took hold of Erusichthon:* We might say, "when the
good fortune of Erusichthon, the son of Triopas, turned to bad."

43. *Nikippê:* "Horse-tamer," otherwise unknown.

45–46. *a poppy . . . a key:* The poppy was special to Demeter. Temple keys were very
large, more like cranks, and are often illustrated on Greek pots.

53. *Tmarian Mountains:* Near DODONA in northwest Greece, that is, in a remote area.

So spoke the youth, and Nemesis° made a note of his
wicked pronouncement. Demeter became unspeakably angry,
60   and she showed herself as a goddess. Her feet were on the ground
but her head touched the sky. The followers, half-dead with fear,
fled, leaving their axes in the trees. She let the others go,
for they followed by necessity a tyrant's hand, but to their
overbearing king she answered: "Yes, yes, make your house,
65   you dog, you! Make your frequent banquets there, your feasts
in the future, following one upon another in quick succession!"
      Having so spoken, she fashioned an evil fate for Erusichthon.
Immediately she cast a savage and wild hunger in him
—fiery, overwhelming!—and he was ruined by a desperate
sickness.
70   What a wretch—however much he ate, he again felt the same
hunger.
Twenty men worked to prepare his feast, twelve men poured
out the wine: whatever infuriates Demeter also infuriates
Dionysos, for Dionysos shares the anger of Demeter.
Erusichthon's parents, in shame, no longer sent him
75   to banquets nor common-meals—they found every excuse!
The sons of Ormenos came, inviting him to the games
in honor of Athena of Itonê°—his mother put them off:
"He's not here . . . he went off yesterday to Krannon°
to fetch a hundred cows in payment of a debt." Poluxo
80   came, the mother of Aktorion,° arranging the marriage
of her son. She invited both Triopas° and his son. Weeping,
with a heavy heart, she answered: "Triopas will come,
but Erusichthon has been wounded by a boar in the fair
valleys of the PINDOS,° and he's been laid up for nine days."

---

58. *Nemesis:* A daughter of Night, she punishes mortals for impious acts.

76–77. *The sons of Ormenos . . . Itonê:* Ormenos was a local Thessalian king. Athena
was celebrated in Itonê, a Thessalian town.

78. *Krannon:* A town in Thessaly.

79–80. *Poluxo came, the mother of Aktorion:* These names are unknown.

81. *Triopas:* The father of Erusichthon, named here for the first time.

84. *PINDOS:* The mountain range that runs down the center of mainland Greece.

85   Wretched mother who loved her son, what lies
       did she not tell? Someone is giving a feast: "Erusichthon
       is out of town." Someone is arranging a wedding: "A discus
       has wounded Erusichthon," or, "He's fallen from a horse,"
       or "He's counting his flocks on Mount Orthrys."°

                                                    In the inmost
90   recesses of his house, an all-day diner, he ate
       ten thousand things. His evil stomach leaped up
       as he forever ate more, and all that food ran down
       as it were into the depths of the sea, in vain,
       unappreciated. As the snow on Mimas,° as a wax
95   doll in the sun—more than these!—he wasted away
       down to his sinews. Only skin and bone remained
       to the wretched man. He mother wept, his two sisters
       mightily wailed, and the breast that gave him to drink,°
       and many tens of female slaves.

                                          Triopas himself
100   tore his gray hair and cried out to Poseidon° (who wasn't
       listening) such things as these: "False father! Look at this
       man here, third in descent from you, if in fact I am
       the child of you and Kanakê, daughter of Aiolos,°
       and this wretch is a child is mine. I wish that he had
105   died at Apollo's hands° and that my hands had given
       him honorable burial! But as it is, a ravenous hunger
       sits in his eyes. So either remove this wretched disease
       from him or take him and feed him yourself—my own tables
       have had it! My cattle stalls are widowed, my pens for four-legged
110   beasts are long since empty, for the cooks have denied
       him nothing. They even unhitched the mules from the big

89. *Mount Orthrys:* In north-central Greece.

94. *Mimas:* Two mountains bore this name, one in Thessaly and one in Ionia
opposite the island of Chios.

98. *the breast that gave him to drink:* That is, his wet-nurse.

100. *Poseidon:* Triopas' father.

103. *Aiolos:* A son of Hellen (himself the son of Deukalion and Pyrrha) and founder
of the Aiolian branch of the Greek race, which lived in Thessaly.

105. *died at Apollo's hands:* When male infants died, they died at the hands of Apollo,
as female infants died at the hands of Artemis.

honored, torch-bearing, holy, rejoicing in the crops of summer.
You spring from the earth, you are brilliant, you are gentle
to all! You are kind to children, a lover of youths, holy,
15   a daughter who nurses the young. You yoke your car
to bridled dragons,° you whirl and swirl around
your throne, crying Euhoê!° You are an only child
but a goddess with many children,° with many powers
over mortals. You have many shapes, you appear in many
20   blossoms, your blooms are sacred.
                                    Come, blessed one,
holy one, brimming with summer fruit, bringing
on peace and lovely good government. And wealth
in abundance, and prosperity, together with Queen Health!

ORPHIC HYMN 41: TO MOTHER ANTAIA

*Demeter, here called Antaia, who suffered looking for Persephone, brings
blessings to those initiated in her mysteries.*

Queen Antaia,° goddess, many-named mother
of the deathless gods and of mortal humans,
who once, searching in unbearable agony, gave up
your fasting in the valleys of Eleusis—you came
5   to Hades for noble Persephone, taking as your guide
the innocent son of Dusaulos,° who announced the news

15–16. *yoke your car to bridled dragons*: Triptolemos' chariot is drawn by dragons (see Figure 14).

17. *Euhoê*: The cry of the followers of Dionysos in ecstasy.

18. *with many children*: Demeter is usually said to be the mother of Ploutos, "wealth," but otherwise her only child is Persephone. The poet must mean that Demeter is the author of fruitfulness generally.

1. *Antaia*: Another name for Demeter. It means "opposite, hostile," perhaps because Demeter was once hostile to humankind and to the gods.

6. *son of Dusaulos*: In the "Homeric Hymn to Demeter," it is Hermes who goes into the underworld to recover Persephone. Dusaulos, according to another tradition, is the husband of Baubo who—not Iambê—causes Demeter to laugh as she sits disconsolate in the Eleusinian palace, in this case by exposing her genitals. Pausanias (1.14.3) says that Dusaulos' sons Triptolemos and Eubouleus inform Demeter of Persephone's abduction, in return for which she teaches them the arts of agriculture. One of these sons must be meant here.

of the holy marriage of the pure Zeus of the underworld.
You gave birth to the divine Euboulos, yielding to mortal
need.° But goddess, queen to whom many pray, I beg
10   of you—come graciously to your pious initiate!

ORPHIC HYMN 29: TO PERSEPHONE

Persephone, queen of the dead, is also the source of life.

O Persephone, daughter of great Zeus, come blessed one!
Sole offspring,° goddess, accept this gracious sacrifice!
Much-honored wife of Plouton,° true-hearted, life-
    giving,
you command the gates of Hades beneath the depths
5   of earth. Lovely-tressed Praxidikê, holy bloom
of Deo, mother of the Erinyes,° queen of those
who dwell beneath the earth, whom Zeus begot
in secret concourse, his daughter.
                            Mother of loud-roaring
Eubouleus, who takes many forms, playmate of the Seasons,°
10   radiant, of beauteous form, holy, almighty,
maiden swelling with fruits, shining, horned,°
sole one desired of mortals, in springtime taking
your joy in the meadow of breezes, showing forth
your holy form in the shoots rich with green fruit,

8–9. *You gave birth . . . need:* This line has never been explained. Perhaps the "Euboulos" here is Ploutos, the son of Demeter and Iasion, but it is a common epithet; he is certainly not the "Eubouleus" possibly referred to as son of Dusaulos in the preceding line. Or something is wrong with the text.

2. *sole offspring:* Of Demeter.

3. *Plouton:* Not Ploutos, said to be Demeter's child, but another name for Hades, though it too means "wealth."

5–6. *Praxidikê . . . mother of the Erinyes:* Praxidikê, "exacter of Justice," is an obscure epithet of Persephone. The Erinyes are the Furies, the spirits of blood vengeance and avengers of the violation of oaths. Their parents are variously named, but in Orphic myth they are, as here, the children of Hades and Persephone.

9. *Eubouleus . . . the Seasons:* Eubouleus, "good counsel," is an epithet of Dionysos (also of Hades), a "loud-roaring" god (as such he is also called Bromios). The Seasons are the Horai, goddesses of the natural portions of time.

FIGURE 15. Ares and Aphrodite. The beardless and nearly naked handsome war-god reaches around with his left arm to remove Aphrodite's clothing while he holds her breast in his right hand. Turning toward him, she assists with her left arm. To Ares' right, a naked winged Eros (Cupid) plays with his helmet. A spear and shield lie on the bench propped against the wall. To the right of the picture, a second Eros holds a jewel box. Roman fresco, AD first century, from the Casa di Meleagro, Pompeii. Museo Nazionale Archeologico di Napoli. Photograph by Marie-Lan Nguyen / Creative Commons.

to all the gods: 'Father Zeus, and you other blessed gods
who last forever, come here!—to see a laughable business,
285 a matter not to be endured! Aphrodite the daughter of Zeus
always scorns me because I am lame. She loves this pestilent
Ares because he is handsome and strong of foot,
whereas I was born a weakling. But who is to blame?
My two parents,° who ought never to have begotten me!

289. *two parents:* Here Hera and Zeus; in other traditions, Hephaistos was the child of Hera alone.

290 But you will see where these two have gone, up to my bed
to make love, and I am troubled to see it. But I doubt that they
will lie in this fashion for long, no, not for a minute, even though
they enjoy the sex. Soon they will both lose the desire
to sleep! The snare and the bonds will hold them until her father
295 gives back all the wedding gifts that I gave him for his bitch
daughter! She may be good-looking, but she can't contain her lust!'

    "So he spoke, and the gods gathered at the house
with the bronze floor. Poseidon the earth-shaker came,
and Hermes the helper, and Lord Apollo came, who works
300 from a long ways off. (But the lady goddesses stayed at home
for shame, each in her own house!) The gods, givers of good
things, stood in the forecourt, and an unquenchable laughter
arose among the blessed gods when they saw the art
of wise Hephaistos.

             "Thus would one say, glancing at his neighbor:
305 'Evil deeds never prosper! The slow catches the swift! As even
now Hephaistos, though slow, has caught Ares, the swiftest
of the gods who live on Olympos. Though he is lame, Hephaistos
has caught him by guile, and Ares owes an adulterer's fine!'

    "They said things like this to one another. Then Lord Apollo,
310 the son of Zeus, said this to Hermes: 'Hermes, son of Zeus,
messenger, the giver of good things, wouldn't you like to share
a couch with golden Aphrodite, even though bound in powerful
chains?'

    "The messenger, the Slayer of Argos,° answered him:
'Would that this might come about, O Lord Apollo who shoots
315 from afar, that three times as many endless bonds might bind me,
and all you gods look on and all the goddesses too, if only
I might lay beside golden Aphrodite.'

                  "So he spoke
and laughter arose among the deathless gods. But Poseidon
did not laugh. He begged Hephaistos, the famous craftsman,

---

313. *Slayer of Argos:* "Slayer of Argos" (Argeïphontes) refers to Hermes as killer of a
hundred-eyed giant named Argos who guarded the princess Io, one of Zeus's girl-
friends, after Hera had turned Io into a cow.

320 to let Ares go. And he spoke to him words that went like
arrows: 'Release him! And I promise this to you, just as
you bid, that he will pay all that is right in the presence
of the immortal gods.'

"The famous god, strong in both arms,
then said: 'Do not ask this, O Poseidon, shaker of the earth.
325 Pledges given on behalf of a worthless fellow are worthless!
How could I put you in bonds among the deathless gods
if Ares should avoid the debt and the bonds and escape?'°

"Poseidon the holder of the earth then said to him:
'Hephaistos, even if Ares avoids the debt and runs off, I will
330 pay it for him.'

"The famous god of two strong arms replied:
'All right, I cannot refuse you.'

"So speaking, the mighty Hephaistos
loosed the bonds, and the two lovers, when the strong bonds
were relaxed, leaped up. Ares went off to Thrace
and laughter-loving Aphrodite went off to CYPRUS,
335 to PAPHOS,° where her estate and her fragrant altar are.
There the Graces° bathed her and anointed her flesh with
immortal oil such as gleams on the gods who are forever,
and around her they placed lovely clothing, a wonder to see."

This song the famous singer sang, and Odysseus was delighted
340 to hear it, and so were all of the oar-loving Phaiakians, men
famous for their ships.

Homer's jocular tale of adultery and hijinks among the Olympian
gods disguises Aphrodite's origin as one of most exalted and powerful
gods of ancient Near Eastern religion, where she was known variously
as Inanna, Ishtar, Ashtoreth, and Astartê. Somehow the name "Aphro-
dite" derives from these Eastern names, though we cannot trace the

---

326–27. *How could I put you . . . and escape:* Hephaistos' point is that Ares would be
sure to default on the pledge, but Hephaistos could not very well move against Posei-
don, the older god who stands up for respectability and due process while the younger
gods, Hermes and Apollo, find the situation a cause for laughter.

335. *PAPHOS:* Where Aphrodite had a famous shrine.

336. *Graces:* The Charites, minor goddesses of female charm and beauty, usually
three in number, who accompany Aphrodite.

details. She was the divine consort of the Near Eastern king who united in sexual intercourse with a woman playing her role in an Eastern rite called in Greek *hieros gamos*, "sacred marriage," whose purpose was to guarantee the fruitfulness of the land. The Eastern goddess was called "queen of heaven," even as Aphrodite was sometimes called Ourania, "the heavenly one." The Eastern goddess was worshipped with incense altars and the sacrifice of doves, as was Aphrodite. She was also a god of war, and occasionally Aphrodite too grants victory in war. Most notably, the Eastern goddess was celebrated by temple prostitution wherein respectable women would take on her role and have intercourse with strangers to guarantee the woman's fruitfulness. An allusion in the Greek geographer Strabo (64 BC–AD 24) claims a similar practice for the temple of Aphrodite at Corinth (8.6.21). Aphrodite's Eastern origins are in any event affirmed by her association with the island of Cyprus, where she had a famous temple at Paphos in the west of the island, and by Hesiod's story that she was born from the foam *(aphros)* that gathered around the severed penis of Sky when it fell into the sea, then washed past the island of Kythera and ashore on Cyprus (*Theogony,* 154–206). Thus her common poetic names were Cythereia, "she of Cythera," and the Cyprian.

Aphrodite's great power is reflected in the story of the Judgment of Paris, when the Trojan prince chose Aphrodite over Hera and Athena as the fairest, the decision that caused the Trojan War. In the *Iliad,* Zeus, too, succumbs to her power by means of a love-charm that Aphrodite gives to Hera. But the most charming testament to her power is an ode of Sappho (c. 630–c. 570 BC):

> O deathless Aphrodite, who sits on a shimmering throne,
> daughter of Zeus, weaver of wiles—I beseech you!
> But do not overcome my spirit with torment
> and suffering—O queen!
>
> Come here, if ever in the past you have heard
> my voice from afar and came,
> leaving the golden house
> of your father,
> yoking your chariot, and beautiful swift sparrows,
> whirring with their wings, brought you above

the dark earth from heaven through
the middle of the air,

and swiftly they arrived. And you, O blessed one,
a smile on your deathless face, asked me what
was the matter *this* time, and why had
I called you *this* time,

and what did I most wish would come to pass
in my crazed heart. Whom am I to persuade,
this time, to lead you back into her heart? Who,
O Sappho, has done you wrong?

Well, if she runs away, she shall soon pursue.
If she will not take your gifts, soon she shall give them.
If she does not love you, soon she *shall*
—though unwilling.

So come to me now again, free me
from my grievous pain. All the things
that my heart desires, fulfill. And you
yourself, be my ally!

Here, from a cosmic force that pervades all creation, the terrible power
that emerged in gore and violence around the severed penis of Kro-
nos, Aphrodite has become the sponsor of personal affection, of the
passion that has always characterized human relationships.

HOMERIC HYMN 5: TO APHRODITE

The long "Homeric Hymn 5: To Aphrodite" is probably the oldest of the
Homeric Hymns, *to judge by its diction and its closeness to Homeric
stories about the Trojan War. Some scholars have even speculated that it
was composed by Homer himself. The story is about Aeneas, one of the
major figures in the* Iliad, *and in fact a prophecy of the greatness of the
descendants of Aeneas, similar to the prediction at the end of the hymn,
appears both in the* Iliad *(20.307–8) and in the hymn (179–80):*

> "You will have a dear son who will rule over the Trojans
> and his children's children, begotten continuously."

*Most commentators have taken both predictions to refer to a family of
Aeneadae prominent in the Troad, though no historical documents have
established the existence of such a family. This hymn celebrates these
descendants more than it celebrates the power of Aphrodite, whose
weakness is revealed by having her own power turned against her in her
passion for Anchises, a prince of the Trojan royal house. After this
shameful incident, she will no longer be able to compel the other gods to
sleep with mortals.*

Tell to me, Muse, of the deeds of golden Aphrodite,
who came from Cyprus, who arouses sweet desire
among the gods and overwhelms the tribes of human
beings who die, and the winged birds, and all the wild beasts
5   that the dry land nourishes, and the sea: all are concerned
with the doings of Cythereia of the lovely crown.
    But three hearts there are that she cannot persuade or
       deceive:
The daughter of Zeus who carries the aegis,°
flashing-eyed Athena, who takes no pleasure in the acts
10   of golden Aphrodite, who finds her pleasure in wars
and the doings of Ares and in battles and fights and in fostering
beautiful crafts. She was first to teach man-the-maker, who dwells
on the earth, to make chariots and cars fancy with bronze.
She taught young girls in the house, whose flesh is tender,
15   how to make beautiful handicrafts, informing the minds of
    everyone.
    Nor does laughter-loving Aphrodite ever master in love
Artemis of the golden shafts and the shriek of the hunt. For she
    delights
in archery and the killing of wild beasts in the mountains, and
    the lyre,
and dances, and the thrilling cry, and shadowy woods, and the city

---

8. *aegis:* The aegis, a shield or cape fringed with serpents, often bearing the head of
a Gorgon, terrifies all who behold it. Both Zeus and Athena carry it, though in art it is
usually worn by Athena (see figure 7). The root is probably *aix*, "goat," probably because
it was originally a made of a goatskin.

20   of just men.

Nor does Hestia,° the chaste maid, take pleasure
in the doings of Aphrodite, whom wily Kronos begot first, yet she
—so revered!—is also the youngest° by the will of Zeus who carries
the aegis, whom Poseidon and Apollo wished to marry.
But she was in no way willing. Decidedly she turned them away.
25   She swore a great oath, that marvelous goddess, that has come to
pass,
touching the head of her father Zeus who carries the aegis
—that she would remain a virgin for all her days. Her father
Zeus gave her a noble privilege in place of marriage, and
receiving fat
she took her place in the middle of the house.° She is honored
30   in all the shrines of the gods, and she is fashioned as preeminent
among all mortals.

Of these goddesses Aphrodite is not able
to persuade nor deceive their minds, but of the others there
is nothing that can escape Aphrodite, neither among
the blessed gods nor among humans who die. Even the mind
35   of Zeus, who delights in the thunderbolt, she has led astray,
who is greatest and greatest in honor. And yet she beguiles
easily his wise mind whenever she wishes, and couples
him with mortal women, putting Hera out of his mind,
his sister and bedmate, who is best in appearance among
40   the undying goddesses, the noblest daughter of wily
Kronos and her mother Rhea. And Zeus, whose counsels
are forever, made her his chaste wife, trusty in her thoughts.

It was in Aphrodite's heart that Zeus cast sweet desire
to have intercourse with a mortal man, so that as soon

20. *Hestia:* The goddess of the hearth (see chapter 13).

22–23. *begot first . . . the youngest:* The tyrannical god Kronos swallowed his children as they were born, beginning with Hestia; but Zeus, the last-born, escaped this fate when Kronos' consort, Rhea, gave Kronos a stone wrapped in swaddling clothes and hid Zeus in a cave on Crete. When Zeus came to maturity, he compelled his father Kronos to vomit up his children in reverse order. Hence Hestia was both first conceived, the eldest, and last born, the youngest.

28–29. *receiving fat . . . of the house:* Hestia, the hearth, is at the center of the house and receives the fat of sacrificed animals that drips down when the animals are roasted.

FIGURE 16. Zeus and Aphrodite. A bearded Zeus, his head crowned with a bough of ivy, sits on a folding stool holding his scepter in his right hand. An elaborately coiffured Aphrodite, clad in a see-through gown, stands before him, dangling a circular love charm from her wrist. The figures are labeled. An Eros (Latin, Cupid), standing for the power of sexual attraction, chucks her beneath the chin. The columns indicate that this is an interior scene, no doubt in the palace on Olympos. Red-figure vase from southern Italy, c. 330 BC. J. Paul Getty Museum, Malibu, CA. Photograph © Dave and Margie Hill Kleerup / Creative Commons.

45   as possible even laughter-loving Aphrodite would not be apart
       from a mortal's bed, and that she might not one day boast,
       smiling sweetly among all the gods, that she had made
       the gods to couple with mortal women so that they bore
       mortals to the deathless gods, and that she had compelled
50   the goddesses to sleep with mortal men.
                                        And so he cast into her heart

51. *Anchises:* A descendant of Tros, who gave his name to TROY, and a cousin to Priam, king of Troy during the Trojan war.

sweet desire for Anchises,° who at that time herded his cows
in the steep mountains of IDA° with its many fountains,
like in his appearance to the undying ones. When laughter-loving
55 Aphrodite saw him, she fell in love, and desire utterly seized
her heart. She went to Cyprus, to Paphos, where her precinct is,
and her fragrant altar, and she entered her fragrant shrine.
She entered there and closed the shining doors. The Graces
washed her and anointed her with immortal oil such as blooms
60 upon the gods who are forever—a divine oil that she filled
with perfume. Then laughter-loving Aphrodite covered her flesh
with beautiful raiment and decked herself out with gold,
and she left fragrant Cyprus and hastened to Troy, making
her way swiftly and high among the clouds.
                                        She came to Ida,
65 rich with its many springs, the mother of wild beasts. She crossed
the mountains. She went straight to the homestead, and with her
went fawning gray wolves and fierce-eyed lions and bears
and swift leopards, ravenous for deer. When she saw them
she took delight in her heart and she cast desire into their
70 breasts so that they all lay down in pairs amidst the shadowy
    haunts.°
    Then she herself came to the well-built hut, and she found
the mighty Anchises left alone apart from the others in the
    steading,
made handsome by the gods. All the other herdsmen were
    following after
the cattle in the grassy pastures while he, left alone apart from them
75 in the steading, went back and forth playing loudly on his lyre.
    Aphrodite, the daughter of Zeus, stood before him, like in
        stature
and appearance to an unmarried girl, so that when he beheld
her he would not be frightened. And when Anchises saw her,
he took stock and wondered at her appearance and her height

---

52. *Ida:* A massif southwest of Troy (not the Mount Ida on Crete).

70. *they all lay down ... haunts:* She is like the ancient Eastern Mistress of the Animals: followed by wolves, leopards, and bears, who forget their savage natures when they lie down together, caught in the net of sexual attraction (see figure 17).

FIGURE 17. The Mistress of the Animals on a Greek gold pendant, c. seventh century BC. The Mistress of the Animals is an aspect of what is sometimes called the Great Goddess or the Great Mother. From very early times she is shown standing between two animals, in this case two leopards. Her wings indicate her divinity. The poet of the Homeric "Hymn to Aphrodite" seems to be thinking of this goddess, although usually the Great Mother is identified with Artemis. Metropolitan Museum of Art, New York.

80 and her shining clothes. For she had put on a robe more brilliant
than the blaze of fire, and she had spiral bracelets and shining
  earrings
and around her tender neck were beautiful necklaces—golden,
elaborate!—and there was a shining like the moon over her tender
breasts, a marvel to see.
                    Desire took hold of Anchises,
85 and he spoke this word: "Hail, my queen, whoever of the blessed
ones you are, who have come to this dwelling—Artemis,
or Leto, or golden Aphrodite, or well-born Themis, or flashing-
  eyed
Athena—or whether you are one of the Graces who have come
  here,
who consort with all the gods and are called deathless,

90 or you are one of the nymphs who dwell in the beautiful forest,
    or one of the nymphs who inhabit this beautiful mountain
    and the springs of the rivers and the grassy meadows. I will make
    for you an altar in a lookout, a place that is cleared all around,
    and I will make for you beautiful sacrifices in every season.
95 But do you, with a friendly heart, let me be an outstanding man
    among the Trojans, and give me a flourishing offspring in days
    to come, and let me live a long life, seeing the light of the sun,
    rich among the people, and may I arrive at the threshold of
        old age."
    And Aphrodite, the daughter of Zeus, answered him:
100 "Anchises, most noble of men who dwell on the earth, know that
    I am no goddess! Why do you compare me to the deathless ones?
    I am mortal and the mother who bore me is a woman. My father
    is renowned Otreus,° if you have heard of him, who rules over all
    PHRYGIA with its mighty walls. I know your language, as well as
        my own,
105 for a Trojan nurse raised me in my halls. She attended me from
        when
    I was a small child, taking me from my mother. So I know your
        tongue
    as well as my own.°
            "Now the Slayer of Argos, who carries a golden wand,°
    has snatched me up from a dance to Artemis of the golden shafts
    and the cry of the hunt. There were many of us playing, brides
110 and marriageable girls, and a large crowd encircled us.
    Then the Slayer of Argos with the golden wand snatched me up,
    He carried me over the many farms of men who die, and much
    land unalotted and untilled across which flesh-eating wild animals
    wander through the shadowy woods. And I did not think that

---

103. *Otreus:* In *Iliad* 3.186, Otreus is a chief of the Phrygians, assisted by Priam in an invasion of the Amazons. PHRYGIA is an inland territory northeast of Troy.

106–7. *your tongue as well as my own:* This is the earliest reference in Greek to bilingualism.

107. *golden wand:* Hermes, the Slayer of Argos, carries the caduceus, a golden wand intertwined with copulating serpents.

115 I could touch the grain-bearing earth with my feet. He said
that I would be called the wife wedded in the bed of Anchises
and that I would bear you glorious children. Then when he had
    shown
you and instructed me, away went the powerful Slayer of Argos
to the families of the deathless ones.

                                    "And then I came to you,
120 and powerful necessity overcomes me. I beseech you by Zeus
and your noble parents—for I don't think that lowborn folk
begot you! Take me now, unsubdued and ignorant of love,
and show me to your father and your careful mother and your
brothers, whose parents are the same. I shall not be an unfitting
125 daughter-in-law, but a fair one. Quickly send a messenger
to the Phrygians of the swift steeds and say to my father and
    worried
mother, and they will send you much gold and woven cloth.
Take these as a right and splendid dowry. Do this, and prepare
the lovely marriage banquet, honoring men and the deathless
    gods."

130   So speaking the goddess cast sweet desire into his heart,
and sexual passion took hold of Anchises and he spoke this word
and addressed her: "If you are a mortal, and a mortal woman gave
you birth, and renowned Otreus is your father, as you say,
and you have come here through the will of Hermes, the
    deathless
135 messenger, and you will be called my wife for all time,
then no god, and no mortal man will hold me back from
our making love—right now, straightaway!—not if Apollo
    himself,
who shoots from afar, should send forth his groaning arrows
from his silver bow. For willingly would I plunge into the house
140 of Hades, if I could enter your bed, O woman like unto the
    gods!"
    So speaking, he took her by the hand, and laughter-loving
Aphrodite, casting her beautiful eyes downwards, turned and
    moved
slowly toward the bed, well covered by cloth, which the lord kept
already spread with soft blankets, and on top lay the skins

145 of bears and roaring lions that he himself had killed in the high
     mountains. And when they had mounted the well-made bed,
     first he took off the jewelry from her shining flesh, the brooches
     and twisted earrings and necklaces. Anchises loosed
     the band around her waist and took off her shining clothes
150 and placed them on a silver-studded stool. Then by the will
     of the gods, and through fate, the mortal bedded the immortal
     goddess, not knowing what he had done.
                                   At the time when
     herdsmen turn aside their cattle and their fat sheep into
     the fold, away from the flowery meadows, then Aphrodite
155 poured sweet and tender sleep over Anchises. She herself
     put on her beautiful robes. And when the divine goddess
     had covered all her flesh, she stood at the bedside, and her head
     touched the roof beams of the well-built chamber. An immortal
     beauty showed forth from her cheeks, such as belongs to
       Cythereia
160 of the lovely crown, and she woke him from sleep and spoke
     and addressed him:
                  "Rise, O descendant of Dardanos!°
     Why do you sleep so soundly? And tell me, if I seem to you
     to be like I was when you first set eyes upon me?"
     So she spoke, and he came swiftly out of his slumber
165 and responded to her. But when he saw the neck and beautiful
     eyes of Aphrodite, he was frightened, and he turned his eyes
     aside and again hid his handsome features in the blanket.
     Pleading, he spoke to her winged words:
                          "When I first
     beheld you with my eyes, O goddess, I knew immediately
170 that you were divine. But you did not speak to me the truth.
     I beg you, before Zeus who carries the aegis,
     not to leave me to dwell as a feeble man among men,
     but take pity on me: For he who has sex with goddesses
     is no fit man afterwards."
                    Aphrodite, the daughter of Zeus,

---

161. *Dardanos:* An early king of Troy, a son of Zeus and father of Ilos.

175 then answered him: "Anchises, most noble of humans
     who die, take heart. Do not have so much fear in your heart,
     nor fear that you will suffer harm from me, nor from
     the other blessed ones, for you are dear to the gods.
     You will have a dear son who will rule over the Trojans
180 and his children's children, begotten continuously.
     His name will be Aeneas, because I suffered terrible sorrow [*ainos*]
     when I fell into the bed of a mortal man. Of all humankind
     who die, those are most like the gods in appearance
     and stature who come from your family.

                                   "So Zeus the Counselor
185 snatched blond-haired Ganymede because of his beauty,
     so that he might go among the deathless ones and carry
     wine to the gods in the house of Zeus—a marvel to see!—
     honored by all the deathless ones as he pours out red
     nectar from a golden bowl. Unremitting sorrow took hold
190 of the heart of Tros,° and he did not know where the divine
     wind had taken his beloved son. He mourned him then
     constantly, every day, and Zeus took pity on him and gave
     him high-stepping horses, such as carry the deathless ones,
     as recompense for his son. These he gave him as a gift.
195 And the Slayer of Argos told him every detail at the behest
     of Zeus, how he would be deathless and ageless, like unto the gods.
     And when Tros heard this message from Zeus, then he no longer
     grieved, but he rejoiced in heart, and joyfully he raced with
     his storm-footed horses.

                                   "Thus too Dawn of the golden throne
200 snatched Tithonos,° who belongs to your family, like unto
     the deathless ones. She went to the dark-clouded son of Kronos
     and asked that he be deathless and live forever, and Zeus nodded
     agreement and granted her wish. Fool! Queenly Dawn
     did not remember in her heart to ask for youth and to strip

---

190. *Tros:* The founder of Troy and father of Ganymede. Troy is also called Ilion, after Ilos (the father of Dardanos), another son of Tros.

199–200. *Dawn of the golden throne snatched Tithonos:* Dawn (Eos) was known for her lasciviousness. Tithonos, a brother to Priam, was a son of Laomedon, grandson of Ilos, and great-grandson of Tros.

FIGURE 18. The handsome naked Ganymede, son of Tros, holding a hoop, symbolizing his youth, and a cock, a traditional gift in Greek pederasty. Cupbearers were often the object of male affection in the Greek symposia. The other side of the vase shows Zeus in pursuit. Athenian red-figure vase, c. 500–490 BC. Musée du Louvre, Paris. Photograph by Bibi Saint-Pol / Creative Commons.

205 him of evil old age. So long as lovely youth possessed him,
     he lived delightfully with Dawn of the golden throne, the early-
          born,
     by the waters of Ocean at the end of the earth. But when the first
     gray hairs poured down from his beautiful head and his noble
     chin, queenly Dawn kept away from his bed, though she kept him
210 in her mansion and nourished him, giving him food and ambrosia
     and lovely clothes. When bitter old age fell upon him utterly,

and he was not able to move or lift his limbs, this seemed to her
the best plan in her heart: She placed him in a chamber and
    she shut
its shining doors. And there his voice runs on unceasingly,
215 and there is no strength at all, such as once was in his supple
    limbs.°
    "Certainly I would not wish that you be deathless like that
among the deathless ones and live for all your days like that.
If you could live being such in appearance and stature
as you are now, and be called my husband, then grief
220 would not enfold my subtle mind. But as it is, wretched
old age, ruthless, will soon engulf you, which stands beside
all men—pitiless, exhausting!—which even the gods despise.
And it will be a reproach to me for all time because
of you among the undying gods, who earlier feared
225 my sweet-nothings and deceits by which I compelled
the deathless ones to have intercourse with mortal
women; for my purpose overcame them all. But now
my mouth will no longer open wide to recount
this among the deathless ones, for I have gone quite mad
230 —awfully, dreadfully—quite out of my mind! and I have
engendered a child in my belly by sleeping with a mortal man.
    "As for the child, when he first sees the light of the sun,
wild nymphs of the mountain, with their deep bosoms,
will raise him, who live on this great and blessed mountain.
235 They belong neither to those who die nor to those who do not die.
They live a long time and eat divine food and they dance
the lovely dance with the immortals. Sileni° and the keen-eyed
Slayer of Argos mate with them in the depths of lovely caves.
At their birth pines or high-topped oaks spring up with them
240 on the earth that feeds mankind. Beautiful, flourishing,
they stand high on the lofty mountains. Men call them precincts
of the gods, and they never cut them down with the ax.
    "But when the fate of death stands at their side, first

214–15. *his voice runs on unceasingly . . . his supple limbs:* According to later reports,
he was changed into a cicada, whirring constantly.
    237. *Sileni:* Creatures of the forest, elder satyrs.

those beautiful trees wither on the earth, and the bark
245 shrivels round about them, and the branches fall, and at the same
time the breath-souls of the nymphs leave the light of the sun.
These nymphs will keep my son by them and rear him.
Then when lovely youth will first come upon him,
the goddesses will lead the child here and show him to you.
250 When you first behold your child with your eyes, you will delight
at the vision, for he will be very like a god. Straightaway
you will take him to windy Ilion.° And if anyone of mortal
men should ask you which mother placed your son
in her belly, remember to answer what I command:
255 Say that he is the child of one of the flowery nymphs
who live on this forest-dressed mountain. But if
you speak out and boast in your mad mind that you
have slept with Cythereia of the lovely crown, Zeus
in his anger will strike you with his smoking thunderbolt.°
260   "All has been spoken. Take heed in your mind.
Take control, do not name me. Have respect for the wrath
of the gods."
        So speaking, she went off to windswept heaven.
I greet you, O goddess, who presides over well-cultivatcd
Cyprus! After beginning with you, I will shift to another song!

HOMERIC HYMN 6: TO APHRODITE

*"Homeric Hymn 6" was evidently composed for a contest (lines 19–20)
but it cannot be dated or placed in a locale. Though some have suggested
Cyprus as a place of performance, the hymn's references to the island are
conventional.*

Of Aphrodite—august, golden-crowned, beautiful!—I will sing,
who rules the bastions of all sea-girt Cyprus, whither the watery

---

252. *Ilion:* Another name for Troy.

258–59. *Zeus in his anger. . . thunderbolt:* According to later reports, this did happen,
leaving Anchises lame and unable to walk (e.g., Vergil, *Aeneid* 2.649).

strength of the blowing West Wind bore her in a soft foam°
across the waves of the much-resounding sea. And the Hours°
5   with their golden frontlets welcomed her eagerly, and cast
about her immortal clothing, and placed on her deathless
head a well-wrought crown—beautiful, golden! And from her
    pierced
ears they hung ornaments of yellow copper and costly gold.
They adorned her tender neck and her silver-white breasts
10   with golden necklaces such as the Hours themselves with their
golden frontlets wear when they enter the lovely dance of the gods
in the house of their father.
                And when they had fully adorned her flesh,
they brought her to the deathless ones, who welcomed her when
15   they saw her, and took her by the hand. And each of them
longed to lead her to his house as his wedded wife,
greatly amazed at the beauty of violet-crowned Cythereia.
    Hail, O goddess with the twinkling eyes, sweet and gentle!
Grant me to carry off the prize of victory in the contest.
20   Prepare my song! But I remember you, and another song too.

HOMERIC HYMN 10: TO APHRODITE

The short "Homeric Hymn 10" *was a prelude to some longer poem.*

I shall sing of Cythereia, Cyprus-born, who gives
to mortals sweet gifts, on whose lovely face smiles
ever play, and a lovely bloom dances across it.
    Hail, goddess! You rule over well-built
5   Salamis° and all of Cyprus. Give me lovely song.
I will remember you, and another song too.

---

3. *bore her in a soft foam:* Hesiod (*Theogony,* 188–200) says that when Kronos cut off
his father Sky's genitals they fell into the sea and Aphrodite arose from the foam *(aph-
ros)* that gathered around them. It is a folk etymology of the sort that the Greeks were
fond of. The name Aphrodite is really a distortion of a Near Eastern name. She was
borne past the island of Kythera to Cyprus, and so is called Cythereia or the Cyprian.

4. *Hours:* The Hours or Seasons, Horai, were the personification of the seasonal
aspects of nature. Like the Graces, they often accompany Aphrodite.

5. *Salamis:* Not the island near Athens, but the town of Salamis, an early Greek col-
ony in eastern Cyprus.

FIGURE 19. The birth of Aphrodite, on the so-called Ludovisi Throne, found in southern Italy; probably it was an altar. The relief seems to show Aphrodite rising from the sea, assisted by two Hours. Marble, c. 460 BC. Museo Nazionale di Roma. Photograph © Becks / Creative Commons.

ORPHIC HYMN 55: TO APHRODITE

The author of the hymn follows earlier celebrations of the goddess, showing her to be the lovely force behind all generation, making her the mother of Necessity, a divine personification.

Heavenly Aphrodite, subject of many songs, ever-smiling,
born of the sea, generative goddess, lover of the night,
blessed, joining lovers in the night, wily mother of Necessity
—from you comes all that is! You have yoked the world,
5   you reign over the three realms,° you have given
birth to all that is, all that is in heaven and on the rich
earth, and in the depths of the sea. Blessed companion
of Bacchus, delighting in festivities, bride-like mother
of the Erotes!° O Persuasion,° who enjoys the pleasures

5. *the three realms:* Probably the sky, the earth, and the sea.
9. *Erotes:* Plural of Eros, "Love," the child of Aphrodite; here the winged attendants of the love-goddess.
9. *Persuasion:* Peitho, an abstraction often said to accompany Aphrodite.

10   of the marital bed, secretive giver of joy visible and invisible,
      with lovely locks, well-born, bridal companion at the feast
      of the gods, holding a scepter, she-wolf, giver of heirs,
      lover of men, most desirable, giver of life who joins
      mortals in unbridled necessity and the many tribes
15   of wild beasts, driven mad by love-potions.

                                   Come,
      divine child of Cyprus, whether you are in Olympos
      —a divine queen—rejoicing in your beautiful face, or whether
      you are attended in your shrine in Syria° with its fine incense,
      or whether, riding in your golden chariot, you possess
20   the fertile baths of holy Egypt,° or whether, passing over
      the swelling of the sea in your swan-drawn carriage,
      you rejoice in the circling dance of sea-beasts, or whether
      you take delight in the dark-eyed nymphs upon the divine
      earth as they lightly leap on the sandy beaches of the seashore
25   —or whether, queen, you are in Cyprus that nourished you,
      where beautiful virgins and unwedded nymphs sing your
      praises for all the year, blessed one, and they sing of immortal
      holy Adonis°—

                      Come, blessed goddess, with your comely face.
      For with pure words I summon you, and with my devout soul.

---

18. *Syria:* The author explicitly equates Aphrodite with a Near Eastern goddess, probably Astartê.

20. *Egypt.* The hymnist equates Aphrodite with the Egyptian goddess Isis.

28. *Adonis:* Adonis is Semitic for "lord." He was another mortal lover of Aphrodite. His mother, Myrrha, lusted after her own father, Kinuras of Cyprus, and secretly slept with him. When discovered, she was changed into a myrrh tree from which the handsome Adonis emerged. Aphrodite became the lover of Adonis but he was gored by a boar and died in Aphrodite's arms, his blood becoming the anemone flower. The Adonia festival was celebrated every year in midsummer. Greek women would plant "gardens of Adonis," pots containing fast-growing plants that they set out in the hot sun where the plants would wither and die. Then the women would mourn the death of Adonis, tearing their clothes and lacerating their breasts in a display of grief.

FIGURE 20. Aphrodite on a swan, by the Pistoxenos Painter. The goddess was much associated with birds, especially sparrows and doves, here a swan. She holds a flower in her right hand, perhaps a lotus. Athenian white-ground wine-drinking cup. From Kameiros in Rhodes, c. 460 BC. British Museum, London. Photograph © Marie-Lan Nguyen / Creative Commons.

PROCLUS HYMN 2: TO APHRODITE

Proclus' hymn to Aphrodite tries to show that Aphrodite is the connection between the visible material world and the invisible realm.

We hymn the lineage of many names, of she born from the
     foam,
the mighty royal fount from which all the deathless winged

Erotes° have sprung. Some shoot at souls with transcendent
arrows so that, receiving the spiritual goads of desire, they may
5   long to see the fiery courts of their mother.° Some, because
of the evil-averting wishes and designs of their father,° wanting
to increase the endless world with its progeny, place desire in souls
for an earthly life.° Still others look always toward the varied
paths of wedding songs so that they might fashion from
10   mortal stock a deathless race of long-suffering humans°—
but all are concerned with the deeds of Cythereia,
the begetter of love.
                    But goddess—for you are far-hearing
no matter where you are, whether you embrace the great heaven
where they say that you are the divine soul of the everlasting
15   cosmos, or whether you dwell in the upper air beyond
the rims of the seven orbits,° pouring your unconquerable
strength into your lineage—hear me! Straighten the painful
course of my life, O mistress, with your just shafts,
putting an end to the icy thrust of my unholy desires.

PROCLUS HYMN 5: TO THE
LYCIAN APHRODITE

Though born in CONSTANTINOPLE, *Proclus was taken to* XANTHOS *in*
LYCIA *in south-central Turkey as a small child. His parents were Lycians*
of high birth. The Lycians were an Indo-European people with their own

---

3. *Erotes:*. Here the Erotes are the manifestation of Aphrodite's activities in the world.

3–5. *Some shoot at souls . . . their mother:* These Erotes represent a force that leads
one upwards to spiritual insight, in Stoicism called an "anagogic" ("upward leading")
force, guiding the soul to a vision of divine beauty, "the fiery courts of their mother."

6. *wishes and designs of their father:* Their father is the stoic Demiurge ("worker of
the people," hence "producer"), which Plato calls "the Father and Maker of this uni-
verse" (*Timaeus*, 28c3). It is the will of the Demiurge that maintains the universe, avert-
ing the evil of the end of the cosmos.

7–8. *desire in souls for an earthly life:* These Erotes direct the soul downward in the
cosmic force of attraction that produces all material things.

9–10. *fashion from mortal stock . . . long-suffering humans:* The Erotes are the force
that leads to human procreation.

16. *the seven orbits:* Of the planets. Aphrodite is here thought of as the world-soul,
vivifying all that is.

FIGURE 21. The Roman theatre and monumental Lycian tombs in the center of Xanthos, Lycia, Turkey. Photograph © Carole Raddato / Creative Commons.

long history. Proclus' "Hymn to the Lycian Aphrodite" celebrates a goddess prominent in the Hellenized town of Xanthos. Abundant ruins survive there, including a pillar inscribed partly in the poorly understood Lycian language. The base of a statue was found in Xanthos inscribed in Greek "To Aphrodite Who Listens" (Aphroditê epêkoô); it may be the statue referred to in this poem. It is not clear what Proclus intends by the evil that threatened Xanthos. Perhaps he simply means that Aphrodite, the goddess of divine love, was a protective deity in the city.

We sing a hymn to the Young Maid Aphrodite,° queen
of the Lycians!° Once the leaders of our fatherland–divinely
inspired, overflowing with her assistance that averts evil—
erected a holy statue to her in our city,° holding the symbols

1. *Young Maid Aphrodite: Kouraphroditê,* a name that appears only here, perhaps a cult name for a statue that was erected in Xanthos in Lycia, Proclus' hometown. The name may refer to Aphrodite's unaging qualities, or to her assistance to brides *(korai)* in wedding ceremonies.

1–2. *queen of the Lycians:* Nothing is known of the cult of Lycian Aphrodite.

4. *our city:* Xanthos.

5   of spiritual marriage, of the spiritual wedding between fiery
     Hephaistos and Aphrodite, the daughter of Sky.°
     And they called the goddess Olympian on account of whose
     power they often escaped the man-destroying arrow
     of death. They held their eye on excellence and a stalwart
10   bright-minded race sprouted up from fertile beds, and
     everywhere was a bountiful sea-calm in their lives.

      But do you now accept the sacrifice° of our eloquence,
     O goddess! For I am myself of the blood of the Lycians.
     Lift up my soul again from ugliness into a greater beauty,
15   fleeing the ruinous goad of earth-born desire.°

5–6. *spiritual wedding . . . the daughter of Sky:* Plato (*Symposium,* 180c) distinguishes two Aphrodites: Ouranian Aphrodite, the daughter of Ouranos, Sky, who represents noble love; and Aphrodite Pandemos ("of the people"), the daughter of Zeus and the goddess Dionê, who represents the cheap love of sexual relations. The "spiritual marriage" (*noeric,* that is, coming from Nous) of Ouranian Aphrodite and Hephaistos is symbolic of the alliance of "Unities" *(henads)* that causes the material basis for living beings (see the introduction). Proclus thus rejects the trashy story of the adultery between Ares and Aphrodite told in Homer, which also Plato rejected from his ideal city (*Republic,* 390c6–7). It is not clear, however, what the "symbols" of this marriage are.

12. *sacrifice:* That is, this very hymn.

15. *earth-born desire:* Souls that fall in love with the material realm forget the beauty of the divine realms, to which Aphrodite can exalt one.

7

Hephaistos

Hephaistos, a son of Zeus and Hera (or Hera alone), is the god famous for his clever creations in metal, including the shields of Herakles and Achilles, as well as self-moving tripods, female androids, bellows that blow themselves, and watchdogs made of gold and silver. He is the smithy-god, husband of Aphrodite in the *Odyssey* where he figures in the famous story about Aphrodite's adultery with Ares (see chapter 6). He is the subject of the only myth told twice in the *Iliad*, when he is thrown from heaven either for helping Hera against Zeus or because he was born lame. His gift of a special chair to Hera that imprisoned her, and as a result, Dionysos' luring of Hephaistos back to Olympos, drunk, on a mule, was the subject of many artistic illustrations (see figure 33). His association with fire is always close, and to the Orphics fire was the element from which the world was made, and the element to which (at least in the Stoic formulation) it would one day return. As god of craftsmanship he oversaw Athens together with Athena, and a famous temple, still standing, was built to him just off the agora (formerly called the Theseion, by a mistaken identification). He helped to birth Athena from Zeus's head, famous in artistic representations (see figure 6).

HOMERIC HYMN 20: TO HEPHAISTOS

Hephaistos is joined with Athena as the divine force underlying the making of crafts.

Of Hephaistos, famous for his cleverness, you shall sing,
O clear-voiced Muse, of he who taught humans who live
on the earth how to fashion glorious crafts. Before,
they lived in caves in the mountains like wild animals.
5   But now, thanks to Hephaistos, famous for his cleverness,
they pass the entire year at their ease in their own houses.

ORPHIC HYMN 66: TO HEPHAISTOS

Hephaistos is a powerful god who can both help and harm the aspiring initiate.

O Hephaistos, mighty of spirit, powerful, inexhaustible
fire, shining with flaming rays, light-bringing spirit,
torch-bearer, with prodigious strength in your hands,
eternal, living in art, worker, part of the cosmos,
5   perfect element, devourer of all, conqueror of all,
highest of all, consuming all—ether, sun, stars,
moon, purest light: these shine forth as the limbs
of Hephaistos. You possess every house, every city,
all peoples. You dwell in the bodies of mortals,
10   very rich, and formidable.
                              Hear, O blessed one!
I summon you to this holy libation that you might
come, gentle, to joyful deeds. End the savage rage
of tireless fire that you hold as nature in our bodies.

8

Apollo and the Muses

Apollo is sometimes said to be the most Greek of the gods. He is also the most complicated. There are really no gods like him in earlier, Eastern traditions. Although in later religions, especially the Roman, he was associated with the sun, he was not in origin a solar deity. He is the archer god, who cuts down with his arrows all who oppose him, though he is not a hunter god. He protects the flocks from predators. He is the plague god, who shoots from the invisible realms to kill without mercy. Because he can make you sick, he can make you well: he is a doctor, curing the sick. He is the father of Asklepios, the god of healing. He is the god of prophecy, presiding over the famous oracle at DELPHI, where he slew monstrous Python with his arrows and brought order to a chaotic world. He is the god of music and poetry because he brings inspiration, and knowledge, from the other world where he dwells.

He is the son of Leto, the daughter of the Titans Phoebê and Koios, and the twin brother of Artemis, who was born with him, or slightly before so she could assist their mother Leto in Apollo's birth on the island of Delos. In art he is a handsome usually beardless youth. His name is a mystery, in spite of elaborate attempts to explain its origin. It may be pre-Greek. It does not appear in the Mycenaean Linear B records, though a god called Paiawon does appear. Later, as *paieon,* the word designates a hymn to Apollo, or sometimes, in the *Iliad,* a separate god. Apollo is often called Lycian, but whether this means the "wolf god," the "god of LYCIA," or "the god of light," all possible explanations, cannot be determined. He is also often called Phoibos, apparently meaning "bright." He has long been associated with ASIA MINOR where, in the *Iliad,* he protects the Trojans and in classical times had major sanctuaries, but he also had important sanctuaries in mainland Greece, at DELPHI especially, where his oracle was located, and on the central island of DELOS. One of the earliest temples in Greece (at ERETRIA) was built to him. Many Greeks bore names that included "Apollo." One scholar attaches his name to an assembly of young men in northwest Greece called *apellai,* as if he embodied the aspirations and talents of young men, but Apollo's derivation from this association cannot be proven. As with so much in early Greek culture, facts are few.

As god of the Delphic oracle, Apollo earned moral authority over the Greek imagination, and two famous maxims were carved over his temple: *meden agan,* "nothing too much," and *gnothi seauton,* "know yourself." Good advice for a people who often went too far and forgot that they were only human!

Closely associated with Apollo were the Muses (of uncertain etymology), usually said to be the daughters of Zeus and Mnemosynê (nē-**mos**-i-nē), "Memory." Apollo was called Mousagetês, "Muse-Leader." Either three or nine in number, the Muses inspired poetry and literature of all kinds. Homer, and many others, began their poems with an invocation to the Muses.

HOMERIC HYMN 3: TO APOLLO

The Homeric hymn to Apollo seems to be one of the oldest in the collection. It is the second longest. An ancient commentator says it was composed by one Kynaithos from CHIOS, who first recited the poems of Homer in SYRACUSE in 500 BC. Many think that Kynaithos was responsible for joining two preexisting poems, oral in origin: one to Apollo of DELOS, which tells of the god's birth, and one to Apollo of DELPHI, which tells of his killing the monstrous Python and the establishment of his oracle there. Such scholars think that the Delian portion was the earlier, from the seventh century BC, and that the Delphic portion is from the sixth century, but others argue for an original unity. In any event, the poem that we have, from the seventh or sixth century BC, celebrates two great events in this famous god's career.

I shall remember, and I shall not forget, Apollo
who shoots from afar! As he goes through the house
of Zeus, the gods are atremble, and they all leap up
from their seats as he comes near, when he stretches
5   his brilliant bow. Leto alone remains at the side
of Zeus who delights in the thunderbolt. She unstrings
his bow and closes his quiver. With her hands she takes
the bow from his powerful shoulders and hangs it up
on a pillar in his father's house, from a golden peg.
10   She leads him to a chair and makes him sit on it.
His father gives him nectar in a golden cup, toasting
his dear son. Then the other gods do likewise from where
they sit, and the lady Leto is glad because she has borne
an archer and a mighty son.
                                        Rejoice, O blessed Leto!
15   You have borne splendid children, King Apollo
and Artemis who delights in arrows—her in Ortygia,
and him in rocky Delos, as you leaned against
the high mass of the hill of Kunthos, near the palm-tree,
beside the streams of Inopos.°
                                        But how shall I sing
20   of you, who are in so many ways worthy of song?
The fields of song are everywhere laid down for you,
O Phoibos,° both on the mainland that nourishes cows,
and throughout the islands. Every lookout is pleasing to you,
and the steep headlands of high mountains, and the rivers
25   flowing to the sea, and the beaches up against the water,
and the harbors of the sea. Shall I sing of how Leto bore you,
a delight to mortals, as she leaned against the hill of Kunthos
in the rocky isle, in sea-girt Delos? And a dark wave

16–19. *in Ortygia . . . streams of Inopos:* Ortygia, "quail island," is often said to be
another name for Delos, "bright," but here is applied to a nearby island, perhaps Rhe-
neia to the west. Kunthos is the name of a hill in the center of Delos. In Latin, Cynthia
is a name for Diana (that is, Artemis), the origin of this name. Inopos is a stream that
flows at the base of Mount Kunthos. On Delos, a palm tree grew beside the temple to
Apollo and Artemis, said to be the tree mentioned in the hymn.
    22. *Phoibos:* "Shining," that is, Apollo.

rolled from either side up on the shore, driven by the keening
30   winds—and you went forth from there to rule over all mortals.
  As many as are in CRETE, and the people of ATHENS,
  and the island of AIGINA, and EUBOIA famous for its ships,
  and Aigai and Eiresiai and Peparethos near the sea, and Thracian
  ATHOS, and the high peaks of PELION, and SAMOTHRACE, and
    the shadowy
35   mountains of IDA, and well-cultivated IMBROS, and inhospitable
  LEMNOS, and most holy LESBOS, the seat of Makar, son of Aiolos,°
  and SKYROS and Phokaia and the steep mount of Autokanê,
  and CHIOS, which lies the most shining of islands in the sea,
  and craggy Mimas, and the high peaks of Korukos, and gleaming
40   KLAROS and the steep mountain of Aisagea, and well-watered
  SAMOS and the steep peaks of Mukalê, and MILETOS and KOS,
  the city of the Meropes, and steep KNIDOS and windy
  KARPATHOS, and NAXOS and PAROS and rocky Rheneia°—
  so many places did Leto traverse, struggling to give birth
45   to the Far-Shooter, if only some land would be willing
  to be a home to her son. But they greatly trembled
  and were afraid, and not one dared to receive Phoibos,
  even the richest of them, until Lady Leto landed on Delos,
  and she asked her the following, speaking winged words:
50   "Delos, if only you would be willing to be the seat
  of my son, Phoibos Apollo! For no other will touch you
  or honor you. I do not think that you will be rich in cattle
  or in sheep, and you will grow no grapes, nor will you
  bear ten thousand kinds of fruit. But if you sponsor
55   the temple of Apollo who works from afar, all humans
  will bring you great sacrifices as they gather here,
  and the smoke of offerings will forever rise, and you will feed
  the people who live here from the hands of strangers;
  for your soil beneath is not rich."
                                            Thus she spoke, and Delos

36. *Makar, son of Aiolos:* A legendary king of Lesbos. His name means "blessed."
  31–43. *As many as are in Crete . . . and rocky Rheneia:* See map 2 for most of these
places, all centers of the worship of Apollo.

60 rejoiced, and answered her: "Leto, most glorious daughter
    of great Koios,° gladly would I receive the birth
    of the Far-Shooter, the king. For it is very true that I have
    a bad reputation among men. But in this way I would become
    greatly honored. Only I fear this saying, Leto, and I will not
65 hide it from you: they say that Apollo will be too reckless,
    that he will lord it greatly over the deathless ones
    and over mortal men upon the rich earth. So I fear
    terribly in my heart and spirit that, when he first sees
    the light of the sun, he will spurn this island, for my soil
70 is hard and rocky, and he will overturn me with his feet
    and shove me down into the depths of the sea. Then
    a great wave of the sea will wash over my head forever.
    And he will go off to another land that will please him,
    and he will build his temple and plant his wooded groves.
75 Octopi and black seals will make their houses in me,
    undisturbed, bereft of people. But if, goddess, you might
    dare to swear a great oath, that first he will build
    a glorious temple here to be an oracle for humans,
    and only later will he go to all men, for he will be greatly
80 renowned . . . ?"
                        So Delos spoke, and Leto swore
    the powerful oath of the gods: "Know this, O Earth
    and broad Sky who are above, and the dribbling water
    of Styx (which is the greatest and most awesome oath
    for the blessed gods), surely here will be forever
85 the fragrant altar and precinct of Phoibos, and he will
    honor you above all others."
                        But when she had sworn
    and completed her oath, Delos greatly rejoiced in the birth
    of the far-darting king. Leto was pierced with unutterable pangs
    for nine days and nine nights. All the chief goddesses
90 were with her—Dionê and Rhea and Themis of Ichnai

---

61. *Koios:* One of the twelve Titans born to Earth (Gaia) and Sky (Ouranos). He has
no other myths.

90–92. *Dionê and . . . Hera of the white arms:* Dionê, the feminine form of Zeus
("Mrs. Zeus"), is sometimes said to be a wife of Zeus and the mother of Aphrodite. Rhea

and groaning Amphitritê and the other deathless goddesses,
except for Hera of the white arms;° for she sat in the halls
of cloud-gathering Zeus. Only Eileithyia,° goddess
of birth-pangs, had not learned of it: She sat on the top
95   of Olympos beneath the golden clouds, by the contriving
of white-armed Hera, who held her back, from envy,
when Leto of the beautiful hair was about to give birth
to a blameless and powerful son.
                                                But the goddesses sent forth
100   Iris° from the well-cultivated isle to fetch Eileithyia,
promising her a great necklace strung with golden threads,
fifteen feet long. They urged her to call Eileithyia apart
from white-armed Hera so that Hera might not dissuade
her from coming. When swift Iris, quick as the wind,
105   heard this, she ran off, and swiftly she crossed the intervening
space. But when she came to the seat of the gods
in steep Olympos, immediately she called out Eileithyia
from the hall to the door and spoke winged words,
telling her everything the goddesses who have their houses
110   on Olympos had instructed her. She persuaded the heart
within her breast, and they went off like shy doves
in their going.
                        When Eileithyia, goddess of birth pangs,
came to Delos, then the pangs took hold of her,
and she longed to give birth. She cast her arms around
115   a palm tree and braced her knees on the soft meadow.
And the earth beneath her laughed. The child leaped forth
to the light and all the goddesses cried out aloud.
Then, O Apollo of the joyous cry, the goddesses washed
you in beautiful water, purely, cleanly, and they swathed

---

is the wife of Kronos and the mother of Zeus and his siblings. Themis, "right, law," is a
Titan and Zeus's second wife. Ichnai is a town in Macedonia. Amphitritê, a Nereid, is
wife to Poseidon. She is "groaning" perhaps because of the sound of the sea.

93. *Eileithyia:* The goddess of childbirth, a child of Zeus and Hera (along with Ares).
She is probably pre-Greek, worshipped in Crete.

100. *Iris:* "rainbow," the messenger of the gods (along with Hermes), a granddaugh-
ter of Ocean.

FIGURE 22. Apollo and Artemis on Delos, by the Comacchio Painter. Artemis stands to the left of an altar, pouring out an offering from a vase. Apollo stands in the center, holding a laurel branch, sacred to his cult, in his left hand and an offering dish in his right. An attendant stands at the far right holding a vine. Behind the altar grows the palm tree that Leto clung to while giving birth. Such a tree grew on Delos, near the temple to Artemis. Athenian red-figure vase, c. 450 BC. Museo Arqueológico Nacional, Madrid. Photograph © Marie-Lan Nguyen / Creative Commons.

120 you in a white cloth— fine, fresh!—and tied a golden cord
around you. Leto did give suck to Apollo of the golden
sword, while Themis offered nectar and lovely ambrosia
with her deathless hands, and Leto rejoiced <that she had
given birth to a powerful son, an archer.>° But surely
125 as soon as you, O Phoibos, had tasted that immortal food,
then no longer could the golden cords restrain your wriggling,
nor did the fastenings restrain you, but all the ties came undone.
　　Straightaway Phoibos Apollo spoke to the deathless
goddesses: "May the lyre and bent bow be dear to me,
and I will reveal to humans the unerring will of Zeus."
130 So saying, he walked upon the wide-wayed earth, long-haired

123–24. <that she had . . . an archer>: Some words are missing here.

Phoibos who shoots from afar. All the deathless goddesses
were astounded, and all of Delos° bristled with gold
when she saw the child of Zeus and Leto, joyous
that the god had chosen her to make his home instead
135 of the other islands and the mainland, and that he loved
her more from his heart.
                                     And you, O King Apollo
of the silver bow, far-shooter, sometimes you went
on craggy Mount Kunthos, sometimes you wandered through
the islands among the men. Many are your temples and
140 wooded groves. Every place of lookout is dear to you,
and the peaks of the high mountains and the rivers
that flow to the sea, but, O Phoibos, Delos most
delights your heart. There the Ionians with their trailing
robes gather with their children and their wives on your
    avenue.°
145 Thinking of you, delighting you, they compete in boxing
and dancing and oral song, whenever they come together.
You might say that they were deathless and ageless
if you came upon them, when the Ionians gather there.
You would see the charm of them all, and delight
150 in your heart seeing the men and the well-belted women,
and the swift ships and all their abundant wealth.
There is a great wonder too, whose renown will never
    perish:
the young Delian girls, handmaidens of the Far-Shooter,
who sing first of Apollo, then of Leto and Artemis
155 who thrills to arrows. Remembering the men and women
of old, they sing a song and delight the tribes of men.
And they know how to reproduce the speech of all men—

132. *and all of Delos . . .* : The text has an alternative version for the rest of the sen-
tence, which reads: "bloomed as a mountain top with flowers of the woods when she
saw" et cetera.

143–44. *the Ionians . . . on your avenue:* Beginning evidently in the eighth century
BC, Ionians—that is, Greeks from the coast of Asia Minor—and inhabitants of the
Greek islands gathered in Delos for a great festival. The poem goes on to describe events
at this festival.

and their babbling! You would each say that you yourself
were singing, so cannily does their beautiful song imitate
160 your accent.

But come, be gracious, Apollo and Artemis,
and hail all you maidens! Remember me in aftertimes,
when some long-suffering stranger comes here and asks,
"O maidens, which man comes here as the sweetest singer,
and in whom do you most delight?" Then do you answer
165 all together, in one voice, "A blind man. He lives
in rocky Chios. His songs will forevermore be the best."°
As for me, I will bear your fame for as far over
the earth as I travel, visiting the well-ordered cities of men.
170 And they will be persuaded, because this is the truth.
And I myself will never cease to sing the praise
of Apollo, the Far-Shooter, he of the silver bow, whom
fine-haired Leto bore.°

O king, you inhabit Lycia
and lovely Maeonia and MILETOS,° delightful city
175 of the sea, but over wave-washed Delos you yourself
rule with power. The son of glorious Leto goes
to rocky Pytho,° playing upon his hollow lyre
clad in immortal clothing, sweetly-smelling.
His lyre gives forth a charming sound as he strikes
180 it with his golden plectrum. From there, from the earth,
he springs to Olympos—like thought!—to the house

165–66. *A blind man . . . will forevermore be the best:* These lines gave rise to the story
that Homer was a blind poet from the island of Chios, but this poem is too late to be by
Homer. Homer probably was not blind and it is doubtful that he came from Chios. The
composer of these lines may be Kunaithos, who may have belonged to a guild of poets
on Chios called the Homerids, who claimed descent from the great poet. Whether they
really were or not, cannot be known.

173. *Leto bore:* Here ends what many take to be, in origin, a separate poem to the
Delian Apollo. The next words begin the poem to the Delphic Apollo.

173–74. *Lycia and lovely Maeonia and Miletos:* Lycia is an area of southern Asia
Minor; many think that Apollo's epithet "Lycian" comes from his association with this
area (but it may also mean "wolf-like"). Maeonia is a region of Asia Minor near the
HERMOS RIVER. Miletos is a great and ancient Greek city further down the coast.

177. *Pytho:* That is, DELPHI, so called after the serpent that Apollo killed there, which
rotted *(puthein)*.

of Zeus, to the assembly of the other gods. At once
the music of the lyre and song are the god's preoccupation.
At the same time all the Muses,° trading beautiful song
185 back and forth, sing of the immortal gifts of the gods
and of the sufferings of human beings, how they live
stupidly and helplessly at the hands of the deathless gods,
and they cannot find a cure for death or a defense
against old age.
                              But the Graces, with their fine hair, and the
190 friendly Hours and Harmonia and Hebê° and Aphrodite,
the daughter of Zeus, dance holding one another by the wrists.
And among them sings one who is not plain, nor small, but tall
to see and noble in her bearing—Artemis who delights in
        arrows,
the sister of Apollo. Among them dances Ares and the Slayer
195 of Argos,° while Phoibos Apollo plays his lyre in the middle,
stepping fine and high. A splendor shines about him,
the gleaming of his feet and his finely woven tunic.
And they rejoice in their great hearts—golden-haired Leto
and Zeus the Counselor—when they see their dear son
200 sporting among the deathless gods.
                                    How shall I sing
of you, who are in every way worthy of song? Perhaps
I will tell of how you went as a wooer in the field of love,
how you pursued as a suitor the daughter of Azan,
in rivalry with godlike Ischus, son of the horseman Elatios?°

184. *Muses:* The nine (or three) Muses inspired song of all kinds.

189–90. *the Graces . . . Hebê:* The Graces (Charites) are the daughters of Zeus and
Eurunomê, an Oceanid; they embody feminine charm. The Hours (Horai), the daugh-
ters of Zeus and Themis, a Titan, are goddesses of the seasons. Harmonia was the
daughter of Ares and Aphrodite; she married Kadmos of Thebes and gave birth to
Semelê, the mother of Dionysus. Hebê (**hē**-bē), "youth," is the daughter of Zeus and
Hera. She married Herakles after his death and exaltation to Olympos.

194–95. *Slayer of Argos:* Hermes.

203–4. *daughter of Azan . . . the horseman Elatios:* The daughter of Azan was Koronis,
the mother of Asklepios by Apollo. He became the god of medicine. Ischus, son of Ela-
tios, was his rival and married Koronis when she was pregnant with Asklepios.

205 Or with Phorbas, the son of Triopos, or with Ereutheus?°
Or with Leukippos and the wife of Leukippos—you on foot
and he on a chariot, but he did not fall short of Triopos.°
Or how, seeking an oracle for humans, you first traveled
over the earth, O Far-Shooter Apollo!

You first came down
210 from Olympos to Pieria. You passed by sandy Lektos
and the Ainianes and you went through the Perrhaiboi. Swiftly
you came to IOLKOS, and you went to Kenaion on EUBOIA,
famous for its ships. And you stood on the Lelantine Plain,°
but to build a temple there and plant wooded groves was not
pleasing
215 to your heart.

From there you crossed the EURIPOS, O Far-Shooter
Apollo, and you went up the green, holy mountains, and soon
from there you came to Mukallesos and Teumessos with its grassy
beds.° Then you came to the site of THEBES, clad in woods.
For as yet no man lived in sacred Thebes, and not yet
220 were there paths or road crossing the wheat-bearing plain,
but all was wooded.

From there you went further, O Far-Shooter
Apollo, and you came to ONCHESTOS,° the glorious wood
of Poseidon. There the colt, just broken, takes breath
though struggling as it draws the beautiful chariot.

205. *Phorbas . . . Ereutheus:* Perhaps also suitors of Koronis, but it is not clear.

206–7. *Leukippos and the wife of Leukippos . . . Triopos:* The references in these lines are unknown.

210–13. *to Pieria . . . on the Lelantine Plain:* Pieria is the region north of MOUNT OLYMPOS in THESSALY; it was the first place that gods landed on earth and the birthplace of the Muses. Lektos is a town among the Ainianes, a tribe of southern Thessaly. The Perrhaiboi lived between Mount Olympos and IOLKOS, which is at the head of the gulf embraced by Mount PELION: Jason and Argonauts set sail from here. Across the channel on Euboia was Kenaion. The Lelantine Plain lies between ancient CHALKIS and ERETRIA, the site of the first historical war in Greece. See map 2.

215–18. *Euripos . . . with its grassy beds:* Euripos is the narrow strait between BOEOTIA and EUBOIA. Mukallesos and Teumessos are towns in Boeotia.

222. *ONCHESTOS:* A Boeotian city northwest of Thebes, at the southern end of LAKE KOPAÏS (now drained). There was a famous shrine to Poseidon there.

225 The driver, though he is a good one, leaps to the ground
from the chariot and walks while the horses rattle along
the empty car, having thrown their driver. If the chariot
smashes in the wooded grove, they take care of the horses,
but tilt up the car and leave it: thus was the rite established
230 from the beginning. The drivers pray to the god
but they then leave the car as the portion of the god.°
Then you went on further, O Far-Shooter Apollo,
and came then to the beautiful streams of the Kephissos,
which sends its fair-flowing water forth from Lilaia.
235 Crossing it, O Worker from Afar, you passed Okelea
rich in wheat, and from there you came to grassy
Haliartos.°
              And then you went to Telphousa,°
and there the kindly site seemed good to build your temple
and plant your wooded grove. You stood near to the nymph
240 and spoke these words: "O Telphousa, I am minded to build
here a most beautiful temple as an oracle for humans,
who forever will bring perfect animals for sacrifice, both
those who live in the fertile PELOPONNESOS,° and those
who live on the mainland and in the islands, washed
245 by the sea, who come to seek an oracle. And I would give
faultless advice to all, giving oracles in my rich temple."
       So speaking, Phoibos Apollo laid out his foundations,
broad and in very long continuous lines. But Telphousa,
seeing them, became angry in her heart and said: "Lord Phoibos,

---

230–31. *The drivers pray . . . the god:* The ritual here is unknown and obscure. Evidently drivers in Poseidon's grove jump from their chariots and allow the horses to run loose. If the chariot is smashed, they leave it leaned against a tree in the grove as an offering to the god.

233–37. *streams of the Kephissos . . . Haliartos:* The Kephissos flows from Lilaia, a town at the foot of MOUNT PARNASSOS, to enter Lake Kopaïs at its northern end. Okalea and Haliartos lay along the western shore of the lake, northwest of Onchestos, so that Apollo would not really have crossed the Kephissos in traveling from Lilaia to Haliartos.

237. *Telphousa:* A spring at the foot of MOUNT HELIKON, as well as the nymph who inhabits the spring.

243. *PELOPONNESOS:* "The Island of Pelops," that is, all of southern Greece, south of the Isthmus of Corinth. This is the first appearance of the word in Greek literature.

250 Worker from Afar, I will say something, and you should take
     it to heart, because you are minded to build a very beautiful
     temple to be an oracle for humans, who will forever bring
     perfect sacrificial animals. But I will tell you, and you lay up
     my words in your heart. The constant pounding of swift horses
255 will forever pain you, and the sound of mules watering
     at my holy spring. Here a visitor will wish to watch
     the finely crafted chariots and listen to the pounding
     of swift-footed horses rather than look at a great
     temple and the many treasures within. But if you will be
260 persuaded—of course you are greater and better than I,
     O lord, and your strength is supreme—make it at Krisa°
     in the fold of Parnassos. There no beautiful chariots
     will clash, nor will there be the pounding of swift-footed
     horses around your well-built altar, but just the same
265 the famous tribes of humans would bring their gifts
     to Iê-Paieon° and you would delight to receive the fine
     gifts of surrounding peoples."
                              So speaking, she persuaded
     the mind of the Far-Shooter, so that she alone should
     be famous in this place, and not the Far-Shooter.
270   From there you went still further, O far-shooting Apollo.
     You came to the city of the overbearing Phlcgyan men,°
     who, having no respect for Zeus, dwell on the earth in a beautiful
     valley near the marshes of Kephissos. From there
     you swiftly rushed on up to the ridge and came to Krisa
275 beneath snowy Parnassos, a spur facing west, and a rocky
     cliff hangs over it and a hollow valley runs beneath it,
     rugged. There the lord Phoibos resolved to build

---

261. *Krisa:* The port of Delphi on the Gulf of Corinth. Delphi is built on the southern slope of Mount Parnassos.

266. *Iê-Paieon:* The "Iê" is of uncertain meaning, but perhaps means "Hail." Paieon is an old name for Apollo as a healing god.

271. *Phlegyan men:* A Thessalian tribe.

273. *Kephissos:* There is a river in Attica with the same name, but this is the river that flows from the foot of Mount Parnassos into Lake Kopaïs.

his lovely temple, and he said:

"I am minded to build
here a most beautiful temple as an oracle for humans,
280 who forever will bring perfect animals for sacrifice, both
those who live in the fertile Peloponnesos, and those
who live on the mainland and in the islands, washed
by the sea, who come to seek an oracle. And I would give
faultless advice to all, giving oracles in my rich temple."
285   So speaking, Phoibos Apollo laid out his foundations,
broad and in very long, continuous lines. And on these
Trophonios and Agamedes, the sons of Erginos,°
dear to the deathless gods, laid a floor of stone.
And the numberless tribes of humans lay down a temple
290 of stones set in place to be a subject of song, forever.
         Nearby was a spring of beautiful flowing water, where
the lord, the son of Zeus, killed a she-serpent with his powerful
bow—bloated, enormous!—a savage monster that had done
many evils to humans upon the earth, to them themselves
295 and to their long-shanked sheep, for she was a blood-reeking
affliction. Once she accepted for nurture from Hera of the
     golden
throne the terrible and pernicious Typhaon,° a curse to mankind.
Hera once bore him in anger at Father Zeus because he, the son
of Kronos, gave birth to glorious Athena out of his head.°
300 Lady Hera at once grew angry, and she spoke to the assembled
     gods:
         "Listen to me, all you gods and all you goddesses,
how cloud-gathering Zeus begins to disrespect me,
without cause, after he made me his doting wife.
For he has given birth to flashing-eyed Athena without

287. *Trophonios and Agamedes:* Trophonios and Agamedes were legendary archi-
tects. Pausanias says (10.15.13) that this temple was burned down in 548 BC.

297. *Typhaon:* Also called Typhoeus, he is usually said to be the youngest offspring
of Earth (Gaia) and Tartaros, but this hymn claims that Hera was his mother. He had
one hundred fire-breathing heads that made a cacophony of sounds.

299. *gave birth to glorious Athena out of his head:* A prophecy said that the child of
Metis ("Mind") would overthrow Zeus, so Zeus swallowed the pregnant Metis and Ath-
ena was born from his head, thus Zeus's child alone and no longer a threat. See figure 6.

FIGURE 23. The temple of Apollo at Delphi on the steep slopes of Mount Parnassos, with several reerected columns. The Pythia, the elderly woman who pronounced the oracles, sat on a tripod in a room at the right of the picture. Krisa was located at the base of the valley in the background, to the right of the picture, on the GULF OF CORINTH. Above the temple, to the left of the picture, was a theater and above that a race course. Photograph © Luarvick / Creative Commons.

305 my participation, she who stands out among the blessed
    deathless ones, while my son Hephaistos has turned out
    to be a weakling, with shriveled feet, whom I myself bore.
    I picked him up in my hands and threw him into
    the broad sea. But Thetis, the silver-footed daughter
310 of Nereus,° took him in and cared for him with her
    sisters. Would that she had done some *other* service
    for the blessed gods!
                     "You wretch! with your fancy designs!
    What are you up to now? How did you dare to give birth
    to flashing-eyed Athena all by yourself? Would not *I* have
315 borne you a child? She would *still* have been called

309–10. *Thetis, the silver-footed daughter of Nereus:* Thetis is the most famous of the Nereids, the fifty daughters of Nereus, the Old Man of the Sea, and the Oceanid Doris. Thetis is the mother of Achilles.

your daughter among the deathless ones, who inhabit
broad heaven. You better watch out that I don't plan
some wickedness in the future! I think, in fact, that I will
give birth to a child who will be called *my* son, who will
320 stand out among the deathless gods, and who will not
bring shame to your bed, nor to mine! In fact I will have
nothing to do with your bed, but will keep company with
the undying gods far away from you."

                                 So speaking
she went apart from the gods with an angry heart. At once
325 cow-eyed lady Hera prayed, and she struck the ground
with her hand turned down and said:

                                "Hear me now,
Earth and broad Sky up above, and the Titan gods who live
beneath the earth around great Tartaros, from whom
are born both gods and men. Listen now, all of you, and give
330 me a son apart from Zeus who is every bit as strong as Zeus—
nay, let him be as much stronger than Zeus as far-seeing
Zeus is stronger than Kronos!"

                          So speaking, she flogged
the earth with her powerful hand. The life-bearing earth
shifted, and when Hera saw it she was delighted in her heart,
335 for she thought that her prayer would be fulfilled. And after that
for a full year she did not go to the bed of Zeus the Counselor,
nor to her fancy carved throne, as before she would sit there
and give wise counsels. Instead, cow-eyed Lady Hera remained
in her temples filled with prayers and delighted in the sacrifices
340 offered there. But when the months and the days were fulfilled,
as the year rolled around and the new seasons came, she gave
    birth
to a creature unlike the gods or any mortal—the awesome
and savage Typhaon, a curse to the gods. At once cow-eyed
Lady Hera took him up and carried him and gave him,
345 one evil, to the evil she-serpent,° and she accepted him.

344–45. *gave him, one evil, to the evil she-serpent:* That is, she delivered the infant
Typhaon to Python to be nurtured at Delphi, to which the narrative now returns.

And she° did great harm to the famous tribes of
    human beings.
Whoever went up against her, she brought to him a day of
    doom,
until the lord, far-shooting Apollo, loosed his powerful arrow
at her, and she, broken by terrible pain, lay gasping out her life,
350 rolling upon the earth. A wondrous screaming filled the air,
indescribable, and she rolled continually round and round
among the trees, and she gave up her life, gasping out blood.
    Phoibos Apollo then boasted: "Now rot° here
upon the man-nourishing earth. Nor shall you live to be
355 a scourge to mortals who, feeding on the fruit of the nurturing
soil, will bring here perfect sacrificial animals. Nor shall
Typhoeus, nor the hateful Chimaira° fend off cruel death
from you, but the dark earth and the blazing sun will set
you to rot."
        So he spoke, boasting. Darkness covered
360 over her eyes. And there the holy power of Helios°
made her to rot, from which the place is now called *Pytho.*
And men call the Lord Apollo *Pythian* because there
the power of keen Helios made the monster to rot.
It was then that Phoibos Apollo saw in his heart that
365 the spring with its beautiful flowing waters had deceived him.°
In anger he went to Telphousa, and quickly he was there.
He stood very close to her and said these words: "Telphousa,

346. *and she:* Pytho is meant.

353. *Now rot:* "rot" here is *peutheu,* whence the title, Pythia, given to the oracular priestess and the name, Pytho, given to the serpent and to the oracular shrine.

357. *Typhoeus, nor the hateful Chimaira:* Here Typhaon is spelled Typhoeus. Chimaira (ki-**mī**-ra) was the daughter of Typhaon. She had the body of a lion, the tail of a serpent, and a goat's head growing from her back, breathed fire, and was killed by Bellerophon.

360. *Helios:* The sun-god.

365. *the spring . . . had deceived him:* That is, Telphousa had told Apollo that he would find a better place for his oracle than her own spring, then sent him up against a dangerous demonic being.

you were not after all going to get away with tricking me
and holding onto this lovely place to pour forth your
370 clear-flowing water! Here too, truly, will I be renowned,
and not you alone!"
                              So spoke the lord, far-darting Apollo,
and he pushed over a jutting crag in a shower of rocks,
and he hid her streams. He set up an altar in the wooded grove,
quite near to the spring with its clear waters. There all men
375 pray to the god by the name Telphousios, because he disfigured
the streams of holy Telphousa.
                              And then Phoibos Apollo
pondered in his heart which men he should bring in as priests
to serve him in rocky Pytho. While he was thinking this over,
he espied a swift ship on the wine-dark sea. There were many
380 men in it of noble descent, Cretans from KNOSSOS,
the city of Minos, who perform sacrifices to the god
and announce the oracles of Phoibos Apollo of the golden
sword, whatever he should say, giving his oracles from the laurel
tree down in the valleys of Parnassos.°
                              These men were sailing
385 for business in their black ship toward sandy PYLOS°
and the men who live in Pylos. But Phoibos Apollo
intercepted them: he took on the shape of a dolphin
and sprang upon their swift ship in the open water
and lay there, a huge and fearsome monster. Whenever
390 any one of them thought in his heart to notice him,
he would toss him off in any direction, and shake
the timbers of the ship.° In terror they sat silently in the ship.
They did not loosen the ropes along the hollow black ship,
nor did they lower the sail of their blue-prowed ship,

383–84. *from the laurel . . . Parnassos:* The laurel was sacred to Apollo, and other
sources tell us that his first temple was constructed of laurel. Oddly the hymn does not
mention the Pythia, the priestess who, in classical times, sat on a tripod and gave out
oracles while holding a laurel branch, after chewing laurel leaves.

385. *PYLOS:* On the southwestern coast of the Peloponnesos.

389–92. *Whenever any one of them . . . of the ship:* The meaning of the Greek is very
obscure.

395 but as they first had rigged it with oxhide ropes they sailed on.
     A rushing south wind pushed on the swift ship from behind.
         First they passed by CAPE MALEA,° then along
     the Lakedaimonian coast they came to the city of TAINARON,
     crowned by the sea, the country of the sun-god who gladdens men,
400 where the thick-fleeced sheep of Lord Helios ever graze,
     living in a delightful country. There they wished to put ashore
     and disembark to contemplate the great marvel and to see with
     their eyes if the beast would remain on the deck of the hollow
     ship, or whether it would leap again into the salty deep
405 that teems with fish. But the well-built ship would not obey
     the rudder, and it went on its way past the rich Peloponnesos.
     For the lord, far-shooting Apollo, easily guided it with his breath.
         The ship ran on its course and came to Arenê and lovely
     Argupheê, and Thruon, the ford of the ALPHEIOS, and well-built
410 Aipu and sandy Pylos and the people who dwell in Pylos.
     The ship passed Krounoi and Chalkis and past Dumê and past
     marvelous ELIS, where the Epeians rule. As it headed for Pheia,
     exulting in the breeze from Zeus, there appeared to them
     beneath the clouds the steep mountain of ITHAKA and Doulichion
415 and Samê and wooded Zakynthos. But when they had passed by
     the whole of the Peloponnesos, and the vast gulf leading to Krisa
     loomed into view that cuts through the rich Peloponnesos
     and divides it off, up came a great west wind, clearing
     all before it, sent at Zeus's command, furiously blowing
420 from the sky so that the ship coursed with all speed across
     the briny sea. So they sailed back eastward and toward
     the sun, and the Lord Apollo, Zeus's son, led them, and they
     arrived at sunny Krisa, land of vines, into the harbor,
     and the seafaring ship came to land on the sands.
425   Then, like a star in the middle of the day, the lord, far-shooting
     Apollo, leaped from the ship. Countless sparks flew from him
         and their
     brilliance reached into the heaven. He plunged into the sanctuary,

---

397. CAPE MALEA: See maps 2 and 3 for the itinerary of the Cretan ship around the
Peloponnesos.

going through the priceless tripods. There he lit a flame
   illuminating
his shafts, and a radiance invaded all of Krisa, and the wives
430 and daughters of the Krisaians, with their beautiful girdles,
   cried out at Phoibos' impulse, for a great fear had fallen on each.
     From his shrine he burst forth, swift as thought, and sped
   forth in the likeness of a man—vigorous, powerful!—and his hair
   fell down on his broad shoulders. And he spoke to them winged
435 words: "Strangers, who are you? From whence do you sail
   on these watery paths? For business? Or do you wander aimlessly
   across the deep, like pirates, risking your lives and bringing trouble
   to foreign peoples as you go? Why do you sit so in sorrow
   and do not come ashore, nor do you stow your black ship's
440 tackle? This is the custom, I think, of men who live by bread
   —whenever they come to land from the sea in their black ship,
   worn out with labor, and the desire for sweet food takes
   hold of them straightaway."
                   So he spoke, giving them courage.
   The captain of the Cretans answered him and said:
445 "O stranger—for you are nothing like men who die, in shape
   and stature, but like unto the deathless gods—hail to you!
   And may the gods bless you! But tell me this truly, so that I may
   know: What folk is this? What land? What men live here?
   For we were sailing over the great deep with a different purpose,
450 trying to get to Pylos from Crete, from where we come. As it is,
   we have come here with our ship, and not at all willing
   —on another way, on other paths—when we only wanted
   a safe passage. Surely, one of the deathless ones has brought
   us here, all unwilling."
                    Apollo, who works from afar,
455 answered them in this way: "Strangers, who lived before
   near well-forested Knossos, but who now, each one
   of you, will not again return to your lovely city and your
   beautiful home and your beloved wives—for here you
   shall keep my rich temple, greatly honored by all people.
460 I am the son of Zeus, Apollo is my name. I have brought
   you here over the great gulf of the sea, not wishing you ill,
   but so that you might keep my rich temple, greatly honored

by all people. And you will know the plans of the deathless
ones, and by their will you will be honored forever,
465 throughout all days. But come, obey me quickly
and do as I say. First, lower your sails and loosen
the cables, then drag your swift ship up on the land.
Take out your cargo and the gear of your well-balanced ship,
and build an altar on the shore of the sea. Make a fire
470 on it and a sacrifice of white barley. Then stand side by side
around it and pray. Because I first appeared to you in the guise
of a dolphin, when I sprang on your swift ship from the misty
deep, pray to me as the Dolphin God.° And the altar
will henceforth be called the Dolphin Altar, conspicuous
475 forever. Then have your meal beside the swift black ship
and pour out an offering to the blessed gods who live
in Olympos. And when you have put aside your desire
for sweet food, then follow me and sing *Iê Paieon!*° until
you come to the place where you shall keep my rich temple."
480   So he spoke. They heard him well and obeyed.
First they slackened the cables and they brought down
the sail and they loosened the forestays and let down
the mast into the mast-holder. They themselves disembarked
onto the shore of the sea, and they pulled the swift ship
485 out of the water up onto the land, high up on the beach,
and they stretched a long line of props on its side. And they
built an altar on the shore of the sea. They made a fire
on it and an offering of white barley. They prayed,
as he commanded, standing side by side around the altar.
490 Then they made their meal at the side of the black ship,
and they poured out an offering to the blessed gods
who live in Olympos.
                              But when they had discharged
all desire for drink and food, they set off, and the son
of Zeus, Lord Apollo, led them, holding his lyre in his hands,
495 playing in a lovely way and he stepped fine and high.
The Cretans followed him to Pytho, dancing in time,

473. *Dolphin God:* "Apollo Delphinios," a common epithet.
478. *Iê Paieon:* "Hail, Healer."

and they sang *Iê Paieon!*—like the paeans of the Cretans
in whose breasts the divine Muse has placed sweet song.
   With tireless feet they climbed the hill, and swiftly
500 they arrived on Parnassos and the lovely place where he was
soon to live, honored by many humans. There Apollo
led them and showed them the holy sanctuary and the rich
temple, and their hearts were stirred within their breasts.
   The leader of the Cretans turned to him and asked:
505 "O lord, surely you have led us far from our dear ones
and from our fatherland. I suppose that is what you wanted.
But how shall we now live? We urge you to tell us.
For this land is not friendly to the growing of wheat,
nor to pasturage, so that we might live well from it
510 and at the same time be of service to the public."
   Apollo, the son of Zeus, smiled and said: "Foolish
men! You are much-suffering—who wish for hard troubles
and pains and heartache! I will give you a simple answer
that you might bear in mind. Each of you should keep a knife
515 in your hand, that you might slaughter sheep: there will
be an abundant number, as many as the famous tribes
of men will bring here for me. Guard my temple
and received the tribes of men as they gather here,
and <regard> my will and <. . . . As for you,>°
520 if there shall be any vain word, or deed, or insolence,
as is common among mortal humans, then other men
will be your masters under whose command you will
ever be subject.° I have spoken all. Keep it in your heart."
   And so I salute you, son of Zeus and Leto!
525 But I will remember you and another song too.

---

519. *<regard> . . . <. . . As for you>:* At least one line is missing here.

520–23. *if there shall be . . . be subject:* This is Apollo's first prophecy. Many have
attempted to find a historical basis for Apollo's words. For example, priests in classical
times were said to be autochthonous, not from Crete, as if the Cretans had been dis-
charged for some fault. But the reference is obscure.

HOMERIC HYMN 21: TO APOLLO

The god's song is like the sound of a swan's wings.

> O Phoibos, of you the swan sings too, with clear voice,
> as he beats his wings and alights on the bank beside
> the swirling Peneios.° And of you the sweet-tongued singer
> sings both first and last, holding his clear-voiced lyre.
> 5   So hail to you, lord! I seek your favor with my song.

HOMERIC HYMN 25: TO THE MUSES AND APOLLO

The Muses and Apollo are the inspiration for song.

> I begin with the Muses and Apollo, the son of Zeus.
> From the Muses and Apollo who shoots from afar come
> the singers upon the earth, and the players of the lyre,
> and from Zeus come kings. He is happy whom the Muses
> 5   love, and speech flows sweetly from his mouth.
>   Hail, children of Zeus! And show honor to my song.
> But I shall remember you, and another song too!

CALLIMACHUS HYMN 2: TO APOLLO

The date of this hymn is unclear, though if the reference to "my king" in line 27 is to Magas, a breakaway commander from the Ptolemaic royal house who ruled CYRENÊ between 276 and his death in 250 BC, that would provide a date.

The setting is outside the temple of Apollo in Cyrenê in North Africa. The narrator is speaking to a group of youths who will form a chorus celebrating Apollo, whose approach to the sanctuary is marked by the shaking of the temple and the springing open of its doors. The narrator advises the youths to prepare their song and dance. He celebrates the power of Apollo's song, describes in detail a statue of the god, and reviews the stories of Apollo's birth and ascent to power. The narrator recounts the story of Apollo's foundation of Cyrenê, his marriage to the nymph Cyrenê, and his

---

3. *Peneios:* The central river in the Thessalian plain, where there was a cult to Apollo.

institution of the festival of the Karneia at Cyrenê, a Spartan celebration of great antiquity. The hymn concludes with a sphragis, *"seal," that states Callimachus' famous preference for short sweet poems over long epics.*

How Apollo's laurel sapling shakes!° How all
the shrine does tremble! Away, away, you impure!
Do you not see Phoibos Apollo kicking at the doors
with his fair foot? The Delian palm tree° gently nods
5   its head, of a sudden, and the swan sings beautifully
in the air.° Open, you door-bolts, of your own accord!
Open, you locks! The god is no longer far away.
Young men, get ready for the song and the dance!
         Apollo does not appear to everybody, but to whomever
10   is good. He who sees him, that man is great. Who does not
see him, that man is impoverished. We shall see you,
O Worker from Afar, and we will never be poor!
         The young men should never keep the lyre silent,
nor the dance-step soundless, when Phoibos is within
15   his shrine, if they are going to be married, or if they
are going to dedicate a gray lock of old age, and if the city
is going to remain firm on its ancient foundations.
I admire you young men, whose lyre with tortoiseshell
sounding box° is never idle!
                                          Be silent now, listening to the song
20   for Apollo! The sea is silent when the singers celebrate
the lyre or the bow, the implements of Lukorean° Phoibos,
nor does Mother Thetis mournfully bewail Achilles
when she hears *Iê Paieon, Iê Paieon.*° And the tearful rock

---

1. *How Apollo's laurel sapling shakes:* The poet addresses a tree growing outside Apollo's temple.

4. *The Delian palm tree:* To which Leto clung while giving birth (see "Homeric Hymn 2: To Apollo"). An actual palm grew in the temple on Delos. See figure 22.

5–6. *the swan sings beautifully in the air:* In the first line of "Homeric Hymn 21: To Apollo," Apollo's song is also compared to the sound of the swan's beating wings.

18–19. *lyre with tortoiseshell sounding box:* Compare figure 29.

21. *Lukorean:* Lucoreus was a town on Parnassos above Delphi.

22–23. *nor does Mother Thetis . . . Iê Paieon:* That is, even Thetis does not bewail her son, Achilles, whom Apollo killed by guiding an arrow fired by Paris, when she hears the soothing song of Apollo.

puts off grief that is fixed in Phrygia, a wet stone,
25   a marble rock instead of a woman, mouthing some lament.°
      Sing *Iê, Iê !* It is bad to quarrel with the Blessed Ones.
He who wars with the Blessed Ones, may he war with
my king!° And he who wars with my king, let him war
with Apollo! O Apollo, he will honor the band of dancers,
30   who sing what is pleasing to his heart. He can do this
because he sits at the right hand of Zeus. Nor will the band
sing of Phoibos for one day only, for he is a fine subject
for song. Who would not *easily* sing of Apollo?
      Golden are his garments and his clothes-clasp and his lyre
35   and his Luktian° bow and his quiver and his sandals. For Apollo
is rich in gold and very wealthy, as testified by Pytho.°
And he is always handsome and forever young. Never
has the down of manhood appeared on his blooming cheeks.
His hair drips down fragrant oils on the ground. Not the oil
40   of fat do the locks of Apollo let fall drip by drip, but the essence
of healing. And in whatever city those drops fall to the ground,
in that city all things are free from harm.
                                        No one has so many
skills as Apollo. The archer is his lot, and the singer
too—for to Phoibos belong archery and song—
45   and to him belong those who divine with pebbles,
and who prophesize the future in words. Doctors
have learned from him how to put off death. Phoibos,

23–25. *the tearful rock . . . mouthing some lament:* The reference is to Niobê, a Lydian princess and queen of Thebes, whose six sons and six daughters Apollo and Artemis killed when Niobê boasted that she had more children than Leto. She was turned into a rock from which drops of moisture continually fall (a Hittite relief associated with Niobê can still be seen in Asia Minor). Thus both Thetis and Niobê, who suffered terrible losses from Apollo, are still comforted when they hear his ritual song.

28. *my king:* The reigning king of Cyrenê, but it is unclear whether this would Ptolemy II (reigned 283–246 BC); his half-brother Magas, who broke with Ptolemy II and declared himself king of Cyrenê in 275 BC; or Ptolemy III, who married Magas' daughter Berenice in 246 BC and became king of a united Egypt and Cyrenê.

35. *Luktian:* Luktos was a town in Crete, an island famous for its archers.

36. *very wealthy, as testified by Pytho:* The temple at Delphi was surrounded by a forest of valuable offerings from near and far.

too, we call the God of Flocks from the time when,
burning with passion for the youth Admetos, he raised
50   yoked mares by the banks of the Amprussos.° Without
effort the herd would increase, nor would the goats
lack young when mixed with the sheep, when Apollo
cast his eyes upon them as they grazed, nor were the ewes
without milk or barren, but all would have lambs
55   suckling from them, and whoever had borne one offspring
would soon bear two.
                            Following Phoibos, people
lay out the foundations of cities, for Phoibos always loves
when cities are built, and Phoibos himself weaves
the foundations.° Phoibos was four years old when he first
60   fashioned the foundations on beautiful Ortygia nearby
the round lake.° Constantly hunting, Artemis
brought him the heads of goats from Mount Kunthos,°
and Apollo wove an altar. He made the foundation
of horns, then he fashioned the altar of horns, and he built
65   up walls of horns° all around. Thus Phoibos first learned
to raise foundations.
                            Phoibos also instructed Battos

48–50. *from the time when . . . Amphrussos:* Apollo was compelled to serve Admetos, a king in THESSALY, for one year as a herdsman in punishment for Apollo's having killed the Cyclopes because they killed Apollo's son Asklepios, a god of healing, for bringing a dead man back to life. But the motif of homoeroticism between Apollo and Admetos first appears here. The Amphrussos is a river in Thessaly.

57–59. *for Phoibos always loves . . . foundations:* The oracle of Apollo at Delphi was routinely consulted when a city-state prepared to send out a colony.

60–61. *Ortygia nearby the round lake:* Ortygia is another name for Delos, where there was a round lake.

62. *Mount Kunthos:* The central hill on Delos.

63–65. *He made the foundation . . . of horns:* The horned altar on Delos was famous in antiquity but archaeologists have found no trace of it and there are no details about its actual construction.

66–70. *instructed Battos . . . to our kings:* Battos, "stutterer," from the island of THERA, founded Cyrenê, birthplace of Callimachus, in c. 630 BC in accordance with instructions received from the oracle of Apollo at Delphi when Battos went there to learn how to correct his stammer. His actual name was Aristoteles, but his successors ("our kings") are called the Battiads. The story is told in Pindar (*Pythian 4* and *9*) and in Herodotus (4.145–205).

FIGURE 24. The Apollo Belvedere, Roman copy, c. AD 140, of a Greek bronze original of 330–320 BC. It was found in central Italy in the late fifteenth century and in 1511 was placed on display in the Vatican Palace, where it is today. In the eighteenth century it was thought to be the finest of all ancient sculptures, epitomizing aesthetic perfection, and it remains one of the most celebrated works of art in the world. It was championed by the great German art historian Johann Joachim Winckelmann (1717–1768) as the perfection of the Greek aesthetic ideal, characterized by its "noble simplicity and quiet grandeur" (*edle Einfalt und stille Größe*), as he described it, although the statue's reputation has declined in modern times. The god has just shot an arrow, perhaps the arrow killing the serpent Python. His curly hair flows down his neck and rises to the top of his head, encircled by a band. His quiver hangs from his behind his right shoulder. He is naked except for sandals and a robe. The missing lower right arm and left hand were restored by Giovanni Angelo Montorsoli (1507–1563), a pupil of Michelangelo. His right arm rests on a pillar up which entwines a snake, perhaps indicating the god's mantic powers (or referring to the serpent Python). Musei Vaticani. Photograph © Wknight94 / Creative Commons.

about my city with its fertile fields, and as a crow
—an auspicious omen for the founder!—he led the people
coming to Libya, and he swore that he would give
70   walls to our kings.° Apollo always honors his oaths.

O Apollo, many call you Boedromios, others call you Klarios,
and everywhere you have a different name. But I call you Karneios
in accordance with ancestral custom.° Sparta—O Karneios!—
this was your first foundation, second was Thera, and third
75   the city of Cyrenê. From Sparta the sixth generation from
Oedipus led you to the colony at Thera; from Thera,
the baneful Aristoteles settled you in the Asbustian land°
and gave to you a very beautiful temple, and in the city
set up a yearly festival in which many bulls—O lord!—
80   fall on their loins for the last time.

Iê, Iê, O Karneios,
subject of many prayers! In the spring your altars bear
as many colorful blossoms as the Hours bring when
Zephyr breathes out dew, but in winter sweet saffron.°
Always does your fire last forever, nor do ashes
85   graze around the coal of yesterday.°

Apollo greatly rejoiced

71–73. *many call you Boedromios . . . ancestral custom:* Boedromios is a common
name for Apollo; Athens even named a month Boedromion after a festival to Apollo.
The name seems to mean "the shout of runners," referring to a warrior cry after a suc-
cessful battle. There was a famous festival to Apollo at KLAROS in Asia Minor, near
EPHESOS, especially important during the fourth to first centuries BC. Apollo Karneios
was celebrated at SPARTA, from where the Theran settlers came, in a festival with ancient
roots. The meaning of "Karneios" is obscure.

75–77. *From Sparta . . . in the Asbustian land:* According to the story, the sea-god
Triton gave to a member of the Argonautic expedition a clod of earth from LIBYA and
said "this is your land." According to Pindar (*Pythian 4*), the clod was washed into the
sea. Seventeen generations later, Battos sailed to Libya to claim the Greeks' right to the
land. The six generations from Oedipus are Oedipus-Polunikes-Thersander-Tisamenos-
Autesion-Theras, who led the colony to Thera. The Asbustai were a native people who
lived in the territory of Cyrenê.

82–83. *the Hours bring . . . saffron:* The Hours (Horai) are the seasons personified.
There was shrine to the Hours beside the temple to Apollo Karneios at Cyrenê. Zephyr
is the west wind, always gentle. Cyrenê was famous for its aromatic saffron.

84–85. *nor do ashes . . . of yesterday:* That is, the fire on your altar is always fresh.

when the belted men of war danced with the yellow-haired
Libyan women, when the appointed time for the festival
of Karneios came to them.° The Dorian Spartans were not yet
able to approach the fountain of Kurê, but dwelled in wooded
90 Azilis.° The lord himself saw them, and he showed them
to his bride, while standing on the horn-shaped Hill of Myrtles,
where the daughter of Hupseus killed the lion who savaged
the cattle of Eurupolos.° Apollo has seen no other dance
more godly than that one, nor has he given as many blessings
95 as to Cyrenê, remembering his earlier carrying off of the nymph.
Nor have the descendants of Battos themselves honored
another god more than Phoibos.

Iê, Iê, Paieon! we hear,

because the people of Delphi first invented this refrain
when you showed forth the archery of your golden arrows.
100 When you were going to Pytho a demonic beast met you,
a dreadful serpent. You killed it, shooting one swift arrow
after another, and the people shouted *Iê, Iê, Paieon!*
Shoot the arrow!° You were a savior right away from when
your mother bore you. And ever since then you are celebrated
105 in this way.

Envy spoke secretly into Apollo's ears:

86–88. *the belted men of war . . . came to them:* The belted men of war are the Spar-
tans who took local wives at the time of the Karneia in Cyrenê.

89–90. *the fountain of Kurê . . . Azilis:* Kurê was a stream or fountain in Cyrenê, from
which many derived the name of the town. Azilis was a region near Cyrenê where, accord-
ing to tradition, the Spartan/Theran Dorians lived for six years before moving to Cyrenê.

91–93. *Hill of Myrtles . . . Eurupolos:* The Hill of Myrtles seems to be the acropolis of
Cyrenê. The name of Cyrenê may be derived from the nymph Cyrenê, referred to here
as the daughter of Hupseus. Usually the story places Apollo in Thessaly, the servant of
Admetos, when he espied Cyrenê and fell in love with her. He then transported her to
Libya. Eurupolos was an early king of Libya who promised the kingship to whoever
could kill a savage lion. The nymph Cyrenê did so, and thus gained the kingdom. It is
not clear how this tradition accords with the story of Apollo espying Cyrenê in Thessaly.

103. *Shoot the arrow:* The Greek puns on *Iê,* which looks like a word that means
"shoot."

105–13. *Envy spoke secretly . . . where Envy dwells:* These difficult final lines, called a
sphragis, "seal," have been variously interpreted. According to the usual explanation,

"I do not admire the singer who does not sing as many
things as are in the sea." Apollo pushed Envy off with his foot
and said the following: "Great is the flow of the Assyrian
river, but it drags much filth from the land and much refuse
110 on its waters. The bees do not carry water to Demeter
from any source, but from what emerges pure and undefiled
from a holy fountain, a tiny drop, the crown of waters."

Hail, lord! As for Blame, let him go where Envy dwells!°

CALLIMACHUS HYMN 4: TO DELOS

*The "Hymn to Delos" is the longest of Callimachus' surviving hymns, as
long as the longer of the* Homeric Hymns. *The topic of this hymn is the
island of* DELOS, *a goddess herself, and the birthplace of Apollo. The first
name of Delos was Asteria, "starry one," a goddess who escaped Zeus's
advances by leaping into the sea. There she became a floating island,
wandering in the* AEGEAN SEA. *As the poem begins, Hera has been
greatly angered by Zeus's intercourse with Leto, a daughter of Titans,
and she has set up the war-god Ares and the messenger-god Iris to pre-
vent any place from allowing Leto to give birth. As Leto wanders, Apollo,
still a fetus, first prophesies about the destruction of the Theban princess
Niobê, who boasted that she had more children than Leto, then predicts
the birth of Ptolemy II on* KOS, *under whose reign (283–246 BC) this*

Envy (Phthonos) prefers poetry like the "sea," that is, long complicated poetry like
Homer's. The Assyrian river, taken to be the Euphrates, represents this kind of poetry.
But Callimachus prefers short sweet poems, which he compares to water brought by the
bees to Demeter (the female priests of Demeter were called *melissai,* bees). There was
a shrine to Demeter, with a spring, near the temple to Apollo in Cyrenê. But what
do Envy and Blame represent? Ancient commentators took them to refer to rival poets
who mocked Callimachus because he would not write long poems, but such biographi-
cal explanations are dubious. Modern scholars suggest that Envy refers to Apollo's
potential ill-will, so that the concluding lines are a request that Apollo receive the
poem favorably. Envy is a common theme in ancient poetry, beginning with Pindar's
poems celebrating athletic victory in the sixth/fifth centuries BC, because victory
in athletic contests always excites envy—and hostility—on the part of those who do
not win. So Envy/Blame would apply to any poets who find compositions of praise
distasteful. Such obscurities as these are characteristic of Hellenistic poetry—and of
Callimachus!

poem must have been written, as well as the Gauls' attack on Apollo's
shrine at DELPHI *at this time, which Ptolemy repulsed. Asteria, a wan-*
derer like Leto, then defies Hera and offers herself as a place where Leto
can give birth. Apollo is born and Asteria is his nurse. The island takes
root in the sea and Asteria's name is changed to Delos, "clear" to see.
Finally the hymn narrates the history of cult on the island, beginning
with the legendary Olen, a poet from LYCIA *who wrote the first Delian*
hymns, to Theseus, who stopped on Delos to dedicate a statue of Aphro-
dite when returning from Crete after killing the Minotaur. Together with
the young men and women who accompanied him, he inaugurated the
famous "crane dance," still celebrated on Delos. The poem is rich with the
geographical allusions so popular in the Hellenistic poets, but rather
alien to modern taste.

    At what time—or when?—will you sing of holy Delos,
    O heart of mine, the nurse of Apollo? Surely
    all the CYCLADES,° which of all islands lie most sacred
    in the salt sea, are the frequent subject of song.
5   But Delos would like to win top prize from the Muses,
    because she bathed and swaddled Phoibos, lord
    of song, and first praised him as a god. Just as
    the Muses hate the singer who does not sing
    of Pimpleia,° so does Phoibos hate the singer
10   who forgets Delos. To Delos, then, I shall give
    its allotted share of the path of song, so that Apollo
    Cynthios° may praise me for thinking of his dear nurse.
       Swept by the wind and uncultivated, beaten by the waves
    as she is, she is stuck in the middle of the sea, more
15   a course for gulls than horses. The sea, rolling
    greatly around her, rubs off much foam from
    its Ikarian water.° Therefore fishermen, who roam the sea,
    have made her their home. But, still, no one blames

    3. CYCLADES: The "circle islands," in the Aegean sea between the mainland and
Crete, are arranged in a circle around Delos.
    9. *Pimpleia:* A village in Pieria near Mount Olympos, sacred to the Muses. Orpheus
is said to have lived here.
    12. *Cynthios:* Cynthos, or Kunthos, is the high hill on Delos.

her if she is spoken of among the first whenever
20   the islands gather before Ocean and Tethys, the Titan,
    and she is always leader of the chorus.° Phoenician CORSICA
    follows after in her footsteps, scarcely to be scorned,
    and EUBOIA, where the Abantes live and the Ellopians,
    and lovely SARDINIA, and the island where Cypris first
25   swam ashore from the sea, whose inhabitants she keeps
    safe as payment of a fee for landing there.° Those islands
    are fortified with sheltering towers, but Delos is safe
    because of Apollo. What defense could be stronger?
    Stone walls might fall under assault by the North Wind
30   blowing down from the Strymon River,° but the god
    is forever unshaken. Dear Delos, such a helper protects you!
        If a great many songs circle about you, how
    shall I weave one now? What would be a delight for you
    to hear? Perhaps the time when the great god, striking
35   the mountains, first levered up from their lowest foundations

17. *Ikarian water:* The Ikarian Sea was the stretch of the Aegean between the Cyclades and ASIA MINOR, from CHIOS in the north to THERA in the south. The island of IKARIA is in its center. The sea and island are named for Ikaros, Daidalos' son, who flew too close to the sun, fell into the water here, and drowned.

19–21. *whenever the islands gather . . . of the chorus:* The picture is of the islands forming a choral procession as they visit Ocean and his wife Tethys, both children of Earth (Gaia) and Sky (Ouranos), hence Titans.

21–26. *Phoenician CORSICA . . . landing there:* These four islands are potential rivals for Delos as leader of the chorus: Corsica, Euboia, Sardinia, and CYPRUS, the largest islands in the far west and the far east of the Mediterranean, thus bracketing the entire Greek world. Corsica was settled by Semitic Carthaginians, hence it is called Phoenician. Homer calls the Euboians "Abantes"; the "Ellopians" as a name for the Euboians appears only here. When Kronos castrated his father Sky (Ouranos), he threw the genitals into the sea and Aphrodite was born from the foam that gathered around them. She then came ashore on Cyprus (hence is called Cypris).

30. *Strymon River:* In northeastern THRACE.

34–37. *when the great god . . . into the sea:* The "great god" is Poseidon, who made the islands by striking the mountains with his trident. The Telchines (etymology unknown) were somewhat mysterious primordial beings and the original inhabitants of the island of RHODES. Their origin is variously given, but usually they were the children of Sea (Pontos) and Earth (Gaia). They were known as metallurgists and made the trident for Poseidon, whom they reared. Eventually the gods destroyed them for their violence.

the islands in the water with his three-pronged sword, which
the Telchines made, and rolled them into the sea?°
And he fastened them root and branch in the depths
of the sea so that they might forget their origin on the mainland.
40   But you were not held by necessity: You wandered free
on the open seas!° Your ancient name was Asteria,
for you leapt from heaven into the deep trough of the waters,
fleeing, like a shooting star, from marriage with Zeus.°
As long as golden Leto did not come near you,
45   for so long you were still called Asteria, not yet Delos.
Often sailors going from fair-haired TROIZEN to Ephyra
within the SARONIC GULF would espy you, but going back
from Ephyra they no longer saw you there, for you had run
up along the swift strait of EURIPOS with its deafening roar.
50   On the same day you turned your back on the water
of the sea of CHALKIS and swam to the furthermost promontory
of ATHENS, CAPE SOUNION, or to CHIOS, or to the breast
of Parthenia, drenched in water (it was not yet SAMOS),
where the nymphs of Mukalê, neighbors of Ankaios,
55   were your hosts.°

        But when you gave your soil as a place
of birth for Apollo, sailors gave you this name in return

40–41. *You wandered free on the open seas:* In origin Delos was a floating island, not
anchored.

41–43. *Your ancient name was Asteria . . . from Zeus: Astêr* means "star" in Greek.
The island is treated as a nymph, whom Zeus fancied. At the time of Apollo's birth, her
name was changed to Delos, "bright," but Delos had many names, including Ortygia,
"quail island."

46–55. *Often sailors going from fair-haired* TROIZEN *. . . your hosts:* This is a complex
description of the island's wandering in the course of one day. The sailors first spot her
as they depart from Troizen (the birthplace of Theseus) on the coast in the northeastern
Peloponnesos. They then travel northwest within the Saronic Gulf, the part of the
Aegean Sea that lies between AIGINA, just off Athens, and CORINTH, whose old name
was Ephyra. When the sailors return from Ephyra, she is gone, having first drifted north
to the strait of Euripos between EUBOIA and BOEOTIA, gone past Chalkis, which lies
directly on the Euripos, then drifted east, first to Cape Sounion at the southernmost tip
of ATTICA (there is a famous temple to Poseidon there), then across the sea to the Island
of Chios, to Samos (Parthenia), and to Mount Mukalê, opposite Samos on the mainland
of ASIA MINOR. There she is the guest of local nymphs. Ankaios was a king of Samos
and one of the crew of the *Argo*.

because you no longer sailed about obscurely [*adelos*],
but put down the roots of your feet beneath the waves
of the AEGEAN SEA.
                    Nor did you tremble at Hera

60 who raged, who bellowed fiercely against all those women
who in labor bore children to Zeus, and especially against
Leto: she alone was about to give birth to a son
more beloved than Ares.° And so Hera kept watch
in the upper air, ferociously angry, unspeakably,

65 and she held back Leto who suffered from her birth
pangs. Two guards were set to watch over the land:
the one, sitting on the high peak of Thracian HAIMOS,
bold Ares in his armor, watched over the mainland
while his two horses were stabled in the cave of Boreas

70 with its seven crannies; the other sat as a watcher
over the steep islands, the daughter of Thaumas—
she rushed on to Mimas.° There they remained, preventing
all the cities that Leto approached from accepting her.
Yes, ARCADIA fled, the sacred mount of Augê

75 fled—I mean Parthenion—and old man Pheneios
fled behind, and all that part of the PELOPONNESOS
that is attached to Isthmos fled, except for ACHAIA
and ARGOS. On those paths she did not set her feet,
for Hera possessed the INACHOS.°

59–63. *Nor did you tremble at Hera . . . than Ares:* Hera's anger prevents Leto from
giving birth. Ares was Hera's son by Zeus.

66–72. *Two guards were set . . . to Mimas:* Hera has placed two watchers—Ares and
Iris, the daughter of Thaumas—to prevent Leto from finding a place where she can give
birth. Haimos, the "bloody mountain," is the highest peak in Thrace, where Ares takes
his seat. The cave of Boreas, the North Wind, is here. Thaumas, "wonder," is a primor-
dial sea god, the son of the Titans Sea (Pontos) and Earth (Gaia); he also fathered the
Harpies. Mimas is a promontory in ASIA MINOR opposite the island of Chios.

74–79. ARCADIA *fled . . . the* INACHOS: Parthenion was a mountain special to Athena
between Arcadia—the central Peloponnesos—and the Argolid, the plain on which
Argos stood. Augê was the daughter of a king of Tegea, a town in eastern Arcadia. She
was a priestess of Athena who slept with Herakles (perhaps raped by him) and gave birth
to Telephos on Mount Parthenion. Telephos became a king in Asia Minor and in a
famous incident was wounded, and healed, by Achilles (Euripides wrote two lost plays

BOEOTIA fled

80   on the same course, and Dirkê and Strophiê with
its black pebbles, holding the hand of their father
Ismenos. Far behind came Asopos with his heavy
knees, for he had been defiled by a thunderbolt.°
The earthborn nymph Melia quaked and ceased

85   from her dance. Her face paled, she caught her breath
in fear for the tree that was born when she was,
when she saw the locks of HELIKON tremble.° O Muses,
my goddesses, tell me—is it true that trees were born
at the same time as the nymphs who inhabit them?

90   "The trees rejoice when the rain nourishes them, but
the nymphs lament when there are no longer leaves
on the trees."°

Well, Apollo, though still in his mother's
womb, became exceedingly angry with the nymphs
and threatened Thebê with the following, a threat

---

on the episode). Old man Pheneios is the obscure founder of a town of the same name
in Arcadia. The part of the Peloponnesos attached to the ISTHMOS of Corinth is the
Argolid. Achaia (called Aigalos here in the Greek) is a territory in the northwest Pelo-
ponnesos. Inachos is the river that flows through the Argolid, so Leto avoided this coun-
try (and the adjoining Achaia). Inachos was personified and said to be the first king of
Argos. This sort of learned geographical catalogue is typical of Hellenistic poetry!

79–83. BOEOTIA *fled . . . thunderbolt:* Callimachus' catalogue turns now to central
Greece and Boeotia (called Aonia in the Greek). Dirkê, Strophiê (otherwise unknown),
Ismenos, and Asopos are all rivers in Boeotia. In an obscure myth, Asopos, personified,
was struck by a thunderbolt when he pursued Zeus who was carrying off his daughter,
the nymph Aiginai (after whom the island of AIGINA is named).

84–87. *The earthborn nymph . . . HELIKON tremble:* Melia is an ash-tree nymph,
whose life, like that of the hamadryads, was coeval with the tree she inhabited. Mount
Helikon's locks (that is, his head) tremble either because Helikon is refusing refuge to
Leto or because he too (the mountain personified) is fleeing at her approach.

90–92. *The trees rejoice . . . on the trees:* Evidently this is the Muses' reply. Callima-
chus has interrupted his narrative of Leto's search for a place to give birth with a some-
what pedantic inquiry into the life of nymphs, the sort of aside that occurs in other
Hellenistic poetry.

94–95. *threatened Thebê . . . consequences:* Thebê was a daughter of the river Asopos
and was married to Zethos, the brother of Amphion. These brothers were the founders
of Thebes, a city named after one of the nymphs startled by Leto's appearance.

95   that was to bear consequences:° "O Thebê, you poor
thing, why do you put to the test the fate that shall
soon be yours? Do not yet force me to prophesize
against my will!° The seat of the tripod at Delphi
is not yet my concern, nor has the great serpent
100 with its dreadful jaws yet met his end, but still
he wraps his nine coils around snowy PARNASSOS,
creeping down from the Pleistos River.°

                      But I
shall nonetheless say something more clearly than
when I speak from the laurel branch.° So flee on!
105 I will quickly overtake you and bathe my bow in blood!
You have been allotted children of a foul-mouthed
woman.° You will not be my nurse, nor will Kithairon.°
I am pure! And I prefer to be in the company of those
who are also pure!"

              Thus Apollo spoke, and Leto turned
110 and went back. But when the cities of ACHAIA refused
her as she came along—Helikê, companion of Poseidon,

95–98. *O Thebê, you poor thing . . . against my will:* Apollo refers to the destruction of Niobê's children. Niobê was Thebê's sister-in-law, married to Amphion, the king of Thebes. Niobê had six sons and six daughters and boasted that she was therefore better than Leto, who had only one of each. To punish her, Apollo and Artemis killed all twelve children. In grief Niobê fled to Asia Minor where she was turned into a weeping rock.

98–102. *The seat of the tripod . . . Pleistos River:* Later, the priestess at Delphi sat on a tripod when she uttered Apollo's prophecies. Mount Parnassos is in central Greece above the GULF OF CORINTH, rising above Delphi, which is built on its slopes. Callimachus presents Python as so huge that he (here masculine, but usually feminine) stretches down the mountain and encircles Delphi. The Pleistos River is a small river that runs beneath Delphi.

102–4. *But I shall nonetheless . . . laurel branch:* That is, speak not an *obscure* prophecy, for which Apollo was known. These are spoken from "the laurel branch" because the Pythia, Apollo's female medium in classical times, held a laurel while she prophesied.

106–7. *children of a foul-mouthed woman:* These are Thebê's nephews and nieces, the children of Niobê, who boasted that she had more children than Leto.

107. *Kithairon:* Apollo and Artemis killed Niobê's children on Mount Kithairon in Boeotia.

111–14. *Helikê . . . THESSALY:* Helikê was a city on the coast of Achaia; it had a famous temple of Poseidon. Boura was a town somewhat inland where Dexamenos, a Centaur, kept his cattle.

and Boura, where were the cattle-stalls of Dexamenos,
the son of Oikeus—she turned her feet back
to THESSALY.° Anauros fled, and great Larisa,
115 and Cheiron's peaks, and Peneios, winding through
the Vale of Tempê, fled.°
                 Hera, your heart was still
pitiless, your anger did not relent, and you had
no compassion when Leto stretched out her hands
and spoke as follows—in vain:°
           "   Thessalian nymphs,
120 children of the river, tell your father to put his stream
to sleep. Entwine your hands in his beard and entreat
him that the children of Zeus° be born in his flood.
O Peneios of Phthia,° why do you now contend with
the winds?° You are not mounted on a racehorse,
125 O father! Are your feet always so swift, or is it only
in my case that they are so nimble, that today you have
made them suddenly to fly?" But Peneios did not hear.
"O my burden,° where shall I carry you?
The wretched tendons of my ankles refuse! O Pelion,
130 delivery chamber of Philyra°—you at least stay, stay,
for wild beasts—lionesses!—often on your mountains

114–16. *Anauros fled . . . Tempê, fled:* Anauros is a Thessalian river. Larisa was a town on a tributary of the Peneios River in Thessaly. Cheiron's peaks are MOUNT PELION, where the nymph Philyra gave birth to the Centaur Cheiron. The river god Peneios was grandfather to Cyrenê, the nymph who marries Apollo in Callimachus' "Hymn 2: To Apollo." Tempê is the valley between MOUNT OLYMPOS and nearby Mount Ossa, famous in poetry for its beauty and serenity.

116–19. *Hera, your heart . . . in vain:* The narrator has addressed the implacable Hera, responsible for the hostility to Leto, and next he describes the scene as Leto stretches out her hands in supplication. First Leto will address the Thessalian nymphs, the children of Peneios, then Peneios himself; then Apollo, who is still in her womb; and finally Mount Pelion.

122. *children of Zeus:* Apollo and Artemis.

123. *Phthia:* A territory in Thessaly, the land of Achilles.

123–24. *contend with the winds:* Peneios is fleeing so swiftly from Leto's approach that he is compared with the wind. In fact the Peneios is a slow-moving, sluggish stream.

128. *O my burden:* The unborn Apollo.

130. *Philyra:* The mother of the Centaur Cheiron.

lay down their labor of untimely birth."°

Peneios

answered her, pouring forth tears: "O Leto, Necessity
is a mighty god. It is not I, my lady, who denies
135 your birth pangs. I know that others have washed
their afterbirth in my waters, but Hera has made
her threat abundantly clear. Look who keeps watch
from the mountaintops, who easily would drag me up
from the depths! What am I to do? Is it a sweet thing
140 to you to see Peneios destroyed? Let my day of destiny
come! I shall endure it for your sake, even if I shall
wander forever, thirsting, with ebbing flood, alone
called the most dishonored of rivers. Here I am!
What more can I say! Only call upon Eileithyia!"°
145   So Peneios spoke and stayed his great flood. But Ares
lifted up the peaks of Mount Pangaion from their roots
and was about to throw them into the swirlings of Peneios
and cover up his streams. From on high he thundered
and smashed his shield with the point of his spear,
150 and it rang out with a warlike sound.° Mount Ossa
trembled and the plain of Krannon and the windswept
reaches of PINDOS,° and all Thessaly danced with fear.
Such a sound clanged from his shield. Just as when

---

132. *their labor of untimely birth:* This obscure reference is evidently to the (supposed) helplessness of lion cubs at birth.

144. *Eileithyia:* The birth goddess.

145–50. *But Ares . . . a warlike sound:* Ares is about to cast a mountaintop onto the river Peneios and stop its flow, but he first stops and sounds his shield so that all Thessaly quakes. Mount Pangaion is in Thrace, about 140 miles from Mount Haimos, where Ares first took up his stand.

150–52. *Mount Ossa . . . PINDOS:* Mount Ossa is south of Mount Olympos; the plain of Krannon is in Thessaly; the Pindos Range runs down the center of the Greek peninsula.

153–60. *Just as when . . . his rounded shield:* The shaking of Ares' shield is likened to the shaking caused by the Giant Briareos, imprisoned under Mount Aetna in eastern SICILY, when he turns over on his shoulder. Ares' shield rattling is also compared to the cacophony from the forge of Hephaistos. Briareos was one of the Hundred-Handers according to Hesiod (*Theogony,* 149–5), a demonic being. Usually Typhoeus is said to be imprisoned under Mount Aetna.

the inmost recesses of Mount Aetna, smoldering with fire,
155 shakes because Briareos, the giant imprisoned underground,
turns onto his other shoulder, or the furnaces roar
beneath the tongs of Hephaistos and his other tools
—and the basins, forged in fire, and tripods fall
on one another and ring out—so loud was the clash
160 of Ares on his rounded shield.°
                               Peneios did not draw back,
but in his strength held his ground as before; he stopped
his swirling eddies.° But the daughter of Koios° called out
to him: "Farewell! Save yourself! Save yourself! Do not
suffer evil for my sake, as repayment for the pity
165 you feel! You will be rewarded for your favor."
                                     She spoke
and after suffering much she came to the islands
in the sea. But they did not receive her when she came,
not the Echinades, which have brilliant harbors for ships,
nor Corcyra, a most friendly island to strangers,
170 for Iris, sitting on high Mount Mimas, very much angered
with them all, turned them away. Under Iris' shouted
command they fled with all speed, each island that
she approached, fleeing over the waters.
                               Then she came
to primeval Kos, the island of Merops and the holy
175 sanctuary of the heroine Chalkiopê.° But this word
of her son held her back: "Mother, do not give birth
to me here. I do not blame the island, or have a grudge

161–62. *he stopped his swirling eddies:* So that Leto could give birth.

162. *Koios:* An obscure Titan, the father of Leto.

168–75. *not the Echinades . . . Chalkiopê:* Leto turns away from the inland waters, first to the western islands: the Echinades, "sea urchins," because they are small and prickly, at the mouth of the ACHELOÖS RIVER (including ITHAKA), and Corcyra to the north; then, to ASIA MINOR and the island of Kos, one of the Sporades ("scattered") islands, opposite HALIKARNASSOS. Iris, sitting on top of Mount Mimas on the coast opposite CHIOS, makes the islands flee. Kos was named after the daughter of one Merops. Chalkiopê was the daughter of a king of Kos (named Eurypolos), and a bride of Herakles.

against it, for it is rich with many cattle, as many
as you find anywhere. But another god is destined
180 to be born here by the Fates, the high race of the Saviors.°
Beneath his crown will come—willingly to be ruled
by a Macedonian—both the lands on the continent
and in the sea, as far the ends of the earth and where
the swift horses carry the sun. He will have the disposition
185 of his father.

        "And now, at some later time, a common
struggle will come to us, when late-born Titans,
arriving from the furthest West, will raise up against
the Greeks a barbarian sword and a Celtic war,
rushing like snowflakes, as numberless as the stars
190 when they graze in huge numbers in the Upper Air . . .
[*two lines here are*
hopelessly corrupt]
. . . and the plains of KRISA and the valleys of Hephaistos
are crowded all around, and they shall see the thick
195 smoke of their burning neighbor, and no longer
will they know of the ranks of the enemy through
hearsay, but see at the side of my temple, alongside
my tripods, the swords and shameless war-belts and hated
shields that will cause an evil journey for the Galatians,
200 that mad tribe.° Some of these shields will be my reward,

179–80. *But another god . . . the Saviors:* Callimachus means Ptolemy II, called Phil-
adelphos, the son of Ptolemy I, born on Kos in 308 BC. He died in 246 BC and was alive
when this hymn was written. *Soter,* "Savior," was a title of the Ptolemies. Apollo goes on
to prophesy an attack of the Gauls on his sanctuary at Delphi and Ptolemy's defeat of
them. This prophecy from Leto's womb is unparalleled in Greek poetry.

188–200. *barbarian sword . . . that mad tribe:* From around 300 BC there was a
southward movement of the Celts, called Gauls or "late-born Titans," who inhabited
northern Europe. In 279 BC they invaded Greece, led by one Brennos, and attacked
Delphi, but the Greeks routed them. Shortly afterwards a body of them settled in central
Asia Minor (c. 240 BC) in a district later called Galatia (hence St. Paul's Letter to the
Galatians, c. AD 50). Krisa is the town beneath Delphi, on the Corinthian Gulf, but
the valleys of Hephaistos (this translation depends on an emendation) are unknown.
The tripods are offerings to Apollo, and the Pythia prophesied from a tripod. The Gauls'
weaponry and shields were hung on display at Delphi after their defeat. The "evil jour-
ney" of the Galatians is presumably the path that Brennos took to the sanctuary.

some will be set by the Nile, having seen their bearers
breathing their last in fire, the prizes of a king who
has labored hard.°
                    "O you will be Ptolemy! These are the
prophecies of Phoibos. You will greatly praise the prophet
205 in the womb in the days to come, forever!
                                        "But now consider,
my mother—there is a slender island visible in the sea,
wandering over the waters. Her feet are not
in a single place but she swims with the tides, like
the thistle, wherever now the south wind, now
210 the east wind, now the sea may carry her. Take
me there. She will willingly receive you."
                                When he had said
all these things, the other islands fled across the sea.
But you, Asteria, lover of song, you came down
from Euboia to have a look at the encircling CYCLADES—
215 not long ago, but seaweed from Geraistos followed
behind. When you see° . . . [   ]
bravely you said [   ] when you saw the goddess
in the pangs of labor: "Hera, do to me what you want.
I have paid no attention to your threats. Cross, cross
220 over to me, O Leto!"
                    You spoke, and she gladly
put an end to her sad wandering. She sat down

201–3. *some will be set by the Nile . . . labored hard:* Callimachus has conflated the
Gaulic attack on Delphi with a separate incident in Egypt that took place about the same
time. Magas, a Macedonian nobleman, became a member of the Ptolemaic dynasty
through his mother's second marriage to Ptolemy I. He wrestled independence for
Cyrenê in modern Libya from the Ptolemies and became king of Cyrenê from 276 to
250 BC. Ptolemy II recruited a band of Gauls to fight against Magas, but the band
revolted and attempted to take over Egypt. Ptolemy led them into an island in the Nile
Delta where he left them to die by starvation and mutual slaughter.

213–16. *Asteria, lover of song . . . you see:* Asteria (that is, Delos) visits her sister
islands, gathering seaweed as she goes. Geraistos is a promontory in southern Euboia
where there was a temple of Poseidon. There are a couple of mutilated lines here in the
Greek (sharing the same damage to the mss. as in lines 191–92).

by the flow of the Inopos, which the earth sends
forth, a deep stream, at the time when the Nile comes
down in full spate from the Ethiopian highland.°
225 She loosened her belt and leaned back her shoulders
against the trunk of a palm tree, exhausted by her painful
ordeal. A damp sweat ran down her flesh. Weakened,
she said: "Why, my child, do you burden your mother?
Here, my loved one, is your island, floating on the sea.
230 Be born, be born, child, and come out gently
from my womb!"
O bride of Zeus, heavy with anger,
you were not going to be ignorant for long! So swift
a messenger ran to you, and spoke still panting,
and her report was mingled with fear: "O most honored
235 Hera, by far the greatest of the goddesses, I am yours!
All things are yours! You sit as the rightful queen
of Olympos! We fear no other female's hand,
and you, O queen, will know who is the cause
of your anger. Leda unties her waist-band on an island.
240 All the others hated her and would not receive her.
But Asteria called her by name as she passed by,
Asteria, foul refuse of the sea! You yourself know it!
But dear—for you are able to do it—defend
your servants—O lady!—who walk the earth at your
235 command."
So she spoke, then sat beside the golden
throne like a hunting bitch of Artemis who, ceasing
from the fast chase, sits by her feet, its ears erect,
ever ready to hear the swift summons to the hunt—
like her, the daughter of Thaumas° sat by the throne.

222–24. *flow of the Inopos . . . Ethiopian highland:* The Inopos was a stream on Delos,
dry most of the year but thought to have a subterranean connection to the Nile so that
when the Nile rose in July from inundations in Ethiopia the Inopos flowed too. Accord-
ing to a Hellenistic interpretation Apollo was thought to be the same as the Egyptian
hawk-god Horus whose birth at the beginning of the Nile's rise augured the revitaliza-
tion of the world.

239. *daughter of Thaumas:* Iris.

240 She never forgets her seat, not even when forgetful
      sleep presses his wing upon her, but there
      at the corner of the great throne, leaning her head
      a little aslant, Iris sleeps. Nor does she ever loosen
      her sash or her quick hunting boots, in case her mistress
245 might issue a sudden command.
                                    Hera answered, terribly
      distraught with anger: "So now, you shameful playthings
      of Zeus, you would marry in secret and bring forth
      in darkness, not where the wretched slave corn-grinding
      women suffer in childbirth, but where the seals of the deep
250 breed among the desolate rocks. I am not so angry
      at Asteria for this misdeed, and there is no way that
      I will act heartlessly against her—as I should!—
      for she was quite wrong to do this favor for Leto.
      Still, I honor her exceptionally, because she did
255 not trample on my bed, and preferred the sea
      to Zeus."°
                    So she spoke. The melodious swans,
      singers of the god, left the Paktolos River in Maionia
      and circled seven time around Delos, and they sang
      a spell for the birth of the child—the birds of the Muses,
260 the best singers of all things that fly!° (For this reason
      the child in later days fitted seven strings to his lyre,
      as many strings as swans that sang at his birth.)
      But on the eighth round they no longer sang, for he had leapt
      out. The Delian nymphs, the offspring of an ancient
265 river, loudly sang the holy song of Eileithyia, and right
      away the brazen sky sang in response a penetrating

255–56. *she did not trample . . . to Zeus:* Asteria did not "trample on" Hera's bed because Asteria refused to sleep with Zeus, who at one time had his eye on her.

256–60. *The melodious swans . . . that fly:* Swans are sacred to Apollo, his special bird. The Paktolos River flows down from Mount Tmolos in Asia Minor past SARDIS, the capital of LYDIA (= Maionia), to empty into the river HERMOS. The Paktolos is near the Kaüster River, which Homer says was filled with swans and cranes (*Iliad,* 2.459–65). The Paktolos was rich in gold, a source of wealth for Lydian kings. Seven was a special number for Apollo: he was born on the seventh day, festivals were celebrated on the seventh day of the month, and there were seven strings to his lyre.

cry. Nor did Hera hold a grudge, for Zeus had taken
away her anger.

And then all your foundations, O Delos,°
became gold, your round lake flowed with gold

270 all day long, golden bloomed the shoot of the olive
in answer to your birth, and the swirling Inopos
ran deep with gold. You yourself picked up the child
from the golden earth, and you placed him in your lap,
and you said this:

"O great earth, with your many altars,

275 and your many cities, with great abundance, and your
rich lands and your islands that lie around me,
I am such—hard to plough, but from me Apollo
will be called the Delian One, nor will any other land
be so loved by another god, not Kerchnis by Poseidon

280 or Lechaion, not the hill of Cyllenê by Hermes, not Crete
by Zeus, as I by Apollo.° And I will no longer
be a wanderer."

So you spoke, and he suckled at your
sweet breast. Ever since that time you are called
the most holy of islands, the childhood nurse of Apollo.

285 Nor does Enyo, nor Hades, nor do the horses
of Ares set foot upon you, but every year tithes
of the first fruits are sent to you, and all cities lead
out choruses—those who have allotments to the east,
and to the west, and to the south, and those who

290 have their dwellings beyond the shore of the north wind,
the most long-lived of peoples.° These are the first

268. *O Delos:* Asteria's name changes to Delos at Apollo's birth.

279–81. *not Kerchnis . . . by Apollo:* The two harbors of Corinth are called Kenchreai, that is, Kerchnis (on the east), and Lechaion (on the west). Poseidon was not born in Kenchreai, but he was closely associated with Corinth. Hermes was born on Mount Cyllenê in Arcadia; Zeus was born on Crete.

285–91. *Nor does Enyo . . . of peoples:* Enyo, an old god of war, and Ares stand for war, so there will be no war on Delos. Nor were burials allowed ("nor Hades") there after the Athenian purification of the island in 426 BC. For the annual festival of the Delia, which celebrated Apollo, Athens and many island cities sent choruses of young men and women. Those living "beyond the shore of the north wind" are the Hyperboreans, among whom Apollo was said to have lived for part of the year.

to bring you stalks of wheat and holy sheaves of wheat.°
These the Pelasgians from Dodona first receive
as they arrive from afar, those who sleep on the ground,
295 servants of the cauldron that is never silent. Then
they come to the town of Ira and the hills of the Malian land.
From there they sail into the good Lelantine plain
of the Abantes, and not far is the journey from Euboia,
for their harbors are your neighbors.°
                                        The first
300 to bring these things from the light-haired Arimaspi were
Oupis and Loxo and fortunate Hekaergê, the daughters
of Boreas, and those who were the best of the young men.°
They never returned home, and they were allotted
good fortune,° and their fame shall never die.
305   Yes, the girls of Delos, when the fine-sounding
wedding song threatens their girlish habits, bring
as an offering their virgin hair to the virgins, and boys

292. *holy sheaves of wheat:* The rest of the hymn tells of the events that lie behind the Delian festival: the first time that first fruits were sent and the origin of the choruses. The sending of first fruits, made up of bound stalks of wheat, was attributed to the Hyperboreans, who also sent a chorus of young women.

293–99. *the Pelasgians from Dodona . . . your neighbors:* The hymn traces the course of the Hyperborean first offerings down to Delos. The Pelasgians are the ancient inhabitants of Greece, really the pre-Greeks. Dodona was the famous site of an oracle of Zeus in remote northwestern Greece. According to Homer (*Iliad,* 16.234–35), the inhabitants of Dodona slept on the ground and had unwashed feet. The cauldron that is never silent is the bronze tripod from which prophecies at Dodona were uttered. From Dodona the first-fruits traveled to Ira, a town in southern Thessaly. The Malian Gulf is the part of the western Aegean Sea between Thessaly and the island of Euboia. The Abantes is the name that Homer uses for the Euboians, and the Lelantine Plain lies between the Euboian towns of Chalkis and ERETRIA. It was the site of the first historical war fought in Greece (seventh century BC?). From Euboia to Delos is a straight shot over several islands.

301–2. *Oupis and . . . young men:* Callimachus now names the women who first brought first-offerings to Delos: Oupis, Loxo, and Hekaergê. The Arimaspi were a one-eyed people (!) who lived south of the Hyperboreans (Herodotus 4.27, apparently from Scythian *arima* = "one" and *spou* = "eye"). Oupis was a cult title of Artemis; Apollo was often called Loxias; Hekaergê, "Worker from Afar," is a feminine form of Hekaergos, a cult title of Apollo. Boreas is the North Wind.

303–4. *they were allotted good fortune:* That is, they died: a polite expression.

FIGURE 25. The Terrace of the Lions on Delos. Delos was a Panhellenic cult center starting in the sixth century BC, when Greek states sent representatives there to festivals for Apollo. These festivals included the Delia, a commemoration of Apollo's birth celebrated every four years, and the Apollonia, celebrated annually. In 477 BC, the island became the center for the Delian League, a federation under the leadership of Athens of around 160 states gathered to resist Persian aggression. The federation's treasury was kept here and the island became a center for choruses and poetic performance. Athens lost control of the island in 314 BC, and it fell under Ptolemaic influence around 286 BC, when a festival was established in honor of the Egyptian Ptolemies. Perhaps Callimachus wrote "Hymn 4: To Delos" for this festival. The Terrace of the Lions was built around 600 BC, and today is part of an immense archaeological site on Delos south of the sacred lake where Leto gave birth to Apollo. The lions create a monumental avenue comparable to the Egyptian avenue of sphinxes that preceded Egyptian temples, which no doubt inspired it. There may originally have been twelve lions, but only seven survive in Delos (an eighth is in Venice). The originals are in the local museum; these are reproductions. Photograph © Bernard Gagnon / Creative Commons.

offer as first-fruits to the young men the down from
their chins.°

       Fragrant Asteria, the islands made a circle
310 around you and surround you as a chorus.° Neither silent,
nor soundless are you when Hesperos with his curly locks
looks down on you, resounding on all sides.° The men sing
the song of the old man of LYCIA, which the seer Olen
brought to you from XANTHOS.° The maiden choristers
315 beat with their feet the solid ground. The famous
holy statue of ancient Cypris, which once Theseus
set up, returning from Crete with the youths, is laden
with garlands.° Having escaped the cruel bellowing
and the wild son of Pasiphaë and the twisted seat

307–9. *as an offering . . . their chins:* When girls on Delos are about to marry, they
offer their hair, never before cut, to Opis, Loxos, and Hekaergê. The dedication of hair
before marriage was widespread. Similarly, the boys on Delos offer hair from their chins
to the unnamed children of Boreas who accompanied Opis, Loxos, and Hekaergê from
the far north to Delos.

309–10. *the islands made a circle . . . as a chorus:* Once Delos became stationary, the
nearby islands formed a circle around her, hence they are called the Cyclades, the "circle
islands." Choruses were arranged in circles and the islands are imagined to take on this
shape for that reason.

311–12. *Hesperos . . . on all sides:* Hesperos is the evening star, so the meaning is that
when night falls, the choruses continue to sing the island's praises.

313–14. *the seer Olen . . . XANTHOS:* According to Herodotus (4.35), the prehistoric
singer Olen composed the first song of the Delians as they presented their offerings
to Apollo. Xanthos is the name both of a town and a river in Lycia, in southern Asia
Minor.

316–18. *holy statue of ancient Cypris . . . with garlands:* This statue of Aphrodite (that
is, Cypris) was a small wooden image with a square base instead of feet, supposedly the
work of the Athenian craftsman Daidalos. Ariadnê brought it with her when she fled
from Crete with Theseus. According to the Athenian myth, Theseus led seven young
men and seven young women as sacrifices to the Minotaur to expiate the death of
Minos' son Androgeos during an athletic competition at Athens, but Ariadnê, Minos'
daughter, fell in love with Theseus, helped him overcome the monster, then fled with
him across the sea.

318–22. *Having escaped . . . led the dance:* The reference is to the famous "crane
dance" around the altar of Apollo on Delos, its origin attributed to Theseus and the
Athenian youths on their triumphant return to Athens. It is not clear why it was so
called, but this dance supposedly originated from the dancers imitating their winding
path to escape the labyrinth. This is the first reference to "labyrinth" as the lair of the

320 of the winding labyrinth, my lady, they raised the sounding
  of the lyre and danced the circle dance around your
  altar, and Theseus led the dance.° From that time
  the Kekropidai send the ever-living offerings
  of the Theoria to Phoibos, the rigging of that ship.°
325 O Asteria, with your many altars, and your many
  prayers, what merchant of the Aegean has passed you by
  in his swift ship?° For winds are never so mighty that blow
  upon him, nor does necessity require so swift a voyage,
  but they quickly furl their sails and do not embark again
330 before they wind about your great altar struck with blows
  and bite the sacred trunk of your olive tree with their
  hands tied behind their backs.° These things did the nymph
  of Delos° devise as sport and laughter for the young Apollo!
   O lucky hearth of islands, hail both to you
335 and to Apollo, and she whom Leto bore!°

Minotaur. Labyrinth seems to mean "hall of the double ax," in reference to pre-Greek
Minoan religion. Pasiphaë was the daughter of the sun-god Helios and the wife of
Minos, the king of Crete. Poseidon gave Minos a beautiful bull to sacrifice, the "bull
from the sea," but Minos decided to keep it and sacrificed another bull instead. To pun-
ish him for his impiety, Poseidon caused Pasiphaë to fall in love with the handsome bull.
Daidalos of Athens, who was living on Crete at this time, designed a hollow wooden
cow that Pasiphaë climbed in to have intercourse with the bull. The resulting offspring
was the Minotaur, "the bull of Minos," half-man and half-bull. Minos imprisoned the
monster in the Labyrinth, which Daidalos also designed.

 323–24. *the Kekropidai send . . . of that ship:* The reference is to the ship that Theseus
sailed on to go to Crete, called the *Theoria*, the "sending" ship. This very ship was sup-
posedly preserved by the Athenians (the Kekropidai, so called after the early king
Kekrops) until the fourth century BC and was sent annually to the Delian festival with
ambassadors and choruses. The ship's rigging was a kind of offering, and because it was
continually replaced, it was "ever-living."

 326–27. *what merchant of the Aegean . . . in his swift ship:* Before Delos was fixed in
the sea, sailors barely caught sight of her as she wandered around the Aegean. Now
every passing ship puts in to participate in the rites to Apollo.

 330–32. *before they wind about . . . behind their backs:* No one is sure of the rite here
described, but an ancient commentator (a scholiast) writes: "In Delos it was customary
to run around the altar of Apollo and beat the altar and, with their hands tied behind
their backs, to take a bite from the olive tree."

 332–33. *nymph of Delos:* One of the nymphs of Delos mentioned earlier.

 335. *she whom Leto bore:* Artemis.

ORPHIC HYMN 34: TO APOLLO

The hymn falls into two parts, perhaps in imitation of "Homeric Hymn 2: To Apollo." In the first part the poet lists the god's cult centers, attributes, and epithets. In the second part, he celebrates the god as the sun, controlling the seasons and the harmony of all life.

Come, O blessed Paian, slayer of Tituos—Phoibos,
Lukoreus, illustrious Memphite!°—to whom we cry
Iê!, bringer of wealth, you of the golden lyre, filled
with seed, plowman, Titan and Pythian god,
5   Grunean, Sminthian,° killer of Python, Delphic
prophet, wild, spirit who brings light, lovable,
O noble youth!
            O leader of the Muses, one
who gladdens, Far-Shooter who fires arrows,
lover of Branchos, Didumeus, Worker from Afar,
10 Loxias, holy!° O lord of Delos, your eye sees all
and brings light to mortals!° Your hair is golden,

1–2. *O blessed Paian . . . Memphite:* Paian was originally a separate god (mentioned in the Mycenaean Linear B tablets) but has been subsumed under Apollo as a god of healing and victory. Tituos was a Giant who attempted to rape Leto after she gave birth to Apollo and Artemis, but the twin gods killed him; he is punished in the underworld, stretched out over nine acres, his liver devoured daily by a vulture. Lukoreus is an epithet derived from a village, Lucoreia, atop Mount Parnassos where Delphi was built. Memphite refers to a god of the Egyptian capital at Memphis, either the hawk-god Horus (this identification is standard) or the sun-god.

4–5. *Titan and Pythian god . . . Sminthian:* Apollo was not really a Titan, but because he is identified with the Sun, who was a Titan, he can be called such. Pythian refers to Apollo's slaying of Python at Delphi and the institution of his oracle there. There was a temple and oracle of Apollo at Gruneion, a city in Asia Minor. Sminthian seems to mean "mouse-god," that is, the god of plague because mice bring plagues. Apollo is called Sminthian at the beginning of the *Iliad* where his priest, Chryses, calls down plague on the Greek attackers (1.39).

9–10. *lover of Branchos . . . Loxias, holy:* Apollo leads the Muses in song to entertain the gods. Branchos became a seer at the shrine to Apollo at Diduma near MILETOS and delivered Miletos from a plague (but some manuscripts read "Bacchic one," identifying Apollo with his half-brother Dionysos). Loxias means "crooked, ambiguous," referring to Apollo's puzzling oracles, a common epithet.

10–11. *O lord of Delos . . . to mortals:* Apollo as the Sun-god sees all.

your oracles are pure and useful.
                                    Hear me with kind
heart as I pray for the people. You gaze upon all
the endless upper air and the rich earth through
15   the twilight. In the quiet of night beneath the dark
with its stars for eyes you see the earth's roots
below, and you hold the limits of the whole world.
      Yours is the beginning and the ending that will come.
You make everything blossom! You bring into harmony
20   both poles with your resounding lyre, now reaching
the highest pitch, now the lowest, now with a Dorian
mode you mix together the poles. You make distinct
the living races, mixing harmony in the lot of all men
in the world. You give an equal measure of winter
25   and summer, striking the low notes for winter,
and the high for summer, and for the lovely blossoming
of spring playing the Dorian mode.° For this reason
mortals call you Lord Pan, the two-horned god, who sends
the whistling winds;° because of this you hold the master
30   seal of the entire cosmos.
                                    Hear me, O blessed one,
and save the initiates with their suppliant voice!

ORPHIC HYMN 35: TO LETO

*Leto is the daughter of the Titans Koios and Phoebê and gentle mother
of Apollo and Artemis.*

O Leto of the dark robe, goddess who bore the twins,
holy, daughter of Koios, great of spirit to whom many

24–27. *You give an equal measure . . . Dorian mode:* Apollo brings harmony to the cos-
mos with his playing on the lyre, affecting not only the lives of men, but also the ebb and
flow of the seasons. According to ancient musical theory, there were six musical "modes," a
mode being similar to what we think of as a musical "key": a mode is a group of notes with
fixed intervals out of which you can compose a melody. The manly and dignified Dorian
mode that Apollo played in the spring was said to be steady, calm, and restrained.

28–29. *Lord Pan . . . whistling winds:* The identification of Pan with Apollo seems
odd, but both are associated with music and both are pastoral gods. Some traditions
report that Pan instructed Apollo in divination.

pray, whose lot was to bear the fine offspring of Zeus!
You gave birth to Phoibos and Artemis who showers
5   arrows, the one in Ortygia, the other in rocky Delos.°
    Hear, O goddess, mistress, and with a favoring
heart bring a sweet end to these holy mysteries!

ORPHIC HYMN 76: TO THE MUSES

*Only three major hymns survive that celebrate these goddesses (see
above for "Homeric Hymn 25" and see below for Proclus' hymn to the
Muses). In the Orphic hymn, the Muses are the inspirers of the poetry
that inspires the mind.*

O daughters of Mnemosynê and loud-thundering Zeus, Muses
of Pieria,° renowned, splendidly famous, most longed for by men
whom you visit, having many shapes, you give birth
to blameless virtue in every task. You nourish the soul,
5   you set straight thoughts aright, you are leaders, mistresses
of the power of the mind. You have revealed the mystic
rites to mortals—Kleio, and Euterpê, and Thalea, and Mel-
        pomenê,
and Terpsichorê, and Erato, and Poluhymnia, and Ourania,
with Mother Kalliopê,° very powerful and holy goddesses.
10   But come to the initiates, O goddesses—in your manifold
holiness, bringing glory and lovely fame, sung by many!

5. *the one in Ortygia, the other in rocky Delos:* According to some traditions Leto
gave birth to Artemis on the tiny island of Ortygia, "quail island," just off Delos, "clear
island," then went to Delos to give birth to Apollo; other traditions say that Ortygia is an
alternate name for Delos.

1–2. *daughters of Mnemosynê . . . Pieria:* Mnemosynê is a Titan, Zeus's first consort.
Pieria is a mountain north of Mount Olympos in Macedonia, birthplace of the Muses.
They seem to have had a cult there.

7–9. *Kleio . . . Kalliopê:* In later tradition the nine Muses were associated with spe-
cific artistic productions: Kleio ("celebrator," history), Euterpê ("well-pleasing," flute-
playing), Thalia ("abundance," comedy), Melpomenê ("singer," tragedy), Terpsichorê
("joy in the dance," dance), Erato ("lovely," lyric poetry), Poluhymnia ("many hymns,"
hymns), Ourania ("heavenly," astrology), and Kalliopê ("pretty voice," epic poetry).
Kalliopê was the mother of Orpheus, and so especially endeared in Orphic cult.

PROCLUS HYMN 3: TO THE MUSES

The philosopher, too, was a servant of the Muses. Pursuing the intellec-
tual life, the philosopher could rid himself of passion and after death be
elevated to a divine existence, the major theme of this hymn. Inspiration
by the Muses creates divine possession and a madness that enables the
philosopher to perceive the realm of Nous.

> We sing! We sing of the light that raises men high,
> of the nine daughters of great Zeus with their marvelous
> voices who have rescued from these earthly pains, so hard
> to endure, souls wandering in the depths of life,
> 5   through immaculate rites taken from mind-awakening
> books, and have taught them to hasten over the tracks
> left by deep-waved forgetfulness, to go pure to their rightful
> star from which they were driven when they fell into
> the promontory of birth, mad with the lot of material things.°
> 10   But, O goddesses, put an end to my agitated desire
> and drive me into a Bacchic frenzy through the spiritual words
> of the wise.° Let not the race of men who do not fear
> the gods° drive me away from the holy path, brilliant
> with light and rich with fruit. Ever draw my soul, wandering
> 15   everywhere, towards the holy light, away from the hubbub

3–9. *who have rescued . . . the lot of material things:* The nine Muses, who inspire
poetry such as this hymn, are able to raise the souls of men from the darkness of earthly
pains into the light of perceptions of the Forms in the world of Nous, particularly souls
that are engaged in mystic rites or that study the sacred texts that inspire such rites. The
Muses teach the soul to follow the "tracks," the faint imprint of the eternal Forms on the
world of matter, to rediscover the star, the eternal Form of every soul's being, from
which at birth souls descended into the world of matter, to be driven mad by objects in
the material world.

11–12. *a Bacchic frenzy . . . wise:* Bacchic frenzy, for the Neoplatonists, is a condition
of the human soul. Multiplicity characterizes the fallen human soul which is incapable
of contemplating the Forms that reside in Nous, characterized by unity. The soul
must become unified. The aspirant is called a Bacchant when inspired with the
poetic madness that the Muses bring about through song and poetry, such as this hymn.
Books by inspired philosophers, like Plato, were thought to create the same Bacchic
frenzy.

12–13. *the race of men who do not fear the gods:* Evidently the Christians.

of the confused crowd, with your verse heavy-laden with
spirit-expanding honey from your hives, an everlasting
glory from an eloquence that charms the mind.°

17–18. *honey from your hives . . . mind:* The bee is sacred to the Muses, and the honey
the Muses produce—that is, inspired poetry, an "eloquence that charms the mind"—
imparts spiritual powers to those who eat it, bringing the poet to a state of Bacchic
frenzy and enlightenment.

9

Artemis

Artemis had many cult-sites in mainland Greece and Asia Minor, exceeded in number only by her brother Apollo. He was, however, more important in the literary tradition because of his many sexual attachments and because he was the sponsor of song. Artemis was a virgin goddess of the hunt and the killing of wild creatures, though she also protected them. She sponsored boys and girls not yet initiated into adulthood; girls left their dolls on her altar before marriage. In a cult to Artemis in the town of Brauron on the east coast of Attica, coming-of-age ritual for girls were famously celebrated. She helped women in childbirth, though she was herself a virgin. She was an important protectress of the city who brought to citizens prosperity, abundant domestic animals, and rich yields from crops, but in litera-ture she had close associations with human sacrifice too, as in the story that she demanded the sacrifice of Iphigeneia before she would permit the Greek fleet to sail to Troy. She has much in common with Near Eastern goddesses, especially Astarte and Cybelê, the Great Mother goddess of PHRYGIA, and with Egyptian goddesses, especially Isis. Greeks associated her with Eileithyia, the goddess of childbirth; with Hekatê; and with the moon. She had temples in ARCADIA, SPARTA, ATTICA, BOEOTIA, THESSALY, CRETE, and above all in IONIA at EPHESOS, where her magnificent temple was one of the Seven Won-ders of the World. She had a major sanctuary on the central Cycladic island of DELOS. In CYRENÊ in North Africa an Artemision was built

next to the temple to Apollo, and Callimachus' *Hymn to Artemis* may
have been composed for a festival there.

HOMERIC HYMN 9: TO ARTEMIS

Artemis is a great goddess in Asia Minor.

    O Muse, sing of Artemis, sister of the Far-Shooter!
A virgin who delights in arrows, raised up with Apollo,
who brings her horses to water in the stream of Meles,
deep in reeds, then swiftly drives her golden chariot
5   through Smyrna to Klaros,° drenched in vines, where
Apollo of the silver bow sits and waits for the far-shooting
goddess who delights in arrows.
                        And so hail to you,
Artemis, in my song, and all the other goddesses too.
But I will begin first of all to sing about you, beginning
10   with you, and then I shall turn to another song.

HOMERIC HYMN 27: TO ARTEMIS

Artemis is the great hunter and the sister of Phoibos Apollo.

    I sing of Artemis of the golden arrow-shafts, the rouser
of hounds, the pure virgin, the shooter of stags, who delights
in arrows, the very sister of Apollo of the golden sword!
    Wandering over the shadowy mountains and windy peaks,
5   thrilling to the chase, she draws her golden bow
and fires her painful arrows. The peaks of the high
mountains tremble, and the thick wood echoes
awfully with the cry of beasts, and the earth shakes
and the fishy seas. But she with bold heart turns
10   every which way as she destroys the race of wild animals.
    But when this huntress, who delights in arrows, has satisfied

3–5. *the stream of Meles . . . Klaros:* Meles was a stream near Smyrna in Asia Minor.
Klaros had a celebrated oracle to Apollo and a temple to the god. Perhaps this hymn
commemorates a procession between the stream of Meles and the city of Klaros.

FIGURE 26. Apollo and Artemis, by the Briseis Painter. Apollo stands on the left, his hair bound by a fillet, holding a staff in his left hand. His name, APOLLON, is written from right to left in front of him (invisible in the photo). Artemis holds her weapon, the bow, in her left hand, while her emblem, the deer, stands in front of her. From an Athenian red-figure wine-drinking cup, c. 470 BC. Musée du Louvre. Photograph by Marie-Lan Nguyen / Creative Commons.

and gladdened her heart, she loosens her curved bow
and enters the great house of her dear brother, Phoibos
Apollo, traveling to Delphi's rich community,
15   where she arranges the beautiful dance of the Muses
and the Graces. There she hangs up her back-bent bow
and her arrows and, having adorned her flesh,
she leads off the dances while in divine voices they
sing of Leto with the delicate ankles, how she gave

20   birth to children in counsel and deed far superior
     to the other deathless ones.
                                    Hail to you,
     children of Zeus and fine-haired Leto! Now
     I will remember you and another song too.

CALLIMACHUS HYMN 3: TO ARTEMIS

*Callimachus' hymn to Artemis begins with the goddess as a child. As she
grows up her roles change from Mistress of Wild Animals to the protector
of cities, manifest in the cultic dance. She begins as a child sitting in her
father's lap, then joins the Olympians as an adult. The young goddess
first selects nymphs to accompany her, goes to the Cyclopes to provide her
with weapons, and to Pan for her hounds. She captures the Ceryneian
deer to pull her chariot. She then arrives on Olympos. Hermes takes her
weapons and Apollo takes her catch—until Herakles takes over this role.
Artemis enters the halls and sits next to Apollo. What island, mountain,
harbor, and city most pleases her? What nymphs? Which men did she
help? On whom did she exercise vengeance? Her chorus of nymphs is
transformed into the Amazons, who dance in her honor at Ephesos, a
famous cult site that receives her protection.*

     We sing of Artemis—for it is no small matter
     for singers to neglect her!—whose great concerns
     are the bow, and the hunting of hares, and the spacious
     chorus and delight upon the mountains, beginning
5   from the time when, still a child, she sat on her father's
     knee and in a childlike fashion said the following:
          "Give me to forever preserve my virginity, O Papa,
     and to have many names, so that Phoibos may not
     outdo me. Give me arrows and a bow—oh, but wait,
10   father, I am not asking you for a quiver nor a big
     bow: the Cyclopes will make me arrows right away,
     and they will make me a back-bent bow—but give
     me to be a light-bearer, and to hitch up my fringed tunic
     as far as my knees so that I might kill wild animals.
15   "Give me sixty daughters of Ocean as my chorus,
     all nine years old, still children, not yet ready for marriage.

Give me twenty Amnisian nymphs as attendants,°
who will take good care of my running boots and my swift
hounds when I'm not shooting at lynxes and deer.
20   Give me every mountain, and as far as cities are concerned,
give me whatever one you wish—it is a rare occasion
when Artemis will go down to a city. For I will dwell
in the mountains, and I will mix with the cities of men
only when women are worn by sharp labor pangs
25   and call out for help. The Fates assigned this role
to me when I was first being born, to help them
because my own mother carried me and gave birth
to me without effort, discharging me from her womb."
      Thus the little girl, having spoken, wanted to touch
30   her father's beard, but in vain she repeatedly stretched
out her hands so that she might touch it. But her father
laughed and nodded assent, and caressing her he said:
      "When goddesses bear me children such as this,
I will care little for the jealousy of an angry Hera.
35   Take, my child, whatever you want, and ask for!
Your father will give other, still greater things. Cities
three times ten will I give, and more than a single
tower! Cities three times ten will know not
to glorify another god but you alone, and will be said
40   to belong to Artemis. And I will give you many cities
that you can share with other gods, both on land
and on the islands. In all there will be altars and woods
sacred to Artemis, and you will be the watcher over
streets and harbors."
                          Having so spoken, he confirmed
45   his promise with a nod of his head. The young girl
went to the White Mountains in CRETE,° overgrown with

17. *twenty Amnisian nymphs as attendants:* Artemis needs twenty personal servants
to care for her clothing and equipment, but sixty Oceanids for the choral dance. The
attendants are daughters of the Cretan river Amnisos, which runs into the sea five miles
east of Knossos.

46. *White Mountains in* CRETE: They occupy a good part of the center of western
Crete. Made of limestone, they are called the White Mountains because they are covered
in snow until late in the spring.

forest, and from there to Ocean. She selected many nymphs,
all of them nine years old, all of them unmarried girls.
The river Kairatos greatly rejoiced, Tethys rejoiced, because
50 they were sending their daughters to be companions to Leto.°
    Then she went to the Cyclopes. She found them
on the island of LIPARI—Lipari now, but then
it had the name of Meligounis—standing at the anvil
of Hephaistos around a mass of molten metal.°
55 They were working a big job, to fashion a watering
trough for horses for Poseidon. The nymphs were frightened
when they saw the huge giants, like the peaks of Mount
Ossa°—under their brows they all had but a single eye,
like a shield made of four oxhides, glowering fiercely—
60 and when they heard the thud of the echoing anvil,
the huge blast of the bellows, and the Cyclopes' immense
groaning. Etna cried out, Trinakria the seat
of the Sikani cried out, neighboring ITALY cried out,
and CORSICA gave forth a loud cry when the Cyclopes
65 raised their hammers above their shoulders and pounded
the sizzling bronze, fresh from the kiln, or the iron,
striking them in turn and snorting loudly.° Therefore

49–51. *The river Kairatos . . . to Leto:* The river Kairatos was a small Cretan river near
KNOSSOS. Tethys is the wife of Ocean. Because Leto was the daughter of the Titans
Koios and Phoibê, whose sister was Tethys, Tethys' daughters, the Oceanids, are
Artemis' cousins.

51–54. *the Cyclopes . . . molten metal:* The Cyclopes (si-**klō**-pēz) are not the pastoral-
ists that Odysseus tangled with, but three children of Earth (Gaia) named for qualities
of the thunderbolt: Brontês ("thunder"), Steropês ("lightning"), and Argês ("flash"). The
nymphs' fear of the Cyclopes contrasts with Artemis' bravery. The Lipari are volcanic
islands off of the northeast coast of SICILY, a traditional location for Hephaistos' forge.
The islands' name-change may be to signal that this is the post-Homeric world.

58. *Ossa:* In Thessaly. The giants Otos and Ephialtes famously attempted to reach
MOUNT OLYMPOS by piling nearby MOUNT PELION on top of Ossa to carry off Artemis
and Hera. Apollo or Artemis killed them.

62–67. *Trinakria . . . snorting loudly:* Trinakria is a name for Sicily. It means "three-
pronged," after the island's shape. According to Thucydides (6.2.1), the earliest settlers in
Sicily were the Cyclopes (Odysseus' enemy, Polyphemos, was thought to reside there),
followed by the Sikani ("Sicilians"), who gave the name Sikania to the island, replacing
Trinakria.

the Oceanids did not dare to look at them straight on
or hear the din without fear.
                                    You cannot blame them—
70 even the daughters of the blessed gods (no children
    they!) cannot look upon them without a shudder.
    But whenever one of the girls is disobedient to her mother,
    the mother will call down the Cyclopes on her child—
    Argês or Steropês.° Or Hermes emerges from the inmost
75 parts of the house, all smeared with burned ashes.°
    Right away he plays the bogeyman to the young girl
    and she runs to her mother's lap, placing her hands
    over her eyes. My child, earlier, when you were only
    three years old, Leto came carrying you in her arms,
80 when Hephaistos summoned you so that he might
    give you a gift. Brontes placed you on his mighty
    knees and you grabbed the hairs on his great chest,
    and you forcefully plucked them out!° Even to this day
    the middle of his chest is hairless, as when scabies
85 settles in on a man's temple and eats away at his hair!
        And so you spoke to them quite forcefully on that day:
    "Cyclopes, come, make for me too a Kudonian
    bow° and arrows and a hollow quiver with a cap
    for my shafts. For I am a child of Leto, just as Apollo.

72–74. *whenever one of the girls . . . Steropes:* To show how terrifying the Cyclopes
are, even for gods, Callimachus inserts an aside in which mothers summon a Cyclops as
a bogeyman to scare a naughty daughter.

74–75. *Or Hermes emerges . . . burned ashes:* Hermes' frightening of children—like the
Cyclopes'—may be an allusion to "Homeric Hymn 11: To Pan" where the newborn appear-
ance of Hermes' son Pan, with his beard, horns, and goat's feet, is so startling that his
mother runs away. In any event, Hermes was the type of the naughty child. First he stole the
cattle of Apollo, his half-brother, and when Apollo in anger entered his cave he pretended
to be sleeping innocently in his cradle, "like embers concealed under wood-ash" according
to "Homeric Hymn 4: To Hermes." As a naughty child, he can scare naughty children.

78–83. *My child . . . a gift:* But Artemis is *not* like such young girls, a fraidy-cat, hav-
ing been taken to the Cyclopes when just a child. Artemis was so fearless that when only
a three-year-old she went with her mother Leto on a visit to Hephaistos, sat on Brontês'
knees, and pulled out his chest hairs.

87–88. *Kudonian bow:* KUDONIA was a city in Crete (modern Chania), and Crete
was famous for its archers.

90 If I should hunt some solitary creature, or savage monster,
with my bow—well, then, the Cyclopes would eat it!"
        You spoke, and they accomplished it. You were
arrayed, O goddess, and immediately, in turn, you went after
your hounds. You came to the camp of Pan in ARCADIA.
95 He was cutting up the meat of a Mainalian lynx° so that
he might feed his breeding bitches. The bearded
one gave you two black-and-white hounds, three ones
brown in color, and one spotted who pulled down lions,
fastening on their throats, and the hound dragged them
100 still alive to Pan's camp. And Pan gave you seven
Spartan bitches, swifter then the wind, who were
the fastest in pursuing fawns and hares (who do not close
their eyes°) and at sniffing out the hiding place of stags
and the lairs of porcupines and following the tracks of deer.
105   Leaving there—and your hounds hurried after you!—
you found skipping deer at the base of Mount Parrhasios,°
a magnificent herd! They always grazed on the banks
of the black-pebbled torrent, larger than bulls, and gold
flashed from their horns. Suddenly you were amazed,
110 and you spoke to your heart: "Now here's a first hunt—
suitable for Artemis!"
                    There were five of them,
but you took four, running swiftly—no need for dogs!—
so they could draw your chariot. The one that fled
beyond the river Keladon, by the order of Hera,
115 you left as a contest for Herakles, yet to be born,
and the Ceryneian hill received her.°
                        O Artemis, virgin,

---

95. *Mainalian lynx:* Mount Mainalos in Arcadia was a special haunt of Pan.
102–3. *who do not close their eyes:* Hares were thought to sleep with their eyes open.
106. *Parrhasios:* A mountain in Arcadia.

114–16. *the river Keladon ... received her:* The river Keladon is a tributary of the ALPHEOS that flows past the site of the Olympic games in the PELOPONNESOS. Ceryneia was a small hill town in Achaea, the territory directly north of Arcadia. Herakles' third labor, to capture the Ceryneian deer, was a common subject of Greek vase painting.

the killer of Tituos,° golden are your arrows, golden
the sash about your waist, and you yoked a golden
chariot, and you put golden bridles on your deer.
120 Where first did your horned team set out to take you?
To MOUNT HAIMOS in THRACE, whence comes the sudden
squall of Boreas, bringing the evil breath of frost
to those who have no cloaks to wear. And where
did you cut down the pine? and from what flame did
125 you kindle it? On Mount Olympos in MYSIA,°
and you placed in it the breath of immortal flame
that your father's thunderbolts distill.

And how many times
did you test your silver bow, O goddess? On the first
time you shot at an elm tree, on the second at an oak,
130 on the third at a wild animal, on the fourth—not an oak—
but you shot into the city of the unjust who did many
wicked things both to themselves and to strangers
—the wretches!—on whom you inflict your savage anger.
Plagues feed on their cattle, frost afflicts their crops,
135 old men cut their hair in mourning for their sons,
women, struck down, die in childbirth or, if they escape,
they breed children who cannot stand up straight.
But to those on whom you look with a gracious smile,
their fields bear much wheat, their four-footed animals
140 are fertile, and their households are rich. Nor do they
approach a tomb, except when they carry the aged there.
Nor does party strife wound their tribes, which
wrecks even houses that are well established,
but the wives of brothers sit down at one table
145 with the sisters of their husbands.

O lady,

---

117. *the killer of Tituos:* The Giant Tituos tried to rape Leto soon after she gave birth, but one or both of her children killed him. He lies in torment in the underworld with a vulture every day devouring his renewed liver.

125. *Mount Olympos in MYSIA:* "Olympos" seems to be a pre-Greek word for "mountain": many mountains in Greece were called Mount Olympos. Mysia was a region east of TROY.

FIGURE 27. Artemis of EPHESOS. One of the statues recovered from the now totally destroyed great Temple of Artemis at Ephesos, one of the Seven Wonders of the World and the second great cult site to Artemis, after Delos. This statue, probably from the first century AD, is a distinctive form of Artemis, owing much to Near Eastern forms. The body and legs are enclosed within a tight-fitting cloak from which the goddess's feet protrude. She wears a special crown, also worn by the Great Mother goddess Cybelê in her role as a protector of cities. From either side of the crown falls a veil covered by animal heads. The oval objects covering the upper part of her body have usually been interpreted as multiple breasts, standing for fertility, but modern scholarship has suggested that they are the scrotal sacs of sacrificed bulls. Above the rows of ovals are a necklace representing the zodiac. Her arms are extended. The lower front of her body is decorated with the heads of animals—lions, leopards, deer, and bulls. Ephesos Archaeology Museum. Photograph © Julian Fong / Creative Commons.

let whoever is my true friend be among this number!
And may I myself, O queen, be among that number,
and may my song be forever my concern!
In that song will be the marriage of Leto,
150 and you will be a principal subject, and Apollo,
and in it all your exploits too, and your hounds
and your bow and your chariots that easily carry you,
splendid, when you travel to the house of Zeus.
Gracious Hermes receives you there in the forecourt
155 and takes your arms, and Apollo takes whatever beast
you bring—at least that used to be the case,
before the mighty Alkides arrived:° Now Phoibos
has this task, because the Tirynthian anvil° ever
sits before the gates, waiting, in case you bring
160 something good to eat.° The gods all laugh without stopping
at that one, and especially his mother-in-law Hera
when Herakles carries a bull out of the chariot, a great
big one, or a wild boar, holding him by the hind
foot as he wiggles around!
                                    With a crafty speech
165 Herakles strongly admonishes you, O goddess:
"Strike down wicked beasts so that mortals might
call you their helper, just as they call me. Let the deer
and the hares feed in the mountains! It's the boars
that wreck the fields, boars that plunder the orchards,
170 and bulls are a big evil for men. Strike them down too!"
So he spoke, and quickly he began to eat the great beast.
Even though his limbs had been made divine under

---

157. *before the mighty Alkides arrived:* That is, before Herakles came to Olympos. His original name was Alkides after his grandfather, Alkaios, the father of his step-father Amphitryon.

158. *Tirynthian anvil:* The anvil is Herakles, so called because Herakles' grandfather, Alkaios, was the king of TIRYNS. When Herakles' cousin Eurystheus inherited the throne of Tiryns, Herakles was forced to serve him.

160. *something good to eat:* Herakles was a famous glutton. This line is meant to be humorous.

the Phrygian oak,° he had not abandoned his gluttony.
He still had the same stomach that he had when he met
175 Theiodamas as he was plowing.°

                    Your Amnisian nymphs°
curry your young deer, once they have been freed
from their yoke, and they cut and carry much swift-growing
clover for them to feed on from Hera's meadow,
the same fodder that feeds Zeus's horses. And they
180 fill golden troughs with water so that there might
be a delightful drink for the deer.

                     You yourself go into
the house of your father. All call out alike, wishing
you to sit with them, but you take your seat next
to Apollo. When the nymphs dance in a circle around
185 you nearby the streams of Egyptian Inopos, or Pitanê
(which also belongs to you), or in Limnai, or where,
O goddess, you came from SCYTHIA to dwell in Halai
Araphanides and you renounced the rites of the Taurians—
then may my oxen not plow a four-acre field
190 for a wage under the hand of a foreign plowman,
surely then they would come to the barn, exhausted
in their necks and limbs even if they were nine-year-

---

173. *Phrygian oak:* Phrygia here is not the territory in Asia Minor, but a hill in TRA-
CHIS, the location of Herakles' funeral pyre. Trachis is just west of the westernmost tip
of the island of Euboea, north of DELPHI. After his body was burned, Herakles became
a god, entered Olympos, and married Hebê, "Youth."

174–75. *the same stomach . . . plowing:* Near Trachis, Herakles asked Theiodamas, an
old man who was plowing his field, for food. When Theiodamas refused, Herakles
killed him, then became guardian of Theiodamas' son, Hulas, who became Herakles'
lover.

175. *Amnisian nymphs:* See line 17.

184–96. *When the nymphs . . . daylight is lengthened:* The references in this very com-
plicated passage go like this: The Inopos river on DELOS was supposed to have a subter-
ranean connection to Egypt. Pitanê was one of the five original villages of SPARTA and
had a temple to Artemis. Another temple in Sparta to Artemis was called the Limnaion,
evidently the reference here. Halai Araphanides was a coastal county in ATTICA with a
temple to Artemis. Orestes and Iphigeneia brought back the cult statue of Artemis from
the Taurian land (today the peninsula of CRIMEA in the north of the BLACK SEA) to
Athens, at Athena's instruction: Artemis rejects the human sacrifice that was part of the

old Stumphaians, drawing by their horns, oxen which
are the best to cut a deep furrow. For the god Helios
195 never passes by that beautiful dance without stopping
his chariot to watch, and the daylight is lengthened.°
    Which island, what mountain do you like especially?
What harbor? What city? Which nymph do you love most?
Which heroines do you have as companions? Tell me, goddess,
200 and I will sing to others!
                Well, of islands, Dolichê;
of cities, you like PERGÊ best; of mountains, TAYGETOS;
and the harbors of EURIPOS.° And you love the Gortynian
nymph, Britomartis, more than the others, the sharp-eyed
killer of fawns.° Once upon a time Minos, excited by love
205 for her, chased her across the mountains of Crete. Sometimes
the nymph hid herself beneath the shaggy oaks, sometimes
she hid in the meadows. For nine months he coursed over
the heights and peaks, and he did not abandon his pursuit,
until, nearly captured, she leaped into the sea from a high

Taurian cult (a theme in Euripides' *Iphigeneia among the Taurians*). Stumphaion was a
region in EPIROS in the northwestern PELOPONNESOS, known for its fine cattle; nine-
year-old cattle are the best. The point of this convoluted passage is that because the
sun-god Helios stops to watch the dancing, daylight is extended so that the time it takes
to plow a field of four acres—a way of saying "a single day's work"—would be length-
ened because one plowed until the sun went down. If the speaker hired a "foreign plow-
man" to work the field for him, the plowman, being foreign, would not be interested in
the oxen's welfare and he would overwork them because of the lengthened day.

200–2. *of islands, Dolichê . . . EURIPOS:* Dolichê was another name for Ikaros, one of
the CYCLADES; the island had a temple to Artemis. Pergê was a city in PAMPHYLIA
famous for its temple and annual festival to Artemis. Taygetos was a mountain range
running the length of the middle peninsula of the PELOPONNESOS; SPARTA lay to its
east. Euripos is the strait between EUBOIA and BOEOTIA; Aulis, which is nearby, had a
temple to Artemis with two statues, one holding a torch, the other firing an arrow. It was
the embarkation harbor of the Trojan expedition, held up when Menelaos killed a stag
in the grove of Artemis.

202–4. *the Gortynian nymph . . . killer of fawns:* "Gortynian" means from Gortyn, a
Cretan town, hence Cretan. Callimachus goes on to tell the story of Britomartis, a
daughter of Zeus, who fled from lustful Minos and jumped into the sea. Saved by a
fisherman's net, she was then called Diktunna, supposedly "lady of the net" (*diktus* is
Greek for "net"). The name probably really means "lady of MOUNT DIKTÊ." Her name is
found in Cretan inscriptions, and seems sometimes to be identified with Artemis.

210 peak and fell into the fishermen's nets that saved her.
Hence afterwards the Cretans call the nymph Diktunna,
and the mountain from which the nymph jumped Diktaion,°
and they set up altars and performed sacrifices. During
the rite their garlands are made of pine or mastic,°
215 but they never touch myrtle because once a myrtle
branch caught up the girl's skirt while she was fleeing,
and for this reason she was greatly angered with the myrtle.
    Oupis°—O queen!—you of the lovely face, bringer
of light, the Cretans also call you Diktunna after
220 that nymph. You also made Cyrenê your companion,
and you gave her two hunting hounds, and with them
this daughter of Hupseus won a contest in games
at the site of the tomb in IOLKOS.° And, my lady,
you made the fair-haired wife of Kephalos, son
225 of Deioneus, one of your companions in the hunt.°
And they say you loved the beautiful Antikleia like
your own eyes.° These were the first women to carry

212. *Diktaion:* That is, MOUNT DIKTÊ, connected with the birth of Zeus, but Calli-machus is in error: Mount Diktê is inland, east of Knossos.

214. *mastic:* A shrub, native to the southern Mediterranean, of the cashew family that has aromatic leaves and fruit, and is closely related to the pistachio. When chewed, the resin of the plant softens and becomes a gum with a pine or cedar flavor.

218. *Oupis:* A cult title for Artemis in her great temple at Ephesos.

220–23. *Cyrenê your companion . . . in IOLKOS:* Cyrenê, the daughter of Hupseus, was the nymph from THESSALY whom Apollo loved and transported to CYRENÊ in Africa (the colony is named after the nymph). Evidently Artemis had an earlier claim on her, but we have no other authority for this myth. The tomb in Iolkos would belong to Pelias, a king in Thessaly, whose funeral games were well attested. Pelias is famous in the story of Jason: he was Jason's uncle, persecuted Jason's family, and sent Jason on the quest for the Golden Fleece. He was murdered by his daughters in a trick contrived by Medea, Jason's lover.

224–25. *wife of Kephalos . . . in the hunt:* The wife of Kephalos, son of Deioneus, was Prokris, a daughter of Erechtheus, king of Athens. When Kephalos was carried off by lustful Dawn (Eos), Prokris spent eight years as companion to Artemis, then returned to her husband.

226–27. *the beautiful Antikleia like your own eyes:* The only person known by the name of Antikleia was Odysseus' mother, but no other account makes her a companion of Artemis.

the swift bows and arrow-filled quivers on their shoulders;
their right shoulders bore the strap of the quivers,
230 and their right breast was always bare.°
                                            And you
praised greatly swift-footed Atalanta, the daughter
of Arcadian Iasios, the slayer of boars, and you taught
her how to hunt with hounds, and fine marksmanship.°
Nor did the hunters summoned to kill the Kalydonian boar
235 begrudge her presence—the tokens of victory came
to Arcadia, and it still has tusks of the boar.° Nor,
I expect, do Hulaios and stupid Rhoikos find fault
with Atalanta's archery, though in Hades they are filled
with hate for her—their flanks, whose blood covered
240 the heights of Mainalos, would hardly support such a lie!°
    O lady of many shrines, of many cities, hail! Lady
of the tunic, dweller in MILETOS, Neleus made you his leader
when he led a fleet from the land of Kekrops.° O lady
of Chesion, O lady of Imbrasia, First Enthroned, to you

230. *their right breast was always bare:* Amazons were shown in art with the right breast uncovered, their name derived from *amazes,* "without a breast," on the theory that these women removed one breast to allow ease in pulling back the bowstring. Artemis is in fact sometimes portrayed as an Amazon.

231–33. *swift-footed Atalanta . . . marksmanship:* Iasios, Atalanta's father, was the son of the Arcadian King Lukurgos of ARCADIA. He exposed Atalanta at birth because he wanted a boy, but she-bears suckled her until hunters discovered her and raised her. Like Artemis, she remained a virgin, caring only for the hunt.

234–36. *the Kalydonian boar . . . tusks of the boar:* Oeneus, the king of Kalydon in southwestern mainland Greece, did not honor Artemis while sacrificing. She punished him by sending the Kalydonian boar to ruin his land. Oeneus summoned a band of heroes to hunt down the boar and allowed Atalanta to participate. She drew first blood, though she did not kill the boar, and was given the tusks and skin as a token of her achievement. The tusks were displayed in a temple of Athena in the town of TEGEA in Arcadia.

237–40. *Hulaios and stupid Rhoikos . . . such a lie:* Hulaios and Rhoikos were two Centaurs who attempted to rape Atalanta. She killed them both in the Mainalos mountain range in Arcadia.

241–43. *Lady of the tunic . . . of Kekrops:* Lady of the Tunic was a cult title of Artemis; she wore a sleeveless hunting tunic *(chiton)* that reached to her knees. Neleus, the son of Kodros, was the king of Athens and the legendary founder of Miletos and other Ionian cities. Kekrops was an early king of Athens, so the land of Kekrops is Athens.

243–49. *lady of Chesion . . . of the Teucrians:* Chesion was a cape on the island of SAMOS. The Imbrasos was a river on Samos. Chesia and Imbrasiê were Samian cult titles

245 Agamemnon dedicated the rudder of his ship in your
    shrine, a charm against bad weather, when you subdued
    the winds, when the Achaeans, angered because of Helen
    of Rhamnous, sailed their ships to harass the cities
    of the Teucrians.° Proitos, surely, dedicated to you
250 two shrines, the one to Artemis of Maidenhood,
    because you gathered up his daughters who were
    wandering in the Azanian mountains, and the other
    in Lousoi to Artemis the Mild, when you took away
    the wild madness from the girls.°
                                    Once the Amazons,
255 eager for war, set up for you an image on the shore
    near Ephesos, beneath the trunk of an oak, and Hippo
    performed a holy rite for you.° And these women,
    O Queen Opis, danced the war dance, first armed
    with shields, then in a broad circle. Clear-sounding
260 pipes, delicately played, accompanied their dance,
    so that they might beat the ground in harmony
    (for they did not yet bore holes in the bones
    of fawns, a work of Athena, for the deer an evil°).

---

applied to Artemis and Hera. A cult of Artemis in Ephesos worshipped her as Prototh-
ronios, "first enthroned." Ship's rudders were often dedicated as offerings after a safe
voyage, in this case for the cessation of the winds that kept the Trojan expedition stalled
at Aulis. Rhamnous was a coastal town in northeastern Attica known for its temple to
Nemesis, the avenging goddess sometimes said to be the mother of Helen, who was also
worshipped there. The Teucrians are the descendants of Teucer, an early Trojan king,
hence the Trojans. Probably "cities" refers to the towns surrounding Troy that Achilles
sacked in the early years of the Trojan campaign.

   249–54. *Proitos, surely . . . from the girls:* Proitos was a king of ARGOS whose daugh-
ters were driven mad because they slighted Hera or Dionysus. Raving, they roamed the
local mountains. The usual story is that the seer Melampos cured them in return for a
portion of the kingdom, but Callimachus makes two aspects of Artemis—"Artemis of
Maidenhood" (Koria) and "Artemis the Mild" (Hemera)—the active agents in the story.
The Azanian mountains are in Arcadia, as is the village of Lousoi.

   256–57. *near Ephesos . . . for you:* Ephesos in Asia Minor was the site of the greatest
ancient temple to Artemis (see figure 27). Hippo, otherwise unknown, is probably Hip-
polutê, a queen of the Amazons.

   262–63. *for they did not . . . an evil:* That is, the dance is accompanied by shepherd's
pipes and not flutes, which were made from the hollow bones of deer and had not yet
been invented by Athena.

An echo ran as far as Sardis and the Berekunthian territory.°
265 They stamped their feet loudly, and their quivers rattled.
Afterwards, a broad foundation was built around the image,
and Dawn saw nothing more divine, nothing richer.
Easily it would surpass Pytho.° Yes, that arrogant Lugdamis,
as he wandered about, threatened to destroy it.°
270 He led an army of milk-sucking Cimmerians, as numerous
as the sands of the sea, those who live beside the Straits
of the Cow, the daughter of Inachos.° Ah, wretched among
kings, how he sinned! He was not destined to return
to Scythia, nor were any others of those whose wagons
275 stood in the meadow of the Kaystros.° Your bow always
stands as a protection of Ephesos!°

O lady of Munuchia,

264. *Sardis and the Berekunthian territory:* Sardis is in Asia Minor, northeast of
Ephesos. Mount Berekunthos is in nearby Phrygia, the home of Cybelê, Mother of the
Gods, whose rites were accompanied by flutes.

268. *Easily it would surpass Pytho:* The temple to Artemis at Ephesos was famous for
its inordinate wealth, even surpassing the rich shrine of Apollo at Delphi.

268–69. *that arrogant Lugdamis . . . destroy it:* Lugdamis was a seventh-century king
of the Cimmerians, from Scythia (southern Ukraine), who attacked the Ionian coastal
cities and, according to some reports, did burn the temple of Artemis at Ephesos.

270–72. *milk-sucking Cimmerians . . . Inachos:* The Cimmerians, that is, the Scythi-
ans, were famous for drinking the milk of mares. The Straits of the Cow are the Bospo-
ros ("cow passage") between Byzantium (modern Istanbul) and Asia, named for Io, the
daughter of the Argive king Inachos. Io was driven by a gadfly across the straits in the
form of a cow, transformed by Hera because she was sleeping with Zeus. The Inachid
line of Argos were supposedly ancestors of the Ptolemies, and Io, though born Greek,
ended her travels in Egypt.

274–75. *those whose wagons . . . Kaystros:* Scythian nomads were noted for traveling
in wagons. The Kaystros is a river in central Asia Minor. The passage imitates a famous
simile in the *Iliad* (2.459–68) where Homer compares the Achaean armies to cranes that
gather in the meadow by the Kaystros.

276. *protection of Ephesos:* The Cimmerians attacked Ephesos in the mid-seventh
century BC but were driven back.

276–77. *O lady of Munuchia . . . hail:* The cult title Lady of Munuchia refers to
Artemis' temple in Attica, near the harbor of Munuchia, or possibly to a temple of the
same name on the Ephesian coast, or to both cult-sites. Mistress of Pherai seems to refer
to Argos, where Artemis' cult statue was brought from Pherai in Thessaly, but she may
have been worshipped with this title in other places too.

guardian of harbors, Mistress of Pherai—hail!°
Let no one dishonor Artemis; for Oeneus dishonored
her altar, and no pleasant contests came his way.°
280 Do not contend with her in the shooting of deer
or in marksmanship, for the son of Atreus boasted
at a very large price.° Let no one court the virgin;
neither Otos, nor Orion, wooed her to their advantage.°
And do not flee from her yearly dance, for not without
285 weeping did Hippo refuse to dance around her altar.°
    Hail greatly, queen, and encounter my song with grace!

ORPHIC HYMN 36: TO ARTEMIS

*Artemis is goddess of the forest and mountains, the great huntress, who
also presides over childbirth and brings prosperity.*

Hear me, O queen, daughter of Zeus, of many names,
of a Titan born,° Bacchic,° great of name, archer,
blessed, bringer of light, torch-bearer,° divine Diktunna,°
helper at childbirth, helper of women in labor,

278–79. *Oeneus dishonored . . . his way:* Oeneus ("wine-man") of Kalydon failed to
offer appropriately to Artemis and she sent the Kalydonian Boar to ravage his land.

281–82. *the son of Atreus boasted at a very large price:* Agamemnon (or Menelaos)
shot a deer sacred to Artemis and boasted of it, which led to the fleet being stalled at
Aulis and to the sacrifice of his daughter Iphigeneia to appease the goddess.

283. *neither Otos, nor Orion, wooed her to their advantage:* Otos and his brother
Ephialtes, giant sons of Poseidon, wanted to storm Mount Olympos and win Artemis
for Otos and Hera for Ephialtes. They piled Mount Ossa on Mount Pelion to reach the
top of Olympos but Apollo killed them. Orion hunted with Artemis in Crete. When he
attempted to rape her, she killed him and changed him into the constellation.

284–85. *not without weeping . . . her altar:* It is not known why Hippo(lutê), who
founded the temple to Artemis at Ephesos, refused to dance around the altar.

2. *Titan born:* Leto was a Titan, daughter of Koios (uncertain meaning) and Phoibê
("bright").

2. *Bacchic:* Like Dionysos (Bacchus), Artemis haunted the mountains, followed by
attendants. She is dangerous, even savage, and is once called a maenad (a follower of
Dionysos).

3. *bringer of light, torch-bearer:* These epithets associate Artemis with the Moon
(Selenê) and with Hekatê.

3. *Diktunna:* A Cretan goddess identified with Artemis.

5   though you yourself have never experienced labor.
O freer of women from virginity,° you love frenzy,
you are a huntress, you dispel care, you are a fine
runner, an archer, a lover of the chase. You roam
through the night, you bring fame, O gracious one,
10   you set us free, in masculine guise, Orthia.°
You are the goddess of quick childbirth, nurturer
of human young, lover of the chase, divine yet
of this earth, killer of wild beasts, blessed one.
You wander the forests and mountains, slayer of deer,
15   exalted, revered, queen of all, fair-blossomed, eternal.
You haunt the woods, driver of hounds, many-shaped
lady of KUDONIA!°

                Come, dear goddess, savior
of all the initiates, accessible to all, bringing
lovely fruits from the earth and a beautiful
20   peace and fair-tressed health. May you drive
disease and pain to the peaks of the mountains!

6. *O freer of women from virginity:* Because she assists in childbirth, the end of virginity.

10. *Orthia:* The sanctuary of Artemis Orthia ("upright," perhaps referring to a primitive cult image) in Sparta was one of the most important religious sites in Sparta. At an annual festival young men would attempt to seize cheeses from her altar while being brutally whipped.

17. *KUDONIA:* A Cretan town where there was a cult of Diktunna.

10

Hermes and Pan

Hermes is the divine trickster and messenger, who connects disparate realms, especially the land of the dead with the land of the living. His name appears to derive from *herma,* a heap of stones, a sort of monument that separates one territory from another. Each passerby casts a stone on the heap and so receives the protection of the spirit of the stone heap, that is, Hermes. In the classical period the stone heaps were translated into stone pillars with a head on top and an erect phallus, which turns away evil (figure 28). Every neighborhood in ATHENS had such herms, and local rites were often celebrated in front of them.

In myth Hermes is a thief and accompanies men on dangerous journeys, for example, in the *Iliad* he accompanies Priam when he travels through the Greek forces to Achilles' hut to ransom his dead son Hector. He appears to Odysseus on Circe's island and warns him against her sorcery and gives him a protective plant. He travels to the distant island of Kalypso, in the "navel of the sea," to free Odysseus from bondage. As Argeïphontes, "the killer of Argos," he frees the princess Io from the many-eyed monster who guards her. In the *Odyssey,* as Psychopompos, "soul guide," he leads the souls of the dead suitors with his staff into the underworld. In the "Homeric Hymn to Demeter," he fetches Persephone back from Hades. As god of boundaries and the transgression of boundaries, he rules over herdsmen, thieves, and heralds. He carries the *kerukeion,* the caduceus, a staff entwined with copulating snakes, and in real life heralds carried such a staff as a token of Hermes' protection. He is the god of merchants,

FIGURE 28. A herm from Arcadia, c. 490 BC. Usually they were made of stone, but this one is of bronze. The bearded god has an erect phallus, to turn away evil. The "wings" on either side are perhaps to hang offerings from. Metropolitan Museum of Art, New York. Creative Commons.

who travel widely to market their wares, and the god of clever speech and persuasion, a merchant's best tool. The name of Mercury, his Roman equivalent, comes from *merces*, "pay, reward."

As a herdsman's god, a protector of sheep, he was closely associated with Pan, the wild spirit of the woodland, and he is sometimes said to be Pan's father. Both gods had important cults in ARCADIA, the remote central PELOPONNESOS. Pan does not come into prominence until the end of the fifth century BC and is never a major god, though he gained influence when he fought with the Athenian troops against the Persians at Marathon (490 BC). He was after all the incarnation of irrational blind fear that paralyses the mind and ruins judgment—*pan*ic. He is the only Greek god traditionally represented as a biform, a goatman. In the European Middle Ages he became the model for the devil in popular Christianity.

HOMERIC HYMN 4: TO HERMES

The hymn is the longest of the Homeric Hymns and one of the latest, probably from the sixth century BC. It tells of Hermes' first twenty-four hours during which he invented the lyre, stole his older brother Apollo's cattle, and at last became incorporated into the group of Olympian gods, controlling various spheres of activity: minor forms of divination, the protection of animals, and communication between men and gods. The tone of the poem is lighthearted and humorous, appropriate to the trickster god who is an accomplished liar and thief, and the genius of many deceptions.

    Sing of Hermes, O Muse, the son of Zeus and Maia,
    ruling over CYLLENÊ° and ARCADIA with its many flocks,
    the swift messenger, whom Maia bore, a fair-tressed
    nymph, who mixed in love with Zeus—a modest nymph,
5   who shunned the crowd of the gods, living within a shadowy
    cave. There the son of Kronos used to unite in love

1–2. *Maia . . . CYLLENÊ:* Maia means "mother." She is a daughter of Atlas and figures only in this myth. Cyllenê is a mountain in northeast Arcadia, eight thousand feet in height, the second highest mountain in the Peloponnesos.

with the fair-tressed nymph in the dead of night, unseen
by the deathless gods and mortal men, while sweet sleep
held white-armed Hera.

                            Now when the plan of great Zeus
10   had been fulfilled, and the tenth month and her tenth
moon was fixed in the sky,° she brought forth,
and notable things came to pass: she gave birth to
a child of many turns, very crafty, a robber, a driver
of cattle, a bringer of dreams, a watcher by night,
15   a thief at the gates who would soon show forth amazing
deeds among the deathless gods. Born at dawn, he played
the lyre at midday, and in the evening he stole the cattle
of Apollo the Far-Shooter on the fourth day of the month,
when Lady Maia bore him.

                          When he leapt forth from
20   his mother's immortal thighs, he stayed not long
in his holy cradle, but he jumped up and sought out
the cattle of Apollo. As he stepped over the threshold
of his high-roofed cave, he found a tortoise there,
and from it he gained endless delight; for it was Hermes
25   who first made the tortoise a singer. He came upon him
outside the doors of the courtyard, feeding on the rich
grass in front of the house, waddling along on his legs.
When he saw him, the swift son of Zeus laughed and said:
    "What a fine portent this is! I don't mind it at all.
30   Hail, you lovely in shape, you dancer, you friend
to the feast, nicely met! Where'd you get this pretty
plaything, this blotchy shell that you wear, being
a tortoise who lives in the mountains? But I shall
pick you up and carry you into the house. You will be
35   of some use to me, and I will not disrespect you.
I will be the first to profit from you! 'Better
to be in the house, for it is harmful to be outside.'°

10–11. *the tenth month . . . in the sky:* The Greeks counted inclusively, counting both
the first and the last unit of time in calculating an interval, so "ten months" is "nine
months" in our own reckoning.

36–37. *Better to be . . . outside:* A proverb, also in Hesiod (*Works and Days,* line 365).

Living, you will be a defense against harmful witchcraft;°
but if you die, then you will sing beautifully."

40   So he spoke, and he took up the lovely plaything
in both hands and carrying him he went back into
his house. Then, probing with a chisel of gray iron,
he cut out the living stuff of the mountain tortoise.
As when swift thought passes through a man's breast,

45   whom pressing cares visit constantly, or when twinkles
flash from one's eyes, thus glorious Hermes made
his action as quick as his word. He cut stalks of reed
to measure and fixed them in, passing through the back
of the stony-hided tortoise.° Over them, most cleverly,

50   he stretched oxhide. He put in arms and fitted a cross-bar
across the two of them, and stretched seven strings
of sheep gut to sound in concord. But when he had made
it, carrying the lovely plaything he tried it out with a plectrum
in a tuneful scale, and it sounded marvelously under his hand.

55   The god sang beautifully, trying out impromptu riffs
such as young men at banquets do when they make
off-color jokes. He sang of Zeus, the son of Kronos,
and Maia with the beautiful sandals, how they used
to exchange sweet-nothings in loving friendship, and he told

60   the glorious tale of his own begetting. He celebrated, too,
the servants of the nymph, and her shining home,
and the tripods scattered about, and the abundant cauldrons.
      While he sang of these things, his mind was on other
matters. And he took the scooped-out lyre and placed

65   it in his holy cradle. Longing for some flesh, he leaped
from the perfumed chamber to a place of outlook,
designing sheer trickery in his heart such as thieves
pursue in the hour of darkest night.

                              The sun was going

---

38. *a defense against harmful witchcraft:* The prophylactic powers of living tortoises
are mentioned several times by ancient authors.

47–49. *stalks of reed . . . tortoise:* It is not really clear what is meant, but perhaps the
reeds are a bridge to support the strings. For the tortoise-shell lyre, see figure 29.

FIGURE 29. Man holding a tortoiseshell seven-stringed lyre. The string also held in his right hand evidently enabled him to change the key he was playing in. Red-figure olive-oil jar, c. 480 BC. J. Paul Getty Museum, Malibu, CA. Photograph © alijava / Creative Commons.

down beneath the earth towards Ocean with his horses
70   and chariot when Hermes arrived at the shadowy mountains
of Pieria,° where the immortal cattle of the blessed gods
have their pasture, grazing on the lovely unmown meadows.
Of these the son of Maia, the keen-eyed Killer of Argos,°
cut out fifty loud-mooing cattle from the herd. He drove
75   them on off-road paths across a sandy place, turning
their hoof prints backwards—he did not forget his skill
in deception!—and he turned their hoofs in opposite
directions, making the front ones to the back, the back
ones to the front, while he himself walked the other way.°
80   Right away, by the sands of the sea, he made sandals
of plaited wickerwork—unimaginable, unheard of!—amazing
things, weaving together tamarisk and myrtle branches.
Tying together an armful of their young growth he bound
the light sandals securely beneath his feet, leaves
90   and all, which the glorious killer of Argos had plucked
from Pieria as he readied his journey, improvising
as one does when setting out on long trip.
      An old man, tilling his flowering vineyard, saw him
as he hastened across the plain through grassy ONCHESTOS.°
95   The glorious son of Maia spoke to him first: "Hey old man,
you with the bent shoulders, digging away at your vines—
I think you'll have a lot of wine, once all your vines bear

---

71. *Pieria:* A mountain north of Mount Olympos, where the gods first stepped when they descended from Olympos. Pieria was the birthplace of the Muses, who had a cult there. Pieria is a long ways from Mount Cyllenê.

73. *Killer of Argos:* The Greek epithet is Argeïphontes, which seems to refer to the myth of Io: Zeus loved her, but Hera turned her into a cow and set up a hundred-eyed monster named Argos to guard her. Hermes put the eyes to sleep with his song and killed the beast.

77–79. *he turned their hoofs . . . the other way:* Hermes marches the cattle backwards, but goes forward himself so as to confuse anyone trying to follow them.

94. ONCHESTOS: Northwest of Thebes in Boiotia, known for its grove sacred to Poseidon.

fruit, but don't see what you've seen, or hear what you've
heard, and keep your mouth shut, so long as it does
100 your affairs no harm."°
                              Having said this, he hurried on
his strong head of cattle. Glorious Hermes drove
them across many shadowy mountains and through
echoing canyons and over flowery meadows. And now
the divine night, his dark ally, was mostly passed, and soon
105 dawn, which sets men to work, would come. The bright
Moon, daughter of Pallas, the son of Lord Megamedes,°
had just reached her place of outlook. Then the mighty
son of Zeus drove the broad-browed cattle of Phoibos
Apollo toward the ALPHEIOS RIVER.° They came unwearied
110 to the high-roofed cave and drinking troughs in front
of the magnificent meadow. Then when he had fed
the lowing cattle abundant fodder, and he had driven
them in a crowd into the cave, chewing clover and dewy
sedge, he gathered a pile of wood and devised the art
115 of fire. He chose a stout branch of laurel and trimmed
it with a knife <and spun it in a hollowed-out piece
of ivy wood,>° holding it in his hand, and the hot
heat blew upward: it was Hermes who first discovered
fire-sticks and fire!
                        Then he took many dried logs
120 and piled all of them—a huge number!—in a pit
he had dug, and the flame showed far around, radiating

99–100. *keep your mouth shut . . . no harm:* The story seems truncated. According
to a folktale motif, Hermes should return in disguise and test the man, then when the
man revealed what he had seen, the god would turn him to stone. But that does not
happen here.

106. *Pallas, the son of Lord Megamedes:* Pallas here is not Athena but a Titan; Meg-
amedes ("very clever") is otherwise unknown.

109. *ALPHEIOS RIVER..* The largest river in the Peloponnesos, it flows west from
Olympia into the sea.

116–17. *<and spun it in . . . ivy wood>:* These words are missing in the text, but some-
thing like this is required.

the blast of the furious fire. And while the might of glorious
Hephaistos° kept the fire burning, he dragged two
of the crumpled-horn cattle that were under the shelter
125 out toward the fire—his strength was very great!—
and he threw both of them, snorting, on their backs
on the ground. Leaning into them, he rolled them
over after piercing their spinal cords. Then, task
following on task, he cut up the meat, rich with fat,
130 and he roasted the flesh fixed on wooden spits
together with the honorable portion along the back
and the black blood stuffed in the intestines.° The rest
lay on the ground. He stretched out the hides on a rugged
rock, and there they remain, even now, after so long
135 a time after these events, a fused mass.° Then Hermes
gladly drew off the rich flesh from the spits and placed
it on a flat slab, and he divided the meat into twelve
portions, determined by lot. He placed a perfect portion
of honor on each.°
                    Then glorious Hermes longed
140 for his own allotment of meat, for the sweet scent made
him weary, though he was a deathless god. But his proud
heart was not persuaded to allow the flesh to pass down
his holy throat, though he greatly desired it.° He put it away
in the high-roofed cave, the fat and all the flesh, and raised

122–23. *might of glorious Hephaistos:* As god of the forge he was closely associated
with fire.

131–32. *honorable portion along the back . . . intestines:* The meat along the back, the
chine, was always considered to be the choicest. The stuffed intestine makes a sort of
haggis.

135. *fused mass:* Perhaps the poet is referring to some familiar feature of the land-
scape near the Alpheios.

138–39. *He placed a perfect portion of honor on each:* Evidently the twelve portions
are for the twelve Olympians, including himself, the earliest reference to the Olympian
gods as a group of twelve. Then, as a sign of honor, Hermes adds to each portion a piece
of the best cut, usually reserved for one person at a feast.

141–43. *But his proud heart . . . desired it:* The gods seem never to eat meat, though
they may desire it. They eat ambrosia ("immortal substance"), which distinguishes them
from mortals.

145 it up high on the wall as a token of his recent theft.
     Gathering up dry logs, he burned up the hoofs and the heads
     in the heat of the fire.
                          When the god finished all that he had
     to do, he threw his sandals into the deep-swirling Alpheios,°
     he quenched the embers and flattened out the dark dust
150 for the rest of the night, while the lovely light of Moon
     shined down. Then at the break of dawn he returned
     to the bright peaks of Cyllenê, nor did any of the blessed
     gods, or any mortal, meet him on the long trip,
     nor did the dogs bark. Twisting sideways, the swift-footed
155 Hermes, the son of Zeus, slipped through the keyhole
     of the house—like an autumn breeze, or a mist. He went
     straight through the cave to the rich inner chamber,
     walking softly on his feet, and he made no noise
     as one usually does on a floor. Speedily, glorious
160 Hermes went to his cradle. Wrapping his swaddling
     clothes about his shoulders, he lay like a little baby, toying
     with the sheet around his knees, keeping his lovely
     lyre beside his left hand.
                          He did not escape his divine
     mother's notice, and she said: "WHAT are you up to,
165 sly one? WHERE have you been in the nighttime, cloaked
     in shamelessness? Now I think that you will soon be going
     out through the porch with your ribs bound helplessly
     at the hands of Apollo—or you will give him the slip
     when he is in the middle of carrying you through the hollows.
170 Get back! Your father has conceived you as a great
     bother for mortal men and for the deathless gods!"
        Hermes answered her with crafty words: "Mother
     of mine, why do you try to frighten me like this,
     as if I were a little babe whose heart knows little
175 of mischief, a terrified one, fearful of his mother's
     reproach? I will undertake the finest of arts, providing

---

148. *threw his sandals into the deep-swirling Alpheios:* Why Hermes discards his san-
dals is not clear, but evidently he first fashioned them not to protect his feet, but to
confuse Apollo's pursuit.

plenty of fodder for myself and for you, forever.
Nor will we tolerate staying here and, alone
180 of the deathless gods, being without offerings
and prayers, as you would have us do. Better to spend
all our days in pleasant conversation with the deathless
ones, rich, wealthy, with heaps of grain, than to sit
185 at home in a gloomy cave. As for honor, I will enter
the same worship as accorded to Apollo. And if my father
will not grant this to me, I will try—and I am able!—
to become the prince of thieves. If that glorious son
of Leto tracks me down, I think I will meet him with
190 something even bigger—I will go to Pytho° and break
into his big house, and I will plunder a big bunch
of tripods, and very beautiful cauldrons, and gold,
and tons of shining iron, and lots of fine cloth: you
will see, if you want to!"

                    So they spoke to one another
195 with these words, the son of Zeus who carries the
aegis, and the Lady Maia. Dawn the early-born, bringing
light to mortals, rose from deep-eddying Ocean, but traveling
Apollo arrived at Onchestos, the lovely grove, sacred
to the loud-roaring Shaker of the Earth.° There he found
200 a slow-moving old man tilling the enclosure for his vines
just off the road. The glorious son of Leto spoke
to him first: "O old man, plucker of thorns from grassy
Onchestos, I have come here looking for some cattle
from Pieria—they were all cows, all with crumpled horns,
205 from a herd. A bull was grazing alone apart from
the others—black in color—and keen-eyed dogs followed
behind, four of them, like men, all of the same mind.
They were left behind, the dogs and the bull, quite a marvel
I'd say, but the cows left just after the sun went down,
210 leaving their soft meadow and their sweet pasture.
Tell me, old man, born long ago, if by chance you have

190. *Pytho:* DELPHI.
199. *Shaker of the Earth:* Poseidon.

seen a man on the road, pursuing these cattle."

The old man
answered him with these words: "My friend, it would
be a hard thing to tell all that one's eyes may see. There
215 are many travelers on this road, some looking for nothing
but trouble, others with good in mind. It is hard to tell
one from the other. Anyway, I was digging all day long
in the slopes of my vineyard, until the sun went down,
and I seem to have seen a child, my good man—
220 but I don't know who this child was, an infant, really,
following long-horned cattle. He had a staff in his hands
and he went this way and that. He was driving them
backwards, and they had their heads facing him."

So spoke
the old man. When Apollo had heard him, he went more
225 quickly on his way. He espied a long-winged bird
and immediately knew by this omen that the thief
was the child of Zeus, the son of Kronos. So King
Apollo, the son of Zeus, hastened toward holy Pylos,°
trying to find his shambling cattle, his broad shoulders
230 wrapped in a purple cloud. The Far-Shooter saw footprints
and he said, "Wow, I think I see a great wonder! These
are surely the tracks of straight-horned cattle, but they
are turned backwards toward the meadow of asphodel.
And I do not think that these footprints are those of man
235 nor woman, nor of gray wolves, nor lions, nor of a shaggy
maned Centaur, whoever makes such monstrous prints
with his swift feet.° A strange business on one side
of the road, and stranger still on the other!"

So saying,
King Apollo, the son of Zeus, hurried off. He came
240 to Mount Cyllenê, covered in forest, to the shadowy
cavern in a rock where the divine nymph gave birth

228. *Pylos:* Not the famous Pylos of Nestor in the *Iliad,* but another town of the same name on the banks of the Alpheios River near Olympia.

236–37. *such monstrous prints with his swift feet:* Apollo now notices the odd prints left by Hermes' curious sandals.

to the child of Zeus. A delightful scent spread across
the holy mountain, and many long-shanked Cyllenian sheep
grazed on the grass. There it was that he then came
245 speeding, and he crossed the stone threshold and entered
the misty cave, Apollo, the Far-Darter, in person.
 When the son of Zeus and Maia saw him, angry because
of his cattle—far-darting Apollo!—Hermes ducked down
into his fragrant swaddling-clothes. Just as wood-ash covers
250 a mass of log embers, even so Hermes curled himself
up when he saw Apollo. He drew together his head and hands
and feet into a tiny space, just as a newly washed babe summons
sweet sleep, though in fact he is wide awake. And he kept
his lyre under his armpit. The son of Zeus and Leto right away
255 recognized the mountain nymph and her very handsome
and beloved child, just a little tyke wrapped in his deceitful
rascalities.
  Apollo inspected every cranny of the great house.
He took the shining key and opened three closets, full
of nectar and lovely ambrosia. Much gold and silver
260 lay within, and many purple gowns of the lady, purple
and silver, such as the sacred houses of the blessed
gods always have inside.
  After he had inspected the recesses
of the great house, the son of Leto said this to glorious
Hermes: "My child, lying there in your cradle, tell me where
265 my cattle are—at once!—or we are going to have a problem!
I shall grab you and hurl you down into misty Tartaros,
into the dismal darkness where there is no hope.
And I don't think that your mother nor father will raise
you again into the light, but you will go to perdition
270 under the earth, the ruler of little children."°
 Hermes answered him with crafty words: "O son

---

270. *the ruler of little children:* Condemned to the underworld as a child, Hermes
will rule only children.

of Leto, why do you say these harsh words? Have you
really come here looking for your cattle, which belong
in the field? *I* haven't see them, nor have I made inquiries,
275 and I've heard nothing. I couldn't reveal their whereabouts,
nor receive a reward for it. Nor do I look like a rustler
of cattle, a powerful man. This is not my business.
I have other things on my mind—like sleep and the milk
of my mother and having swaddling clothes around
280 my shoulders, and warm baths. I hope no one learns
what this quarrel was about. It will come as a great
surprise to the deathless ones that a newborn child
passed cattle of the field through a porch! Your talk
is way out of line. I was born yesterday, my feet
285 are tender, the earth is hard beneath. If you want,
I swear a great oath on the head of my father:
I promise that I am not guilty! Nor have I seen
any other thief of your cows—or whatever cows
are, I have only heard about them."

                                            So he spoke,
290 and glancing slyly from his eyes and brows he tossed
and turned, looking here and there, whistling a long tune,
and treating Apollo's words as hollow. Laughing gently,
Apollo who works from afar said: "Oh boy, you little
cheat, you rat! I think by the way you talk that often
295 you'll be boring into rich men's houses by night,
leaving more than one man sitting in the middle
of the floor while you rob the house, not making
a sound. And you will bring grief to many a field-dwelling
shepherd in the valleys of the mountains when, wanting
300 some flesh to eat, you stumble on his herds of cattle
or flocks of sheep. So come on now—unless you want to sleep
the big sleep!—get out of that cradle, O you companion
of darkest night! Surely this will be your title among
the deathless ones: 'Prince of Thieves for Evermore'!"
305   So spoke Apollo, and he seized the child and made
to carry him off, when the powerful Slayer of Argos,
thinking this through as he was carried in Apollo's hands,

expelled an omen, a steadfast day-laborer of the belly,
a reckless messenger, and right after that he sneezed.
310 When Apollo heard it, he threw the glorious Hermes
from his hands onto the ground.° Apollo sat down in front
of him and, though Apollo was anxious to be on his way,
he spoke in a mocking tone to Hermes: "Be of good cheer,
my little Mister Swaddling Clothes, son of Zeus and Maia.
315 I shall very soon find my strong cattle with these omens.
And YOU shall lead the way."

           So he spoke. Cyllenian Hermes swiftly
leaped up, moving with speed, and he pushed up around his ears
his swaddling clothes that had draped on his shoulders,
and he said, "Where do you think you're taking me, O Worker
320 from Afar, most irascible of all gods!? Are you harassing
me like this because you're angry about some cows?
Well, I wish that the whole race of cows would disappear.
At least it wasn't *I* who stole your cows! Nor did I see
anyone else with them—whatever cows are. I've only
325 heard of them. Put the case before Zeus, the son
of Kronos. Let him decide!"

           When Hermes the shepherd
and Apollo, the glorious son of Leto, had asked all their
questions about everything, being angry on both sides—
Apollo, speaking true, was not unjustly taking hold
330 of Hermes over the matter of the cows, whereas
Hermes was trying to trick Apollo of the silver bow
with his arts and his wily words—so when Hermes
saw that Apollo was as devious as he was cunning,
he straightaway went ahead, walking through the sand,
335 and the son of Zeus and Leto followed behind.

    Quickly the most beautiful sons of Zeus came
to the summit of fragrant Olympos, to the son of Kronos.

308–11. *expelled an omen . . . onto the ground:* First Hermes farts, then sneezes. Sudden expulsions of air from the body were an omen, whether of good or bad it was hard to tell. Apollo is taking no chances.

The scales of justice were set up there for the two of them.
There was an assembly taking place on snowy Olympos,
340 and the deathless gods, who never die, were gathered
after golden-throned Dawn. Hermes and Apollo
of the silver bow took their stand before Zeus's knees.
Zeus, who thunders on high, questioned his shining son
in these words:
             "Phoibos, where do you come from,
345 driving this wonderful spoil, a newborn child
with the look of a herald? This is a weighty matter come
before the assembly of the gods."
                  King Apollo, who works
from afar, answered him in this way: "You shall soon
hear a powerful tale, though you think that I alone
345 am eager for gain. I found this child, this absolute
burglar, after wandering around for a long time
in the mountains of Cyllenê—a real rascal the likes
of which I have not seen among gods nor men,
as many as are burglars themselves upon the earth.
355 He stole my cows from a meadow and drove them
last night along the shore of the loud-resounding sea,
heading straight for Pylos. There were two kinds
of tracks—huge, definitely to wonder at, the work
of a demon! As for the cows, the dark dust showed
360 the hoof prints all going backwards towards the asphodel
meadow, while he himself—the rat!—was crossing
the sandy ground outside the road, neither on his feet
nor his hands—he had some other trick as he lay down
tracks—huge!—as if he were walking on slender oak trees.
365 While he pursued the cattle across the sandy ground,
the tracks were easy to see in the dust, but when
he had finished the long path across the sand,
then you couldn't see the track either of the cows
nor of him across the hard ground. But a mortal
370 man saw him herding the broad-browed cattle
straight toward Pylos. After he had shut them up
quietly and finished his trickery on this side of the road
and that, he lay down in this cradle like blackest night

in the gloom of his misty cave. Not even a sharp-sighted
375 eagle would have spotted him. He rubbed his eyes
vigorously to further his deception, and he right away
spoke most forthrightly: 'I saw nothin', I know nothin',
I've heard nothin', I couldn't tell you nothin'—not
even for a reward!'"

So speaking Phoibos Apollo
380 took his seat. Hermes, for his part, answered in reply,
pointing to the son of Kronos, the boss of all the gods:
"Father Zeus, I am now going to tell you the truth.
I'm a truthful guy and I don't know how to lie.
He came to my house looking for his crumple-horned
385 cows, today, just as the sun was rising. He brought
forth no witnesses nor any of the blessed gods who
had seen these events, but straightaway he ordered
me to confess, and with the threat of much violence.
He threatened to throw me into broad Tartaros!
390 Well, he has the tender bloom of his glorious youth,
while I was born yesterday, and he knows it well.
Nor do I look much like a robber of cattle, a powerful
man. Believe me—for you claim to be my father—I did
not drive his cattle to my house—so may I prosper!—
395 nor did I cross the threshold. I speak the truth.
I have the greatest respect for Helios° and the other gods,
and I love you and I fear him. You know yourself
that I am not at fault. And I will swear a great oath:
by these fancy porches of the gods, I will never pay
400 him compensation for this vile theft, strong though
he is. You really must help those who are younger."

So spoke the Cyllenian Slayer of Argos, looking
askance and holding his swaddling cloth on his arm
and not casting it off. Zeus laughed out loud
405 at his wicked child who made such fine and expert
denials about the cows. He ordered the two of them
to be reconciled and to seek out the cattle, Hermes

---

396. *Helios:* Who sees all that happens on earth.

the guide to lead the way and to show without deception
the place where he had hidden the strong cattle.
410 The son of Kronos nodded his head and glorious
Hermes obeyed, persuaded by the purpose of Zeus
who carries the aegis.
                              Eagerly the two very
handsome children of Zeus arrived at the ford
of the Alpheios, to sandy Pylos. They came to the fields
415 and the high-roofed cave where the stock had been
tended during the night. While Hermes went the length
of the rocky cave and drove out the sturdy cattle
into the light, the son of Leto, looking away, saw
the hides on the steep rock, and quickly he asked
420 glorious Hermes: "How were you able—you rat!—
to flay two cattle, being but a newborn babe?
I dread the strength that will one day be yours.
You had better not go on growing, O Cyllenian,
son of Maia!"
                    So Apollo spoke and with his hands
425 wove strong bonds of willow,° but they straightaway
took root right there in the ground beneath their feet,
and intertwining with one another they grew and covered
over all the field-dwelling cattle—by the tricky wiles
of Hermes! Apollo was totally amazed. Then the mighty
430 Slayer of Argos surveyed the land askance, his eyes
darting fire, eager to conceal . . .°
                              Hermes easily pacified
the glorious Far-Shooter, the son of Leto, just
as he wished, though Apollo was very powerful.
He took his lyre on his left arm and tried a scale
435 with his plectrum, and the sound was wonderful
that came from under his hand.
                              Phoibos Apollo

425. *wove strong bonds of willow:* To bind Hermes.
431. *eager to conceal . . . :* One or several lines are omitted here and there are gram-
matical and logical problems with the text. In the missing section Apollo seems to want
compensation for his loss; Hermes then placates him with his lyre-playing.

laughed for joy as the lovely sound of the godlike
voice went into his heart and sweet desire took
hold of his spirit as he listened. The son of Maia,
440 taking heart, stood on the left side of Phoibos
Apollo and played his lyre. Soon, with the lyre sounding,
he sang of the deathless gods, and the dark earth,
and of how things first came into being, and how each
received his portion.° First of the gods he honored
445 Mnemosynê° in his song, the mother of the Muses,
for she had taken the son of Maia into her following.
Then the glorious son of Zeus honored the other
deathless gods in accordance with their seniority,
and he told how each was born, saying everything
450 in correct order, with the lyre hanging from his arm.°
An unquenchable longing filled Apollo's heart
and he spoke to him in winged words:
                                    "You cow-killer,
you rat! Busy with your companion to the feast,°
you have devised fair compensation for the fifty cows!
455 I think we're going to work this out peacefully.
Only tell me this, rascally son of Maia, did these wonders
follow you around right from birth, or did some god
or some mortal give to you this remarkable gift
and teach you divine song? For I am hearing a marvelous
460 voice—brand-new!—which I don't think that any mortal
or any of the deathless ones who occupy Olympos
has ever known—apart from you, you deceitful son
of Maia! What technique, what a song for troubled times,
what a road! Why, you get three things in one—

442–44. *he sang of the deathless gods . . . his portion:* Hermes' song is like Hesiod's
Theogony.

445. *Mnemosynê:* "Memory," essential for an oral poet.

450. *with the lyre hanging from his arm:* A strap attached to the left wrist supported
the lyre, leaving the fingers of the left hand free to pluck or damp the strings, while the
right hand used the plectrum.

453. *companion to the feast:* The lyre.

465 peace of mind, a little sex, and sweet sleep.
                                        "You know,
    I too am a follower of the Olympian Muses—who love
    the dance and the glorious path of song° and lively
    music and the shrill of the flutes that stimulates desire.
    But nothing else has ever been of such concern to me,
470 like the passing to the right at young men's feasts.°
    I am simply amazed at all this, O son of Zeus, how well
    you play the lyre. But now, because you are little, though
    your mind is filled with big ideas, sit, my boy, and have
    some respect for the views of your elders. For now
475 you will have fame among the deathless gods—
    you and your mother. I declare this emphatically:
    by this javelin of cornel wood I will lead you into
    fame and fortune among the deathless ones and I will
    give you fancy gifts, and I will never deceive you!"°
480   Hermes answered him with crafty words: "You are
    questioning me, O wise Far-Darter. But I don't mind at all
    if you encroach on my art —you will know it today.
    For I wish to be your friend in intent and in word.
    Your knowledge of everything is great! For, O son
485 of Zeus, you sit among the deathless ones, noble
    and strong. Zeus the Counselor loves you as he should
    and he has given you many fine gifts. They say that you
    received the province of possessing prophetic knowledge
    from the utterance of Zeus, and—O Far-Shooter!—
490 the utter revelation of Zeus's will. That you are richly
    endowed with these things has become clear to me,

---

467. *path of song:* Almost a technical term to refer to the course of an oral poet's narrative. In line 464 "road" probably refers to the same thing.

470. *the passing to the right at young men's feasts:* It was the custom at the symposia to pass the lyre from left to right, each participant being expected to come up with some verse. Presumably the *Homeric Hymns* were performed in just this manner.

471–79. *how well you play . . . deceive you:* In historical times Apollo presided over music and musicians. But how did he come to have that role? The hymnist suggests that it is through the invention of Hermes—the lyre—that Apollo acquired his power over music. Apollo has heard Hermes sing and he wants that lyre for himself.

abundantly clear. So it's up to you—learn what you want to.

    "Now since your heart is inclining you to learn the lyre,
play it! Make music! Have a party! *Take* it from me.
495 And, dear brother, give me a little credit. Sing sweetly!
Place your hands on this pure-voiced little escort,
who knows how to speak very well and tidily.° Take
her to the blossoming feast, and the lovely dance,
and the glorious revel, a balm both day and night.
500 If you question her with art and wit, she will tell
you all sorts of pleasant things, easy to play with
in tender closeness, fleeing every unpleasant labor.
But if an ignoramus asks something roughly, then
she sounds useless, discordant. It's up to you,
505 how much you want to learn.

                        "Look, I'm going
to give her to you, O marvelous son of Zeus. We will
be happy to herd our field-dwelling cattle in the pastures
of the mountain and the horse-nourishing plain,
O Far-Darter. Then the cows will submit to the bulls
510 and bear many offspring, both female and male.
There really is no need—though you are greedy!—
to be so extravagantly worked up over all this."
So he spoke and held out the lyre.° And Phoibos
Apollo took it. Then he happily handed Hermes
515 the shining whip and he appointed him keeper of the herds.
And the son of Maia joyfully accepted. The glorious
son of Leto, far-shooting King Apollo, taking
the lyre on his left arm, tried out a little tune
with the plectrum. It rang out marvelously down low
520 and the god sang beautifully to its accompaniment.

    Then the very handsome children of Zeus, the two
of them, turned the cattle toward the sacred meadow,

    496–97. *this pure-voiced little escort . . . tidily:* The hymnist compares Hermes' lyre to a courtesan, a *hetaira,* who can delight her customer with clever speech and sensual pleasure.

    513. *and held out the lyre:* Hermes' gift of the lyre establishes his place among the gods and buys the sponsorship of Apollo, his powerful brother.

FIGURE 30. Apollo with lyre. The god wears an elaborately decorated gown such as lyre-players would have worn at contests. His head is crowned with laurel. This is not the lyre made from a tortoise shell (as in figure 29), but one called a *kithara*, with a wood sounding-box. It is elaborately carved and has seven strings that the god is plucking with his left hand. Fragment from a South Italian red-figure wine-mixing bowl, c. 400 BC. Metropolitan Museum of Art, New York. Photograph © Marie-Lan Nguyen / Creative Commons.

then headed back to snowy Olympos, prancing
all the way and delighting themselves with the sounds
525 of the lyre.
          Zeus the Counselor was glad, and he brought
them together in friendship. Hermes loved Leto's son
constantly, as he still does today, when he had given
the lovely lyre that he played so skillfully to the Far-Darter
as a token of his affection, and Apollo played it under
530 his arm. He himself devised a different artful skill—
he made for himself the sound of the Pan-pipes,
heard from afar.°
          And then the son of Leto spoke
to Hermes: "But I'm afraid, O son of Maia—
guide and rascal!—that you will steal my lyre
535 and my bent bow.° For you have this as a kind
of office from Zeus, to look out over the switching
of property among men upon the much-nourishing
earth. But if you will only swear a great oath of the gods,
either by nodding your head or swearing it upon
540 the mighty water of the Styx,° you would do everything
possible to delight and please my heart."
          And then
the son of Maia promised, nodding in agreement,
that he would never steal anything from all that
the Far-Darter possessed, and that he would never
545 go near his strong house. Apollo, for his part, nodded
in agreement that they would share a close friendship,
that no other would be dearer among the deathless ones,
neither god nor a man born of Zeus's stock.

531–32. *Pan-pipes heard from afar:* The Pan-pipes are so called because of their asso-
ciation with Pan, god of the wilderness, a son of Hermes, known for his playing of them.
So Hermes continues his association with music.

534–35. *you will steal my lyre and my bent bow:* As Hermes in fact does in a poem by
Alcaeus (c. 620–sixth century BC).

540. *the mighty water of the Styx:* An oath sworn on the underworld river Styx can
never be broken.

"And I will make you a perfect contract among
550 all the deathless ones,° trustworthy and honored,
and then I will give you a very beautiful wand of wealth
and riches—golden, with three branches°—that will keep
you free from harm, fulfilling all the dispositions of words
and deeds, as many as I have learned from the voice of Zeus.°
555 "However, as for seership, my darling child of Zeus,
about which you ask, it is not destined that you learn
about it, nor any other of the deathless ones. That
is for Zeus's mind alone. I have given a pledge, and agreed
to it, and sworn a solemn oath, that no other of those
560 who live forever—apart from me!—shall ever know
the shrewd counsel of Zeus.
                              "So my brother who carries
a golden staff do not ask me to reveal the destinies
that far-seeing Zeus contrives. As for humans, this one
I shall harm, and that one assist, as I lead their
565 peoples this way and that. And he shall profit
from my voice, who comes after hearing the cry
or watching the flight of birds of omen—this man
shall profit from my voice, and I will never deceive
him. But he who comes after listening to some
570 garbled twittering common birds, who wishes
to know a prophecy that it is not my intention
to give, wishing to know more than those who live
forever, I say he has traveled an empty road—
but I'll take his gifts!
                          "I will tell you something else,
575 O son of brilliant Maia and of Zeus who carries
the aegis, you swift genius of the gods:

549–50. *And I will make you . . . deathless ones:* Apollo is speaking. This is the meaning of the Greek, but there is something wrong with the text.

552. *with three branches:* Apparently referring to the head of the *kerukeion,* the wand of Hermes, made up of two serpents copulating on a staff (see figure 31). With this wand Hermes puts men to sleep or awakens them.

554. *as many as I have learned from the voice of Zeus:* It is not clear what exactly is meant.

There are three august virgins, all sisters, endowed
with swift wings, their heads sprinkled with white
barley—they live under a ridge on PARNASSOS.
580 They are teachers of a different kind of prophesying,
which I practiced when I was still a tyke, herding
my cattle. But my father didn't care at all for this.
From there they go off flying, now here, now there,
munching away at the honeycombs, then giving
585 their prophecies. When they are inspired by eating
the yellow honey, they are happy, eager, to tell
the truth. But if they are turned away from the gods'
sweet food, then they tell falsehoods, buzzing
around in a bunch.°
　　　　　　　"Yes, I give them to you for the future.
590 Take delight in questioning them closely. And if
you teach a mortal man, he will listen to your voice
often—if he's lucky.
　　　　　　　"Take these methods, O son of Maia.
And care for your field-ranging crumple-horned cattle,
and tend your horses and your hardworking mules . . . "°
595　　<So spoke Apollo, the son of Zeus and Leto,
and Zeus agreed that all would be as Apollo said.
Hermes would be the herald of the gods and he would
rule over every kind of animal, bears and gray wolves>
and savage lions and boars with shining tusks and dogs
600 and sheep, as many as the broad earth nourishes,
and that glorious Hermes will rule over all herd animals
and that he alone will be the official messenger to Hades,
for which he will receive no offerings, yet will he give

577–89. *There are three august virgins . . . in a bunch:* In this odd passage the hymnist seems to have conflated two rather off-beat methods of divination: (a) by the casting of pebbles, performed by priestesses called Thriai, "pebbles," who are mentioned elsewhere in Greek literature; (b) by putting out honeycombs for swarms of wild bees, then interpreting the direction they fly off.

594. *hardworking mules . . . :* A chunk of the text has fallen out here whose content is conjectural. When the text begins again, Zeus seems to affirm the fields of operation that Hermes will have as a full member of the Olympian pantheon, the climax and purpose of the poem.

the greatest of boons.°

So Apollo showed his love

605 for the son of Maia in every way, and Zeus added
his favor. He consorts with all mortals and the deathless
ones too. He brings a rare profit, but constantly he plays
tricks on the tribes of humankind.

Thus I salute you, son

of Zeus and Maia! I will take heed of you and another song.

HOMERIC HYMN 18: TO HERMES

This hymn appears to be a summary of the preceding hymn.

I sing of Cyllenian Hermes, the Slayer of Argos,
lord of CYLLENÊ and ARCADIA rich in flocks,
swift messenger of the deathless ones, whom Maia
bore, the daughter of Atlas, who mixed in love with
5   Zeus, a modest goddess. She avoided the crowd
of blessed gods, dwelling in her shadowy cave. There
the son of Kronos slept with the fair-tressed nymph
in the depths of the night, once sweet sleep had come
over white-armed Hera. Neither deathless god nor
10   mortal man knew of it.

And so hail, O son of Zeus and Maia!

I will begin with you, then pass on to another song.
Hail, Hermes, giver of favor, messenger, granter of blessings!

ORPHIC HYMN 28: TO HERMES

The beneficent Hermes is a master of speech and trade.

Hear me, O Hermes, messenger of Zeus, son of Maia!
You have a heart with every power, master of debate,

602–4. *he alone will be . . . greatest of boons:* As messenger to Hades, Hermes was
called Psychopompos, "soul guide." It was he who led the breath-souls of the dead to the
underworld, presided over by Zeus's brother Hades. This is Hermes' greatest power,
because otherwise the earth would swarm with the ghosts of the dead.

6. *priestly god:* The Greek here is very uncertain.

FIGURE 31. Hermes wearing a typical cloak *(chlamys)* and a broad-brimmed traveler's hat *(petasos)*, and carrying a caduceus *(kerykeion)*. His boots are winged; as a messenger he flies through the air. Red-figure Athenian oil jar, c. 480 BC. Metropolitan Museum of Art, New York. Photograph by Tithonos / Creative Commons.

lord of the dead, of good cheer, wily, guide, slayer
of Argos, who has flying sandals, lover of men,

5   prophet to mortals! You delight in athletic contests
and in wily deceit, you are a priestly god!° You interpret
all there is, you profit from trade, you free us from care.
You hold in your hands the blameless tool of peace.
    Lord of Korukos,° blessed, swift-traveler,

10   skilled in words, a helper in work, a friend to mortals
in need. You are a dreaded weapon of speech,
you are awesome to humankind. Hear me as I pray!
Send us a noble end of life filled with much
industry, pleasant speech, and mindfulness.

ORPHIC HYMN 57: TO CHTHONIC HERMES

Hermes is the Psychopomp, who leads the souls of the dead to the under-
world.

Dwelling on the road of necessity, from which no man
returns, beside Cocytus,° who leads the souls of mortals
into the depths of the earth—Hermes! Child of Dionysos
who revels in the dance, and of Aphrodite of fluttering

5   eyelids, the lady from PAPHOS.° You dwell in the holy
house of Persephone, the guide throughout the earth
for souls doomed to die, the souls you lead when
the time of death has come, charming them with
your sacred wand, bringing them sleep, then rousing

10   them again. The goddess Persephone gave you the duty

---

9. *Korukos:* The southern promontory of a peninsula in CILICIA, perhaps indicating
that the Orphic cult for which these poems were written was located in ASIA MINOR.
Ordinarily it would be "lord of Cyllenê."

2. *Cocytus:* (ko-**sī**-tus), "lamentation," a river in the underworld.

3–5. *Child of Dionysos . . . from PAPHOS:* This genealogy of Hermes is unparalleled
and a puzzle. Nowhere else in Greek literature are Dionysos and Aphrodite said to be
the parents of Hermes; usually he is said to be the child of Zeus and Maia. Paphos on
CYPRUS was the center of an ancient cult to Aphrodite.

to lead the way through broad Tartaros° for the eternal
souls of mortals.

              O blessed one, may you send
to the initiates a noble end to all their endeavors!

HOMERIC HYMN 19: TO PAN

*A son of Hermes is Pan, who like his father loved the outdoors. He is the
god of the wilderness, of shepherds and their flocks. He plays his reed
pipes to the accompaniment of song and dance. He is companion to the
nymphs. He is the only Greek god who is part animal in form, having the
hindquarters and horns of a goat. His natural haunt is remote Arcadia,
the central Peloponnesos. He is associated with sexual activity and so is
connected with fertility and the spring. "Panic" come from his name—
the sense of irrational fear that comes over one in the wild.*

O Muse, you shall sing of the dear child of Hermes, who has
the feet of a goat, twin-horned, noise-loving, who wanders
through the wooded meadows with the nymphs who delight
in the dance. Along the steep crags they tread the summits,
5   crying out "Pan!"
              You are the herdsman's god, with a thick
head of hair, shaggy, who has been allotted every snowy
hill, and the peaks of the mountains, and the rocky paths.
He wanders here and there through the thick brush,
now drawn to the gentle streams, now he passes among
10   the towering crags, seeking the highest peak from where
he can survey the sheep. Often he runs through the tall
white mountains, often he drives the beasts through
the valleys, killing them, keen in his sight. Towards
evening he comes from the chase, sounding his lonely
15   sound, playing his sweet song on his reed pipes.° Not even

---

11. *Tartaros:* Here, simply the underworld.

    15. *reed pipes:* Pan fell in love with the nymph Syrinx and pursued her, but she turned
into a bed of reeds. Hearing the beautiful sound of the wind through the reeds, Pan
cut two of them and made the pipe that he often played. (But another story reports
that Hermes invented the reed pipe: see above, "Homeric Hymn 4: To Hermes," lines
531–32.)

that bird could surpass him in melody who in the many-
flowered spring pours forth her lament, her sweet song,
amidst the leaves.° Then the clear-voiced mountain nymphs,
sing with him, tripping with nimble feet around
20 a fountain of dark water, and the echo wails about
the mountaintop. The god dances on this side and that,
then creeping into the middle he cuts an agile caper,
wearing on his back a brown lynx pelt, delighting
in high-pitched songs in the soft meadow, where crocus
25 and sweet-smelling hyacinth grow randomly, mixed in the grass.
    They sing of the blessed gods and of high OLYMPOS.
They tell of the runner Hermes above all, how he is the swift
messenger for all the gods, and of how he came
to ARCADIA with its wealth of springs, the mother
30 of sheep. It is there that he has his precinct of Cyllenian
Hermes. There, though a god, he tended dirt-encrusted
flocks at the side of a mortal man, for there waxed within
him the surging desire to sleep with the lovely-tressed
daughter of Dryops.° He brought about the fruitful
35 marriage, and she bore in his halls a dear child to Hermes,
a wonder to behold, with a goat's feet and two horns,
a lover of noise, a merry laugher.
                          When the nurse saw
his crude face with its full beard, she was frightened
and leaped up and ran away.° But Hermes the runner
40 took him in his arms, and the god rejoiced exceedingly
in his mind. Quickly he went to the abodes of the deathless
ones, wrapping the child in the thick skins of mountain
hares, and he sat down next to Zeus and the other deathless
ones, and he showed forth his son. All the deathless ones
45 were delighted, above all Bacchic Dionysos. They called
him "Pan," because he delighted them all [*pantes*].°

16–18. *that bird . . . amidst the leaves:* The nightingale.

34. *Dryops:* He was a king in central Greece. His daughter's name was Dryopê,
"oak-girl."

38–39. *she was frightened . . . away:* That is, she was beset by *panic.*

46. *he delighted them all:* "Pan" means "all" in Greek.

FIGURE 32. Pan holding a torch and a wreath. He wears a leopard skin tied around his shoulders and string of beads but is otherwise naked. He is horned and has a grotesque bearded face and goat legs. Illustration on a wine bowl from Paestum in Italy, c. 350 BC. Musée du Louvre, Paris. Photograph © Pandosia75 / Creative Commons.

The other gods could not free her. Ares descended to force Hephaistos to
return but was unsuccessful. Then Dionysos tried his hand, got Hephais-
tos drunk, and led him back to Olympos, drunk and sitting on an ass.
Hephaistos freed Hera and persuaded the other gods to accept Dionysos
as one of their own. This story appears to have been told in the lost por-
tion of the poem. Its surviving portion reports Dionysos' acceptance into
the company of gods.

. . . Some say that it was on Drakanon, some on windy Ikaros,
some on NAXOS—O child of Zeus, bull-god!—some say it was
beside the deep-swirling river of the ALPHEIOS° that Semelê,
pregnant, bore you to Zeus who delights in the thunder.
5   Others say that it was in THEBES, O king—but they lie.
The father of men and gods bore you far from humans,
hiding you from white-armed Hera.
                                        There is a certain Nysa,°
a high mountain, blooming with woods, far off in PHOENICIA
near the streams of Aigyptos°. . .
....
10   ". . . And they will set up many statues in his shrines,
and because there are three,° people will make perfect
sacrifices at your festivals every three years."
So spoke the son of Kronos, and he nodded with
his dark brows. The immortal locks of the king leaped
15   forward from his deathless beard, and great Olympos
trembled.

        Be kind, bull-god, who drives women mad!
We singers sing of you as we begin and as we end.

1–3. Drakanon . . . ALPHEIOS: The hymnist lists various places claimed to be the
birthplace of the god. Drakanon is a cape on the island of Kos; Ikaros is an island near
SAMOS; Naxos is one of the CYCLADES in the central Aegean; the Alpheios is a river in
the northwestern PELOPONNESOS. All these places had important cults to Dionysos.
7. Nysa: Several places in the ancient world bore this name, but the location of this
Nysa seems to be in Egypt, perhaps referring to Dionysos' association with the Egyptian
god Osiris, a god of resurrection who was also the inventor of wine.
9. Aigyptos: The Nile River, not the land of Egypt.
11. . . . are three: Zeus is speaking, but the reference to "three" must be to something
in the missing portion of the poem.

FIGURE 33. The return of Hephaistos, by the Antimenes Painter. In the center stands Dionysos, leading Hephaistos back to Olympos. Dionysos is wrapped in long robes and holds a wine cup in left hand and ivy vines in his right. He is crowned with ivy. On the right, a drunken Hephaistos rides on an ass, holding a horn cup. His hair, too, is wreathed with ivy. Behind Dionysos follows a dancing maenad, one of his intoxicated followers. Athenian wine jug, c. 520 BC. Walters Art Museum, Baltimore, MD. Photograph © Walters Art Museum / Creative Commons.

There is no way to be mindful of holy song, and forget
you. And so Hail, O Dionysos, bull-god, together with
20   your mother Semelê, whom some call Thuonê.°

HOMERIC HYMN 7: TO DIONYSOS

This hymn may reflect the custom in Dionysiac cult of carrying a ship through the streets, the priest of Dionysos seated inside as helmsman, followed by devotees, although such practices seem to be later than the hymn.

20. *Thuonê:* "inspiring frenzy," an alternate name for Semelê, also the name of Dionysos' nurse and of a maenad.

I will remember Dionysos, the son of glorious Semelê,
who appeared on a jutting promontory of the barren
sea in the likeness of a young man in the flush
of manhood. His beautiful dark hair waved about him
5   and he wore a purple cloak over his powerful shoulders.
Suddenly men appeared in a ship with fine benches,
traveling swiftly on the wine-faced sea, pirates
from Tuscany.° An evil doom bore them on.
    When they saw the lad, they nodded to one another
10   and quickly leapt out. Seizing him, they right away
put him on their ship, rejoicing in their hearts.
They thought he was the son of a princely line descended
from Zeus. They wished to bind him with grievous bonds,
but the bonds would not hold him. The withies fell far
15   away from his hands and his feet while he sat there,
smiling from his dark eyes. When the helmsman saw it,
he cried out to his companions, saying:
                                    "Madmen! What
god have you captured and bound—a mighty one!
Our strong ship cannot hold him. Surely this is Zeus,
20   or Apollo of the silver bow, or Poseidon, for he is not
like mortal men, but like unto the gods who live
on Olympos. So come, let us let him go on the dark
earth—right away! And don't lay your hands on him,
or he may become angry and stir up savage winds
25   or even a hurricane."
                            So he spoke, but the captain
rebuked him with a harsh word: "Madman!—watch
the wind! Set up the ship's mast° and gather the sheets
together. As for this fellow, the men will take care
of him. I imagine that he is headed for EGYPT, or CYPRUS,
30   or to the Hyperboreans,° or even further. In the end he will
speak and he will tell us of his friends and of his wealth

---

8. *Tuscany:* Etruria, in Italy.

27. *ship's mast:* Ancient ships had masts that were hinged at the base so they could be
set down into the hull, or raised up, as the weather dictated.

30. *Hyperboreans:* Dwellers in the far north, a mythical people.

FIGURE 34. Dionysos and the pirates. Holding a wand, accompanied by two maenads who hold *thyrsi*, the naked god stands in the stern of the ship. Ivy wreathes his hair. Poseidon, lord of the sea, sits in the prow. A leopard leaps across the gunwales, gnawing on the legs of a sailor whose upper body has been turned into a dolphin. Two other sailors are in the sea, their legs turned to fins. A dolphin, no doubt once a sailor, swims on the far left of the picture, while an octopus swims on the far right. North African Roman mosaic, c. AD 200. Bardo National Museum, Tunis. Photograph © Dennis Jarvis / Creative Commons.

and of his brothers, now that fate has thrown him among us."
So speaking, the captain raised the mast and the sail.
The wind blew full in the sail and the crew tightened
35   the sheets on either side. But immediately amazing things
appeared to them. First, a sweet, fragrant wine ran burbling
through the swift black ship and a heavenly scent
arose. Amazement seized all the sailors when they
saw it. Straightaway ivy vines grew on both sides
40   along the top of the mast and many grape clusters
hung from it. A dark ivy twisted around the mast,
blooming with flowers, and pretty berries grew on it
and all the pegs along the edge of the boat had crowns
upon them.
When the pirates saw this, they told

45   the helmsman to steer the boat ashore. But the lad
turned into a lion, there on the bows of the ship—
    terrible!—
and he roared mightily. In the middle of the ship,
showing forth wonders, he made a shaggy bear to appear.
The bear stood up ravening, while the lion stood on
    the top
50   of the deck, staring fiercely. The sailors fled into the stern
and halted, terrified, around the cautious-minded
helmsman. Suddenly the lion jumped upon the captain
and seized him. The sailors all leapt out into the shining
sea when they saw it, hoping to avoid an evil fate,
55   but they became dolphins. The god, taking pity
on the helmsman, held him back, and pronounced
a blessing, saying:
                "Have courage, [good mariner,]°
you have found favor in my heart. I am Dionysos,
the loud-roarer, born to the daughter of Kadmos,
60   Semelê, after she made love with Zeus."
    Hail, child of Semelê of the beautiful face!
There is no way to adorn sweet song without you.

HOMERIC HYMN 26: TO DIONYSOS

Dionysos and the nymphs of Nysa wander through the forest.

I begin by singing of Dionysos, crowned with ivy,
the loud-roarer, the brilliant son of Zeus and glorious
Semelê, whom the nymphs with fine hair took in their
bosoms from his father, the king, and carefully nourished
5   in the valleys of Nysa. By the will of his father he grew up
in the scented cave, counted among the deathless ones.
    But when the goddesses had raised him up, the subject
of many songs, he took to wandering through the wooded

---

57. *[good mariner]:* The text here is corrupt.

valleys, wreathed with ivy and laurel. The nymphs followed
10   after, and he led the way, and their cry filled the endless forest.
      So hail to you, O Dionysos, crowned with many clusters
of grape. Grant that we may come again in happiness at the right
season, and from that season onward for many years.

ORPHIC HYMN 30: TO DIONYSOS

Dionysos is like the creator god, bringing blessings to his followers.

I call on you, O Dionysos, loud-roarer, who cries *Euhoê!*
First-born, two-natured, born three times, King Bacchus,°
wild, ineffable, secretive, hidden, two-horned,
twin-shaped, crowned with ivy, bull-faced, war-like,
5   wailing, pure!° Eater of raw flesh in triennial feasts,
draped in grapes, wrapped in foliage, resourceful
Eubouleus, child of Zeus and Persephone, product

1–2. *Euhoê! . . . King Bacchus:* Euhoê was the characteristic cry of the followers of
Dionysos in ecstasy. "First-born" in Greek is Protogonos, the name of the creator god in
Orphic theology, with whom Dionysos was identified. "Two-natured" may refer to
Dionysos' androgynous nature; he is both male and female, like Protogonos. "Born
three times" refers to the Orphic story (see note to lines 5–8 just below) that when
Dionysos was a small child (sometimes called Zagreus in Orphic religion, in origin a
separate god) the Titans tempted him with playthings, then tore him apart and devoured
him. Zeus destroyed the Titans with a thunderbolt but rescued Dionysos' heart from the
ashes and reconstituted the god from it. Thus he was born three times: from Perse-
phone, from Semelê, and from Zeus's thigh. Bacchus is an alternate name for Dionysos,
but its original meaning is unknown.

3–5. *ineffable, secretive . . . pure:* The mysterious rites of Dionysos are known only to
the initiates, who are pure of heart and sworn to silence, thus he is "ineffable, secretive,
hidden." Dionysos is often identified with the bull (in Euripides' play *The Bacchae* [405
BC] the king sees him as bull), and bulls were sacrificed in his cult, thus he is "two-
horned . . . bull-faced." He is "twin-shaped" because he is both male and female. Por-
traits of Dionysos usually show him crowned with ivy or carrying an ivy branch (see
figure 33), a vigorous plant that grows around things. Dionysos is "war-like" because he
was involved in famous battles, including the battle of the gods against the Giants.
"Wailing" refers to the cry *Euhoê!* Purity is essential for the initiates into his cult, as it
was characteristic of the god.

of an unspeakable union, immortal god!°

Hear my voice,

O blessed one, breathe sweetly on me with gentleness,

10   having a kindly heart, along with your fair-girdled nurses!°

ORPHIC HYMN 45: TO DIONYSOS
BASSAREUS AND TRIENNIAL

Bassareus is one of the many names of Dionysos, from the Thracian word bassara, *"fox," and refers to the fox-skin often worn by the maenads, sometimes called "bassarids," and by the god himself. One tradition reports that the bassarids tore Orpheus limb from limb, and this is, of course, an Orphic hymn. "Triennial" refers to the performance of his rites every two years.*

Come, O blessed Dionysos, conceived in fire, with the face
of a bull, Bassareus and Bacchus, who has many names,
who can accomplish anything, who delights in swords
and blood, who delights in the maenads! You howl

5   throughout Olympos,° loud-roarer, mad Bacchus! You carry
the *thyrsus,* wrathful in the extreme,° honored by all the gods
and all mortals, as many as dwell on the earth.

Come,

blessed one, leaping one, who brings much joy to all!

ORPHIC HYMN 46: TO DIONYSOS LIKNITES

Liknites means "of the cradle," from the Greek liknon, *really a winnowing fan, a kind of basket often used as a cradle. The* liknon *was a com-*

5–8. *Eater of raw flesh . . . immortal god:* The consumption of raw flesh *(omophagia),* sometimes while the animal was still alive, was in myth and sometimes in reality part of Dionysiac cult, celebrated every two years ("triennial" because the Greeks counted inclusively). Eubouleus, "of good counsel," is an epithet of Dionysos used several times in the Orphic hymns. According to a variant tale of Dionysos' conception, Zeus mated with Persephone, his own daughter, in the form of a snake and so conceived him.

10. *fair-girdled nurses:* The maenads.

4–5. *howl throughout Olympos:* That is, cry *Euhoê.*

6. *wrathful in the extreme:* Many stories were told of those who were destroyed for resisting or denying the god.

mon object in Dionysiac cult, often contained a phallus, and referred to the god's mysterious birth. Dionysos Liknites was worshipped at Delphi, where the god presided during the three winter months while Apollo was away among the Hyperboreans, the "men of the north." Dionysos' strong link with Orphic rites explains the abundance of Orphic hymns to him.

> O Dionysos Liknites, I call upon you with these prayers,
> you of Nysa, blossoming, beloved kind-hearted Bacchus!
> Lovely nursling of the nymphs, and of fair-crowned Aphrodite,°
> who once danced through the forest, striking the ground
> 5   with your dear nymphs, driven on by madness. By the counsels
> of Zeus you were brought to noble Persephone,° who reared
> you, feared of the deathless gods.
>   Come with kindly heart,
> O blessed one, accept this gracious gift of sacrifice!

ORPHIC HYMN 47: TO DIONYSOS
PERIKONIOS

The very obscure epithet Perikonios means "twined around the pillar," and according to a late commentator refers to the tradition that after Zeus blasted Semelê with a thunderbolt, ivy twined around the palace to protect the fetus; the epithet is unknown outside this Orphic hymn.

> I call on Bacchus Perikonios, giver of wine, who
> wrapped around the entire house of Kadmos and with
> his power calmed the heaving earth. When the flashing
> brilliance moved all the land, and the whistling
> 5   of the hurricane, the bonds of all were loosened.°
>   Come, O blessed one, reveler, with joyous heart!

---

3. *Aphrodite:* Evidently mentioned because of her association with sensuality.

6. *Persephone:* Sometimes said to be the mother of Dionysos (in contrast to the story about Semelê). Here she seems to be the name of his principal nurse.

5. *the bonds of all were loosened:* Evidently the "bonds" are a metaphor for the condition of the followers of Orpheus before their liberation through initiation into the mysteries.

ORPHIC HYMN 50: TO DIONYSOS
LYSIOS LENAIOS

This hymn is dedicated to Dionysos Lusios, "looser" from care, also called Lenaios, "of the wine-press," because he is the spirit in the blessed fluid that brings us joy.

Hear me, O blessed one, son of Zeus, Bacchus of the wine-press,
who has two mothers,° seed always remembered, of many
names, spirit who looses us from care, sacred child
of the blessed ones, begotten in secret, Bacchus who shouts
5   *Euhoê!,* well-fed, fruitful, increasing joyful bounty,
bursting from the earth, god of the wine-press, mighty,
with changing form, a cure for men's pain, holy bloom,
a pain-hating joy for mortals, one who takes hold, with
beautiful hair, a looser from care, raging with the *thyrsos,*
10   thunderer who shouts *Euhoê!,* kindly to all, to those mortals
or gods to whom you wish to reveal yourself. I call you now,
O sweetness, come to the initiates, bringer of fruit!

ORPHIC HYMN 52: TO DIONYSOS, GOD OF
THE TRIENNIAL FEASTS

Dionysos (Bacchus) is celebrated as the leader of nighttime revels in the mountains where his followers, clad in fawn skins, devour raw flesh, dance, and are filled with the joyous presence of the god. Along the way the god is called by many familiar epithets: Nysias (raised on Mount Nysa), Liknites (because the winnowing fan, liknon, *was his cradle), Eubouleus ("he of good counsel"), Protogonos (First-Begotten, the name of the first principle in Orphic thought), Erikepaios (a foreign word of unknown meaning), Paian (a name of Apollo; Dionysos resided at* DEL-PHI, *Apollo's sanctuary, during the winter months), Bassareus ("he of the fox skin," a Thracian word).*

I call on you, O blessed one, who has many names, raging,
Bacchus, with horns of a bull, god of the wine-press,
begotten in fire, Nysian, looser, nourished in the thigh,

---

2. *two mothers:* Semelê and Persephone, according to different traditions.

God of the Winnowing Fan, fire-breathing, leader of the mystic
5   rites in the night, Eubouleus, wearer of the fillet, shaker
of the *thyrsos!* Your rites are unspeakable, you are of threefold
nature,° secret child of Zeus! First-begotten, Erikepaios,
father and son of gods! O eater of raw flesh, holder
of the scepter, mad leader of the dance and the revel!
10   You take us into the sacred revel of the triennial feast
that brings peace. You burst from the earth in a fiery
blaze, you seize upon us, O son with two mothers!°
You wander the mountains, horned, wrapped in a fawn-
skin, god of the annual feast.

                      O Paian, holder of the *thyrsos,*
15   nursling, decked in grapes, Bassareus, exulting in ivy,
pursued by many young girls, leader of the host,
come, O blessed one, bursting with joy for the initiates!

ORPHIC HYMN 53: TO DIONYSOS, GOD OF ANNUAL FEASTS

Dionysos is the spirit of returning fructification. That which is dead shall live again.

I call on Bacchus, god of the annual feast, earthly Dionysos
roused together with the well-tressed maiden nymphs, he who,
slumbering in the sacred halls of Persephone, arranges
the holy Bacchic time every three years.°

                          And when he gets up
5   the recurring triennial, he sings a hymn along with his nurses
who have pretty waists, putting to sleep and awakening the dances
in the cycling seasons.

                 But, O blessed one—green fruited, horn-bearing,

6–7. *threefold nature:* Perhaps: beast, human, and god.

12. *two mothers:* Semelê and Persephone.

3–4. *slumbering in the sacred halls . . . three years:* That is, the god is asleep, dormant, during the winter season, when he resides in the underworld, only to come forth as new life, memorialized in the biannual feast for Dionysos; of course he comes forth *every* year in the spring, the god standing for the renewal of seasonal growth, so he is also the god of the annual feast.

abundantly fruiting Bacchus!—come to this most holy rite with
10   joy on your face, teeming with fruit most holy and most perfect.

ORPHIC HYMN 44: TO SEMELÊ

Semelê has become a god, thanks to Dionysos' descent into the under-
world to retrieve her spirit and carry it to Olympos. Here the hymnist
calls for her blessing, especially at the triennial feast.

I call on you, most queenly daughter of Kadmos,
beautiful Semelê, with the erotic hair and deep breasts,
mother of Dionysos who carries the *thyrsos* and gives joy,
who was thrust into pain by a blaze of fire while you gave
5   birth, through the will of deathless Zeus, the son of Kronos.
The noble Persephone gave you honors among men
in the triennial festivals when men reenact the pain you felt
when giving birth to Bacchus: the sacred table° and the holy
mysteries.
Now, O goddess, I beg of you, daughter of Kadmos,
10   queen, call down everlasting gentleness on the initiates!

8. *the sacred table:* The meaning of "sacred table is unknown.

12

Ares

Ares is the god of the war-cry, the blood and guts of battle. Athena, too, is a god of war, but of reasoned strategy, of how to accomplish the objectives of war, of organized military protection of the city (as such she was called Promachos, "she who fights in the forefront," the name of a large bronze statue by Phidias on the Acropolis in Athens). Ares, by contrast, is the emotion of blood-lust that overcomes one in the heat of battle, forgetting oneself in the wild destruction of the enemy. Supposedly he came from THRACE, where wild things live. The Greeks did not like him much (as if they deplored violence!), but admired his role in the story about his adultery with Aphrodite (see figure 15) where he is the tough guy in town, seducing all the ladies, who admire his handsome build.

HOMERIC HYMN 8: TO ARES

This poem seems foreign to the collection because of its late Greek forms, its listing of the god's epithets (as in the Orphic hymns), the identification of the god Ares with the planet Mars, and general references to cosmology. Most commentators think the poem was written by Proclus (AD 412–485) and that it slipped into the corpus. Ares is usually a feared or hated god, but here he inspires the hymnist to escape the desires that bind the soul to the material world.

Ares, great in strength, driver of chariots, wearer of a golden
helm, mighty in courage, bearer of the shield, savior of cities,

FIGURE 35. Ares battles Athena, by Nikosthenes. A famous story about Ares, often represented in painting, told how Herakles encountered the bandit Kyknos ("swan"), a son of Ares, who robbed pilgrims traveling to Delphi. In the fight, Ares joined on the side of his son and Athena on the side of Herakles, until Zeus interfered and parted the two gods. Here Zeus stands in the middle with his thunderbolt, Athena on the left, wearing her helmet and serpent-fringed aegis, and Ares on the right, fully armed in the style of a Greek warrior. Kyknos flees in his chariot on the far right and on the far left Herakles (off the picture) approaches in his chariot. Athenian black-figure wine-mixing bowl, c. 520 BC. British Museum, London. Photograph by Jastrow / Creative Commons.

      clad in bronze with powerful hand, untiring, good with
      the spear, wall of Olympos, father of Victory in the good
5   war, ally of Themis,° master over the revolutionaries, leader
      of the most just men, sceptered lord of manliness, spinning
      your fiery sphere among the seven coursing lights of the *aither,*
      where your fiery horses keep ever to the third orbit°—Hearken,
      O helper of men, grantor of a powerful youth, dripping

    4–5. *father of Victory . . . Themis:* Victory (Nikê) is usually said to be the child of the goddess Styx (also an underworld river); she is the daughter of Ares only figuratively, as the war-god brings victory. Themis, "right, law," is a Titan, Zeus's second consort.

    7–8. *the aither . . . orbit:* The *aither* is the Upper Air. In the geocentric ancient model, Ares (Mars) was the third planet counting inward from the outer firmament. First and second were Zeus (Jupiter) and Kronos (Saturn). Between Ares (Mars) and the central Earth spun Hermes (Mercury), Aphrodite (Venus), Helios (the Sun), and Selenê (the Moon).

10   down your gentle brilliance from above upon our life and our
     martial power, that I might be able to shake bitter wickedness
     away from my brain and turn aside the soul-deceiving influence
     of my thoughts, and hold back the sharp force of desire that
     provokes me to walk in the ways of icy conflict. But grant me
15   the courage, O blessed one, to stay within the harmless laws
     of peace, escaping battle with my enemies, and a grievous death.

ORPHIC HYMN 65: TO ARES

*Savage Ares should give up his bloodthirstiness and be calmed by the
love of Aphrodite, whose loving spirit brings happiness and good har-
vests.*

Unbreakable, powerful of essence, mighty, strong spirit,
lover of weapons, unconquered, man-killer, wall-stormer,
King Ares! You love the din of armor, always spattered in gore,
rejoicing in the blood of men scattered, raising the clamor
5   of war, horrid one! You who want only the songless battle,
the cry of swords and spears! Stop your raging fight! Put away
that anguish that pains the soul! Incline to the desire
of Cypris,° the revels of Dionysos, turning your might
of arms to the yield of Deo,° longing for the peace
10   that nourishes young men, the giver of happiness!

8. *Cypris:* "She of Cyprus," that is, Aphrodite, born on Cyprus.
9. *Deo:* Another name for Demeter; the hymnist means agricultural wealth.

13

Hestia

Hestia means "the hearth." She is the center of the house, the life of the house, where people gather to be together. Most Greek temples, too, began as hearths. She is pure, as fire is pure, and in myth was never married. She was the first child of Kronos and Rhea. Ordinarily she is not represented by an image, is not really anthropomorphized, and rarely appears in literature. Homer does not mention her, but she was the goddess with whom the Greeks had most intimate daily contact, and she was the recipient of offerings at every meal. There were many civic cults to her, in which eternal flames burned. The Orphics seem to have equated her with the Great Mother goddess, so prominent was she in Greek life.

HOMERIC HYMN 24: TO HESTIA

Hestia is pure, as fire is pure, and in myth was never married. She is one of only three goddesses whom Aphrodite cannot persuade into love-making (the others are Athena and Artemis). This hymn is a prayer that Hestia send her presence to bless a house or temple.

O Hestia, who tends the sacred house of King Apollo,
the Far-Darter, in holy Pytho,° with oil oozing from your
locks—come to this house, being of one mind with
Zeus the Counselor: grant grace to this song!

2. *Pytho:* DELPHI.

HOMERIC HYMN 29: TO HESTIA

Hestia, the hearth, receives first and last libations at the feast. She is honored along with Hermes, both gods protective of the house.

O Hestia, who have obtained a seat forever and an honor,
the privilege of seniority, in the high houses of all,
of the deathless gods and of peoples who walk on the earth.
You have a fine honor and a privilege, for not without you
5   do men begin and end the feast, pouring out sweet wine
in honor of Hestia.
                    And I call on you, too, O Slayer of Argos,°
the son of Zeus and Maia, messenger of the blessed ones,
you with the golden wand, grantor of good things, be favorable
and assist with Hestia, whom you respect and love. For both
10 of you dwell in the beautiful houses of people who live
on the earth, friendly toward one another, fine bulwarks
against harm, and you attend intelligence and youth. Hail,
O daughter of Kronos! And you too, O Hermes who carries
a golden wand! I will remember you, and another song.

ORPHIC HYMN 84: TO HESTIA

Hestia can give the initiate wealth and health.

O Hestia, queenly daughter of the mighty son of Kronos,
fire of eternal magnitude, possessing the center of the house,
may you raise up these holy initiates in their sacred rites!
Make them ever young, drenched in wealth, with good sense,
5   pure—O home of the blessed gods, powerful pillar of mortals!
Everlasting, with many shapes, longed for, yellow in color,
smiling, O blessed one, eagerly take these offerings,
breathing out wealth and a gentle-handed health.

6. *Slayer of Argos:* Hermes.

14

Sun, Moon, Earth, Hekatê, and All the Gods

The Greeks had very many gods other than the Olympians, whose nature and deeds were defined by the poetry of Homer and Hesiod. Many were of local importance with little or no development, and in invocations were often included in the formula "all the gods." Hestia (chapter 13), though an Olympian, was such a god, and attracted few stories. Eileithyia, the "coming," was the goddess who presided over childbirth; she was associated with Artemis and Hera, but had no individual character. The god of war Enyalios is already attested in the Linear B tablets of the Bronze Age, but becomes an epithet of Ares in Homer. Hekatê had more importance and was equated with Artemis beginning in the fifth century BC. She carries torches and is the goddess of where three pathways meet. She is also goddess of the moon, accompanied by barking dogs and ghostly powers. Prometheus, the son of the Titan Iapetos, is famous from one of the best-known Greek myths. He is the advocate of humans, whom some say he created, against a tyrannical Zeus. He stole fire from heaven, causing Zeus to fashion the first woman, Pandora, as a curse to men, and was punished by being crucified in the CAUCASUS MOUNTAINS where an eagle every day devoured his liver, until Herakles killed the eagle. Herakles was himself regarded as a god, the only hero in Greek myth to be so *ted. Rivers, the sea, and springs throughout Greece received local *s divinities. Some minor gods received attention in the *le Leto (see chapter 8), who was celebrated in vari-

ous cults, and Pan (see chapter 10), the goat god, whose cult was cen-
tered in ARCADIA.

Gods of nature, too had cults, but enjoyed nothing like the impor-
tance they held in the earlier Near Eastern religions. Nonetheless they
were the subjects of hymns, which I include here as examples of Greek
nature religion. In Greek the sun-god was called either Helios or
Hyperion, but he was rarely anthropomorphized and figures little in
Greek myth. His best-known story, told by the Roman Ovid (43 BC–c.
18 AD) tells how his son Phaëthon borrowed his chariot, then was
struck down by Zeus when Phaëthon lost control. He had little cult
except on the island of RHODES, which built a colossus in his honor
striding the entrance to the harbor, one of the Seven Wonders of the
World. He was considered a foreigner's god, which in fact he was: the
sun-god was always the great god in Egyptian religion. Greek philo-
sophical thought adopted him as a symbol for the creator, the first
source and center, a natural role. The moon-goddess was called Selenê,
which means "bright," or just Menê, "Moon." She had even less prom-
inence in myth and cult, except as she was identified with Artemis or
Hekatê. Earth (Gaia) is a generic mother goddess embodying all the
productive powers of the land. She plays an important role in Hesiod's
Theogony, giving birth without sexual intercourse to Sky (Ouranos),
Sea (Pontos), and Mountains (Ourea). She then unites with Sky to
produce the Cyclopes, the Hundred-Handers, and most importantly
the Titans. She conspires with her son Kronos to overthrown the tyr-
anny of Sky by castrating him, then assists in outwitting Kronos, who
has taken to swallowing his own children. She warns her grandson
Zeus, who is in danger of being defeated by the child of his first con-
sort Metis, "Mind," whom Zeus swallows when pregnant, then gives
birth to the child, Athena, from his head.

HOMERIC HYMNS 31 AND 32: TO THE SUN
AND THE MOON

*These poems go together, and are no doubt by the same hand. They seem
to be the most recent poems in the collection. They must introduce epic
poems, not songs about the gods, to judge from the last lines.*

10   course of the cosmos. You command good deeds, you nourish
the seasons.
           Lord of the world, you play the pipes° in your
fiery circling, bringing the light, coruscating, nurturing life,
fruitful, Paian! You are eternal, unpolluted, the father of time,
deathless Zeus, clear, brilliant, the all-encompassing eye

15   of the world both when you set and when you shine with your
beautiful glorious rays.
                Paragon of justice, water-loving° lord
of the world! You guard pledges, you are forever the highest,
helpmate to all. O eye of justice, light of life—O chariot-driver,
you drive on the four-horsed car with your whistling whip!

20   Hear my words, and reveal sweet life to the mystics!

ORPHIC HYMN 9: TO THE MOON

A prayer for the favor of the beneficent Moon.

Hear, O goddess queen, bringer of light, divine Selenê,
bull-horned Moon, night-runner, air-wandering, night-dweller,
torch-bearer, maid, surrounded by lovely stars, O Moon!
Waxing and waning, female and male, radiant, horse-loving,

5   mother of time, bearer of fruit, amber-colored, melancholy,
illuminator, bringer of children, all-seeing, wakeful, teeming
with beautiful stars, rejoicing in peace and the richness of night!
    Radiant, giver of favors, of fulfillment, jewel
of the night, ruler of the stars, with long cloak, traveling

10   in circles, all-wise maid! Come, O blessed one, kind, star-rich
maid, shining with your inner light, save your new initiates!

11. *you play the pipes:* Not only does Helios play the lyre of Apollo (with whom he was identified starting in the fifth century BC), but he also plays the pipes of Pan. The heavenly bodies create a harmonious sound, the music of the spheres, as they spin.

16. *water-loving:* Perhaps because at the end of the day the sun sinks into Ocean, there to travel, in a cup, back to the east for start of the next day.

PROCLUS HYMN 1: TO HELIOS

When Helios, channel for the Demiurge, has helped the soul escape from the material world to the divine, the soul will not be subject to the fickle Fates but will enjoy the sure happiness of the divine life.

Hearken, O king who is the fire of Mind,° Titan whose
reins are gold,° hear me! Housekeeper of fire, who holds
the key, the life-supporting source who draws off
a rich stream of harmony from above in the orders
5   of the material world.°
                    Hearken! For you hold the middlemost
seat of the *aither,*° and possessing the brilliant disc, the heart
of the cosmos, you have filled everything with your providence
that awakens our intellects.° The planets, binding their waists
with your ever-blooming fires, shed life-engendering drops
10   from their ceaseless and untiring dance. All that is born
blossoms up from the returning ride of your chariot according
to the course of the seasons.° The din of the elements clashing
against one another stopped once you appeared from

1. *fire of Mind:* That is, of Nous. The sun is the king of this world because he is made of Nous, the Mind that underlies all reality.

1–2. *Titan whose reins are gold:* The Sun (Helios), the Moon (Selenê), and Dawn (Eos) are the children of Theia ("divine") and Hyperion ("he who goes beyond") (Hesiod, *Theogony,* 371–74), two of the Titans produced by Earth (Gaia) and Sky (Ouranos) (Hesiod *Theogony,* 134–5). We might say that Helios is a second-generation Titan, but the Greeks were vague about this. Here he rides in his chariot of gold across the sky.

2–5. *who holds the key . . . material world:* The sun is the mediator ("holds the key'") between the creator Demiurge, the source of life, and this world; thus Helios is king of the material world. His harmony establishes order in the different levels of the material world: the heavenly bodies, the elements, music, and health. The fire of the sun, deriving from the Demiurge, is able to impose harmony on the disorderly material realm.

6. *aither:* Here the *aither* is a special kind of fire from which the heavens are made. The Sun is in the center of the heavens and so controls all.

8. *awakens our intellects:* Helios removes the dark clouds that surround the soul and illuminates the soul with light from the Demiurge (or Nous, Mind) so that the soul remembers the divine world, from which it has come but which it has forgotten.

12. *the course of the seasons:* The seasons follow the regular course of the sun, from low in the sky to high in the sky.

your unspeakable begetter.° For you the unshakable
15 dance of the Fates has yielded. When you wish, you unwind
the powerful force of destiny. You are mighty, you rule
with force over all that is around you.° From your chain,
the king of divinely inspired song, Phoibos, leaped forth.
Singing god-inspired songs to the accompaniment of the lyre,
20 he calms the waves of roaring generation.° Paieon
blossomed forth from the band that averts evil,
a giver of sweet things, and he established health, filling
the broad cosmos with harmony that drives away all pain.°
Some praise you in song as the famous father of Dionysos;
25 some praise you as Attis who cries *Euhoê* in the lowest
depths of matter; some as pretty Adonis.° The ferocious
spirits that bring harm to our wretched souls, noxious
to humans, fear your threatening swift whip, so that
our souls suffer forever in the noisy gulf of life,

12–14. *the elements clashing . . . begetter:* The world is made up of the four elements
(air, water, fire, earth), which clash with one another, but the sun's power, derived from
the Demiurge, brings them together through the love that the sun derives from the
Demiurge, which one cannot really speak of.

17. *over all that is around you:* Helios has the power even to change the dictates of
Fate, to unwind the thread of destiny.

17–20. *From your chain . . . generation:* According to Neoplatonic thought, groups of
things that depend on a cause share in the quality that is characteristic of that cause. In
other words, Apollo is one of the things dependent for his existence on the cause repre-
sented by the sun, which is channeling the light, power, and energy of the Demiurge. By
his music he brings harmony to the chaotic noise in the sea of generation.

20–23. *Paieon . . . all pain:* Paieon (sometimes spelled Paian) is the physician of the
gods, sometimes equated with Helios and Apollo, here seen as one of the "series" headed
by Helios ("blossomed forth from the band"). Sickness, according to ancient theories,
comes from discord between the elements, which Paieon removes by instituting harmony.

24–26. *famous father of Dionysos . . . Adonis:* Usually Zeus is the father of Dionysos,
so Proclus seems here to identify Helios with Zeus. Attis is the lover of the Great Mother
goddess, Cybelê, but after adultery with a nymph he goes mad, castrates himself, dies,
then is brought back to life by Cybelê. The story of Adonis is similar. He is a beautiful
youth, a lover of Aphrodite killed by a boar while hunting, then reclaimed from Perse-
phone by Aphrodite. Both stories refer to the annual cycle of growth and death in
nature, in Neoplatonic terms interpreted as the fall into the realm of matter and return
of the soul to the intelligible realm. Helios is the agent of this cycle. Attis' cry of *Euhoê*
associates him with Dionysos, the twice- (or thrice-)born god.

30   fallen under the yoke of the body, and forget the fiery
      hall of their lofty father.°
                              But, O very best of gods, crowned
      with fire, blessed spirit, image of the god who creates all,
      lifter-up of souls, hearken! Ever purify me of all
      defilement, receive my supplication, drenched with tears!
35   Free me from destroying pollution, and keep me far
      from those who punish, softening the swift eye of Justice
      that sees all.° Always provide my soul with holy light,
      so rich with blessings, by means of your assistance
      that chases off evil, having scattered the man-destroying
40   poisonous cloud and imparted to my body the magnificent
      gift of perfect health.
                              Bring me to glory, and may I sing
·   according to the traditions of my forefathers, gifted
      by Muses with their pretty locks of hair. Give me, lord
      —if you wish!—the bliss that cannot be shaken in return
45   for my fine piety. You are able easily to accomplish
      all things, for you have the power and the infinite might.
      And if some ill comes my way from the star-driven
      threads, from destiny's spindles that move in spirals,
      ward it off with the mighty power of your rays.°

30–31. *forget the fiery hall of their lofty father:* Hostile spirits try to imprison souls in
the swamp of matter so that they forget their celestial origin in the "court of the Father,"
that is, the Demiurge, from where they come. Helios can bring salvation because he him-
self originates from the Demiurge and can purify all souls of their material attachment.

36–37. *softening the swift eye . . . sees all:* The soul is saved from the eternal cycle of
rebirth by rejecting the demands of the body—lust, fear, anger—and by being purified
by Helios' rays, transmitted from the Demiurge. This is a life in accordance with Justice
(*Dikê*). The just soul will return to the Demiurge whereas the unjust soul will constantly
be reborn. Because Justice sees every fault, you cannot escape punishment unless
cleansed by Helios of your sins, who thus softens Justice.

48–49. *destiny's spindles . . . your rays:* The spindle of the Fates is the planets which,
according to some explanations, move in spirals rather than circles, explaining the fact
that some planets appear to move backwards at certain times. Helios, as king of the
universe, controls the planets and the Fates by his light and can suppress whatever evil
the Fates may have in store.

HOMERIC HYMN 30: TO EARTH
MOTHER OF ALL

Earth brings all good things.

I will sing of Earth, the mother of all, the base of all,
the eldest, who makes to live all that moves on the shining
land, or in the sea, or everything that flies—you nourish
them from your richness. From you mothers are fertile
5   and the trees bear fruit, O mistress, and it is in your power
to give the means of life or take it away from mortal humans.
　　He is rich whom you favor with your gentle heart.
He has all things in abundance. His plowland bursts
with the support of life, and his fields are rich with cattle.
10   His house is filled with good things. Such men are princes
in their cities of beautiful women, ruled by good laws,
and much good luck and wealth follow them. Their sons
exult with youthful joy and their daughters skip
with happy delight, dancing in flowered dresses through
15   the soft flowers of the meadow—so it is with those whom
you honor, O august goddess, bountiful spirit.
　　Hail to you, mother of the gods! Wife of starry Sky!
May you give a comfortable livelihood, eagerly, in return
for this song, and I will remember you and another song.

ORPHIC HYMN 26: TO EARTH

Earth is the begetter of all things, but also their destroyer.

O goddess Earth, mother of the blessed ones and of mortal
humans, nourisher of all, who gives all things, who accomplishes
all things, who destroys all things. You promote growth,
you bear fruit, brimming in the beautiful season, seat
5   of the deathless cosmos, maiden of many forms,
in the pains of labor you beget every kind of fruit.
You are eternal, much revered, deep-bosomed, blessed,
rejoicing in the sweet-breathing grass, a goddess covered
in every kind of flower. You delight in the rain, and around
10   you spins forever the intricate and awesome realm

of the stars.

> But, O blessed goddess, may you and the rich
> seasons increase the delicious fruits, having a kindly heart!

ORPHIC HYMN 1: TO HEKATÊ

Hekatê receives a long passage of praise in Hesiod's Theogony *(411–452), where she is hailed as a mighty goddess, a Titan, whose beneficent powers protects all kinds of men and endeavors, but she is little known outside this passage until in the Hellenistic Period (c. 332 BC–c. 30 BC) she becomes a sinister goddess of occult practice, mistress of the crossroads, where she received offerings of dog meat, and sometimes identified with Persephone, the goddess of death. She receives the first hymn in the collection of* Orphic Hymns, *appropriately as mistress of the dark mysterious realms to which the initiates hope to gain access. Here she is identified with Artemis as protector of the young, with Dionysos, the herder of bulls, and with Persephone, who consorts with the souls of the dead.*

> I call on Hekatê of the roads, of the crossroads—lovely!
> In heaven and on the earth and on the sea, wrapped in robes
> of saffron, spirit of the tomb, reveling with the breath-
> souls of the dead, daughter of Perses,° lover of solitude,
5 > delighting in deer, nocturnal, accompanied by dogs,
> indomitable empress! Herder of bulls, queen holding
> the key of the whole world, leader, nymph, mountain-
> wandering nurse of the young—I pray, O maid, be present
> at our holy rites, ever with joyous heart favor the oxherd!

PROCLUS HYMN 6: TO THE MOTHER OF THE GODS, HEKATÊ, AND JANUS/ZEUS

Hekatê is like Rhea and Zeus in her power to raise the individual soul from the darkness of the material world into the light of the Demiurge.

> Hail, O mother of the gods, who have many names,
> blessed with beautiful offspring! Hail, O Hekatê,

---

4. *Perses:* A colorless male Titan whose name means "destroyer"; Hekatê also had other genealogies.

frequenter of the porch, powerful! Hail to you too,
O forefather Janus, undying Zeus. Hail supreme Zeus!°
5   Make the passage of my life glorious, bristling with good
things, and drive pain from my body. Draw in my soul,
which rages mad around the material realm, purified
by the rites that awaken the intellect.
                                                    Yea, I pray
to you, give me your hand, show me the way revealed
10   by the gods—I crave it! I will observe the precious light
by which it is possible to escape the evil of a dark birth.
Yea, I pray to you, give me your hand, and bring me,
with your winds, exhausted as I am, to the harbor of piety.°
Hail, O mother of the gods, who have many names,
15   blessed with beautiful offspring! Hail, O Hekatê,
frequenter of the porch, powerful! Hail to you too,
O forefather Janus, undying Zeus. Hail supreme Zeus!

PROCLUS HYMN 4: TO ALL THE GODS

*Proclus invokes the gods as a body to provide protection and guidance
for the soul's ascent to the intelligible realm of the Demiurge.*

Listen, O gods, who sit at the helm of wisdom, who kindle
the fire of the spirit in the souls of mortal men, drawing
them up to the deathless ones, out of the shadowy hole,

1–4. *O mother of the gods . . . Zeus:* Rhea, the wife of Kronos, is the mother of the
gods in Neoplatonic thought. The reference to the Roman Janus, the Roman god of gates
and doorways, is odd but in representations he has two faces just as Hekatê often had
three. Hekatê dwells in the porch of her mother Rhea's palace because she is the link
between the inaccessible divine world and this world. Janus/Zeus, equated with the
Demiurge, also functions on the border between the intelligible world, to which Rhea
belongs, and the material world, of which he is the creator.

13. *to the harbor of piety:* Proclus seems to refer to an allegorical interpretation of the
Odyssey in which Odysseus is the soul adrift in the world of matter, striving to return to
Nous, the Demiurge, the intelligible world whence the soul came and where it can con-
template the pure Forms, even as it is itself a Form. This is the "precious light," whereas
this world is the dark material realm from which one wishes to escape.

purified by the secret rites of hymns.°

Hear, mighty saviors!

5   Scatter the mist and grant me your holy light that comes
from sacred books°, that I might know well the difference
between a man and an immortal god. And do not allow
a spirit, doing evil things, to hold me down in the streams
far from the blessed ones. And let not cold Punishment
10   bind me in the bonds of life, fallen in the waves of cold
becoming, unwilling to wander long.°

But gods, masters of bright

shining wisdom, hear! Reveal to me, as I ascend the path
that leads upwards, the rites and initiations of sacred words!°

1–4. *who kindle the fire . . . of hymns:* The gods energize the divine spark that is in all humans and lead them up into the realm of the Demiurge, where the gods live. Their control is like that of a helmsman on a ship, leading to the possession of the wisdom that makes it possible to leave this dark world of matter and enter the realm of light. The means that the gods use to accomplish this exaltation are literary compositions, such as this very hymn.

6. *sacred books:* The sacred books would be any from which one can discover the hierarchy of the divine world, including Homer, Hesiod, Plato's dialogues, the Orphic poems, and the *Chaldean Oracles,* a (lost) set of texts used intensively by Neoplatonist philosophers from the third through the sixth century AD. Fragments of the *Chaldean Oracles* survive, however, in Neoplatonic quotations and commentary.

9–11. *let not cold Punishment . . . wander long:* An evil spirit (the Greek is *daimon,* sometimes translated as "demon") may persecute the human soul that is fallen into the material world, thought of as a sea. "Punishment" is the personification of this hostile force.

13. *the rites and initiations of sacred words:* The study of scripture that is divinely inspired initiates one into the mysteries.

BIBLIOGRAPHY

TEXTS

Allen, T. W. *Homeri Opera.* Vol. 5. Oxford, 1912.

Bernabé, A. *Orphicorum et Orphicis similium testimonia et fragmenta.* Vol. 2 of *Poetae epici graeci, testimonia et fragmenta.* Munich, 2004–2007.

Giordano, D. *Proclo: Inni.* Florence, 1957.

Pfeiffer, R. *Callimachus.* Vol. 2, *Hymni et epigrammata.* Oxford, 1953.

Quandt, W. *Orphei Hymni.* Berlin, 1955.

Ricciardelli, G. *Inni orfici.* Milan, 2000.

van Den Berg, R. M. *Proclus' Hymns: Essays, Translations, Commentary.* Leiden, 2001.

West, M. L. *Homeric Hymns. Homeric Apocrypha. Lives of Homer.* Cambridge, MA., 2003.

GENERAL

Burkert, W. *Structure and History of Greek Mythology and Ritual.* Berkeley, 1979.

———. *Greek Religion.* Translated by J. Raffan. Cambridge, MA, 1985.

Furley, W. D. and J. M. Bremer. *Greek Hymns.* Tübingen, 2001.

Huxley, G. L. *Greek Epic Poetry: From Eumelos to Panyassis.* London, 1969.

Larson, J. *Ancient Greek Cults.* New York, 2007.

HOMERIC HYMNS

Allen, T. W., W. R. Halliday, and E. E. Sikes. *The Homeric Hymns.* Oxford, 1936.

Athanassakis, A. N. trans. *The Homeric Hymns.* Baltimore, 1976.

Boedeker, D. D. *Aphrodite's Entry into Greek Epic,* Mnemosyne Supplement 32. Leiden, 1974.

Brown, N. O. Hermes the Thief: The Evolution of a Myth. Madison, WI, 1947.

Burkert, W. "Kynaithos, Polycrates and the Homeric Hymn to Apollo." In *Arktouros: Hellenic Studies Presented to Bernard M. W. Knox,* edited by Glen W. Bowersock, Walter Burkert, Michael Putnam, 53–62. Berlin, 1979.

Clay, J. S. The Politics of Olympos: Form and Meaning in the Major Homeric Hymns. Princeton, NJ, 1989.

Faulker, A. *The Homeric Hymn to Aphrodite.* Oxford, 2008.

———. *The Homeric Hymns: Interpretive Essays.* Oxford, 2011.

Faulkner, A., A. Vergados, and A. Schwab. *The Reception of the Homeric Hymns.* Oxford, 2016.

Fontenrose, J. *Python: A Study of Delphic Myth and Its Origins.* Berkeley, 1959.

———. *The Delphic Oracle.* Berkeley, 1978.

Hoekstra, A. *The Sub-epic Stage of the Formulaic Tradition: Studies in the Homeric Hymns to Apollo, to Aphrodite, and to Demeter.* Amsterdam, London, 1969.

Janko, R. "The Structure of the Homeric Hymns: A Study in Genre." *Hermes* 109 (1981): 9–24.

———. *Homer, Hesiod and the Hymns: Diachronic Development in Epic Diction.* Cambridge, 1982.

Kirk, G. S. "Orality and Structure in the Homeric Hymn to Apollo." In *I poemi epici rapsodici non omerici e la tradizione orale,* edited by C. Brillante, M. Cantilena, and C. O. Pavese, 163–82. Padova, 1981.

Lord, M. L. "Withdrawal and Return: An Epic Story Pattern in the Homeric *Hymn to Demeter.*" *Classical Journal* 62 (1967): 241–48.

Miller, A. M. "The 'Address to the Delian Maidens' in the Homeric Hymn to Apollo: Epilogue or Transition?" *Transactions and Proceedings of the American Philological Association* 109 (1979): 173–86.

———. *From Delos to Delphi: A Literary Study of the Homeric Hymn to Apollo.* Leiden, 1985.

Most, G. "Callimachus and Herophilus." *Hermes* 109 (1981): 188–96.

Notopoulos, J. A. "The Homeric Hymns as Oral Poetry: A Study of the Post-Homeric Oral Tradition." *American Journal of Philology* 83 (1962): 337–68.

Parke, H. W. *The Delphic Oracle,* 2 vols. Oxford, 1956.

Parker, R. "The Hymn to Demeter and the Homeric Hymns," *Greece and Rome* 38 (1991): 1–17.

Rayor, D. *The Homeric Hymns: A Translation, with Introduction and Notes,* rev. ed. Berkeley, 2014.

Richardson, N. J., ed. *The Homeric Hymn to Demeter.* Oxford, 1974.

Segal, C. "The Homeric Hymn to Aphrodite: A Structuralist Approach." *Classical World* 67 (1974): 205–12.

———. "Orality, Repetition and Formulaic Artistry in the Homeric Hymn to Demeter." In *I poemi epici rapsodici non omerici e la tradizione orale*, edited by C. Brillante, M. Cantilena, and C. O. Pavese, 1–56. Padova, 1981.

Shelmerdine, S. C. "The 'Homeric Hymn to Hermes': A Commentary (1–114) with Introduction." Ph.D. diss., University of Michigan, 1981.

Smith, P. M. *Nursling of Mortality: A Study of the Homeric Hymn to Aphrodite*, Studien zur klassischen Philologie 3. Frankfurt, 1981.

Thalmann, W. G. *Conventions of Form and Thought in Early Greek Poetry*. Baltimore, 1984.

Vergados, A. *The Homeric Hymn to Hermes: Introduction, Text and Commentary*. Boston, 2013.

West, M. L. "Cynaethus' Hymn to Apollo." *Classical Quarterly* 25 (1975): 161–70.

CALLIMACHUS

Acosta-Hughes, B., and S. A. Stephens. *Callimachus in Context: From Plato to the Augustan Poets*. Cambridge, 2012.

Bing, P. *The Well-Read Muse: Present and Past in Callimachus and the Hellenistic Poets*, 2nd ed. Ann Arbor, 2008.

Bulloch, A. W. *Callimachus: The Fifth Hymn*. Cambridge, 1985.

Cameron, A. *Callimachus and His Critics*. Princeton, NJ, 1995.

Hopkinson, N. *Callimachus: Hymn to Demeter*. Cambridge, 1984.

Lombardo, S., and Rayor, D. J. *Callimachus: Hymns, Epigrams, Select Fragments*. Baltimore, 1988.

Nisetich, F. *The Poems of Callimachus*. Oxford, 2001.

Stephens, S. A. *Callimachus: The Hymns*. Oxford, 2015.

Williams, F. *Callimachus: Hymn to Apollo*. Oxford, 1978.

ORPHIC HYMNS

Athanassakis, A., and B. Wolkow. *The Orphic Hymns: Translation, Introduction, and Notes*. Baltimore, 2013.

Betegh, G. *The Derveni Papyrus: Cosmology, Theology and Interpretation*. Cambridge, 2004.

Burkert, W. *Ancient Mystery Cults*. Cambridge, MA, 1987.

Graf, F., and S. I. Johnston. *Ritual Texts for the Afterlife: Orpheus and the Bacchic Gold Tablets*. London, 2007.

Guthrie, W. K. C. *Orpheus and Greek Religion: A Study of the Orphic Movement*. Princeton, NJ, 1935.

Janko, R. "The Derveni Papyrus: An Interim Text." *Zeitschrift für Papyrologie und Epigraphik* 141 (2002): 1–62.

Linforth, I. M. *The Arts of Orpheus.* Berkeley, 1941.

Segal, C. *Orpheus: The Myth of the Poet.* Baltimore, 1989.

Taylor, T., trans. *The Mystical Hymns of Orpheus,* 1896. Available at www.theoi.com/Text/OrphicHymns1.html, 1896.

West, M. L. "Notes on the Orphic Hymns." *Classics Quarterly* 18, no. 2 (1968): 288–96.

———. *The Orphic Poems.* Oxford, 1983.

PROCLUS

Chlup, R. *Proclus: An Introduction.* Cambridge, 2012.

d'Hoine, P., and M. Martijn, eds. *All from One: A Guide to Proclus.* Oxford, 2016.

Gersh, S., ed. *Interpreting Proclus: From Antiquity to the Renaissance.* Cambridge, 2014.

Johnston, S. I. *Hekate Soteira: A Study of Hekate's Roles in the Chaldean Oracles and Related Literature.* Oxford, 1990.

Layne, D., and D. D. Butorac, eds. *Proclus and his Legacy.* Berlin, 2017.

Siorvanes, L. *Proclus: Neoplatonic Philosophy and Science.* New Haven, CT, 1996.

West, M. L. "The Eighth Homeric Hymn and Proclus." *Classical Quarterly* 18, no. 2 (1968): 288–96.

GLOSSARY/INDEX

ABANTES (a-**ban**-tēz): Homer's name for the Euboeans, 148, 161

ACHAEANS (a-**kē**-ans. Akhaians): a division of the Greek people, Homer's word for the Greeks at Troy, 185

ACHELOÖS (ak-e-**lō**-us): a river in southwestern Greece, the largest river in Greece, 78, 155

ACHERON (**ak**-er-on. Akheron): "sorrowful," river of the underworld, 87

ACROPOLIS (a-**krop**-o-lis): hill in Athens on which the Parthenon is built, 36, 47, 49, 50, 55, 235

ADMETOS (ad-**mē**-tos): "invincible," king of Pherai in Thessaly, son of Pheres, husband of Alkestis, 142, 145

ADONIS (a-**don**-is): son of Kinyras and Myrrha, beloved by Aphrodite, killed by boar, 110, 246

ADRASTEIA (a-dras-**tē**-a): the easternmost city of the Troad, which overlooked the southwestern shore of the Propontis, 23

AEGEAN (ē-**jē**-an): sea between Greece and Turkey, 146, 149, 150, 161

AEGIS (**ē**-jis): "goat skin," a shield with serpent border used by Athena and Zeus, 36, 37, 46, 47, 48, 96, 97, 103, 199, 206, 212, 236

AENEAS (ē-**nē**-as): son of Aphrodite and Anchises, greatest Trojan fighter after Hector, descended from Tros, ancestor of the Roman people, 95, 104

AENEID (ē-**nē**-id): poem by Vergil on founding of Rome, late first century BC, 3, 107

AETOLIA (e-**tō**-li-a): district north of the Corinthian Gulf, where were the cites of Pleuron and Kalydon, 78

AFRICA, 139, 170, 183

AGAMEMNON (a-ga-**mem**-non): son of Atreus, brother of Menelaos, leader of Greek forces at Troy, 185, 187

AIGAI (ē-jē): where Poseidon had his palace, probably in Achaea in the northwestern Peloponnesos, 33, 120

AIOLOS (ē-o-los): eponym of the Aiolians, son of Hellên, king of Lesbos, 82, 120

AKRISIOS (a-**kris**-i-us): father of Danaë, killed accidentally by Perseus, 29

ALCAEUS (al-**sē**-us, Alkaios): Greek poet, 620-sixth century BC, 211

ALEXANDER THE GREAT (356–323 BC), 56

ALEXANDRIA: city in Egypt founded by Alexander the Great, 8, 15, 20, 39

ALEXANDRIAN SCHOLARS, 7, 8

ALKMENÊ (alk-**mēn**-ê): daughter of Elektryon, wife of Amphitryon, mother of Herakles, 29

ALPHEIOS: river in the Peloponnesos and the god of this river, 135, 196, 197, 198, 200, 206, 224

AMAZONS: a race of warrior women, descendants of Ares, 101, 173, 184, 185

AMBROSIA: "immortal," food of the gods, 60, 66, 105, 123, 197, 201

AMPHION (am-**fī**-on): son of Zeus and Antiopê, husband of Niobê, musician brother of Zethus, one of the twin founders of Thebes, 151, 152

AMPHITRITÊ (am-fi-**trī**-tē): a Nereid, wife of Poseidon, 122

AMPHITRYON (am-**fit**-ri-on): descendant of Perseus, husband of Alkmenê, 29, 180

ANCHISES (an-**kī**-sēz): prince of Troy, lover of Aphrodite, father of Aeneas, 96, 98, 99, 100, 101, 102, 103, 104, 107

ANKAIOS: a king of Samos, on the Argonautic expedition, 149

ANTIKLEIA (an-ti-**klē**-a): a companion of Artemis, 183

ANTRON: a coastal town in Thessaly, 75

AOIDOS (a-**oi**-dos, pl. *aoidoi*): Greek word for such oral poets as Homer and Hesiod (contrast with "rhapsode"), 5, 89

APHRODITE: Greek goddess of sexual attraction, related to Inanna/Astartê/Ishtar, equated with Roman Venus, 5, 7, 16, 27, 37, 39, 61, 89–115, 121, 126, 148, 163, 216, 231, 235–38, 246

APOLLONIUS (a-pol-**lōn**-i-us) of Rhodes (third century BC): author of the *Argonautica*, 8

APOTROPAIC (apo-trō-**pā**-ik) device: a magical object that turns away evil, 76

ARCADIA (ar-**kād**-i-a): mountainous region in the central Peloponnesos, 17, 20, 21, 22, 150, 151, 160, 170, 177, 184, 185, 190, 191, 214, 217, 218, 241

ARES (**air**-ēz): Greek god of war, 6, 7, 24, 30, 35, 36, 89–93, 96, 114, 115, 122, 126, 146, 150, 154, 155, 160, 224, 235–37, 240

ARGEÏPHONTES (ar-jē-i-**fon**-tēz): "Argus-killer," epithet of Hermes, 69, 92, 189, 195

ARGÊS (**ar**-jēz): "bright," one of the three Cyclopes, 175, 176

ARGOLID: the easternmost lobe of the Peloponnesos, including the Argive plain, Mycenae, Tiryns, Epidaurus, and Troizen, 150, 151

ARGONAUTS (**arg**-o-notz): Jason and his companions on the *Argo*, 127

ARGOS: "plain," city in the Argive plain in the northeastern Peloponnesos, 38, 40, 41, 45, 69, 70, 92, 101, 102, 104, 106, 126, 150, 151, 185, 186, 189, 195, 202, 205, 206, 214, 216, 239

ARIADNÊ (ar-i-**ad**-nē): "very holy one," Cretan princess, daughter of Minos and Pasiphaë who helped Theseus defeat the Minotaur, 163

ARION (a-**rī**-on): magical horse, 32

ARISTOTLE (384–322 BC): Greek philosopher, 223

ASOPOS (ā-**sō**-pos): the largest river in Boeotia, 151

ASTARTÊ (as-**tar**-tē): Phoenician fertility goddess, like Aphrodite, 170

ATALANTA (at-a-**lan**-ta): female Arcadian athlete, loved by Meleager, 184

ATHENS: main city in Attica, 8, 14, 15, 17, 35, 40, 47, 49, 50, 53–57, 79, 88, 108, 115, 120, 144, 149, 160–64, 181, 183, 184, 189, 235. *See also* Acropolis, Attica, Cecrops, Erechtheus, Erichthonius, Parthenon, Theseus

ATLAS: a Titan, son of Iapetus and Clymenê, father of Kalypso and Maia; holds up the sky, 191, 214

ATREUS (**ā**-trūs): king of Mycenae, son of Pelops, father of Agamemnon and Menelaus, 187

ATTICA (**at**-ti-ka): region in central Greece where Athens is located, 62, 129, 149, 170, 181, 185, 186

ATTIS: beloved of Cybelê, driven mad, castrates himself and dies, a resurrection god, 246

AULIS (**ow**-lis): port in Boeotia from which the Trojan expedition set sail, 182, 185, 187

BACCHAE (**bak**-kē. Bakkhai): female followers of Dionysus, a play by Euripides, 229

BACCHUS (**bak** kus. Bakkhos): another name for Dionysus, preferred by the Romans, 10, 49, 84, 109, 187, 222, 229, 230, 231, 232, 233, 234

BIG DIPPER: the constellation of Ursa Major, "the Great Bear," 22

BLACK SEA: also called Pontus, 181

BLACK-FIGURE: a style in Greek pottery decoration, 37, 236

BOEOTIA (bē-**ō**-sha. Boiotia): "cow-land," region north of Attica, where Thebes was situated, 9, 36, 41, 127, 149, 151, 152, 170, 182

BOREAS (**bōr**-e-as): the North Wind, 14, 150, 161, 163, 178

BRAURON (**braw**-ron): a village in Attica, site of a temple to Artemis, 170

BRIAREOS (bri-**ar**-e-os): one of the Hundred-Handers, 154, 155

BRISEIS: Achilles' war-prize, taken by Agamemnon, 172

BRONTÊS: "thunderer," one of the three Cyclopes, 175, 176

BRONZE AGE: c. 3000–1200 BC, 223, 240

BYZANTIUM: Greek colony at the entrance to the Bosporus (= later Constantinople), 186

CADUCEUS (ka-**dū**-se-us): a wand with two intertwined snakes, carried by Hermes, 69, 73, 101, 189, 215

CALLIMACHUS (ka-**lim**-a-kus. Kallimakhos) (third century BC): Alexandrian poet, 1–9, 21, 23, 24, 41, 43, 78, 80, 83, 140, 142, 146, 151, 153, 156, 157, 161, 162, 171, 173, 176, 182, 185

CALYPSO (ka-**lip**-sō): "concealer," a nymph, daughter of Atlas, who kept Odysseus for seven years on her island Ogygia at the navel of the sea, 72, 189

CANNIBALISM, 223

CASTOR: mortal son of Tyndareus and Leda, brother of the immortal Polydeuces (= Pollux) and of Helen and Clytemnestra, 39

CATULLUS (ka-**tul**-us) (84–54 BC): Roman love poet, 9

CAUCASUS MOUNTAINS: at the eastern end of the Black Sea, 240

CELTS (keltz): a racial and linguistic group that dominated northern Europe, England, and Ireland in the pre-Roman period, 156

CENTAURS (**sen**-towrs. Kentauroi): half-human, half-horse creatures, 29, 184

CERYNEIA (se-ri-**nē**-a. Keryneia): mountain in the Peloponnesos where Heracles caught a magical deer, 177

CHAOS (**kā**-os. Khaos): "chasm," the first thing that came into being, 11

CHARIS: "charm," personification of the quality, the wife of Hephaistos, 89

CHARITES (**kar**-i-tes. Kharites): the Graces, imparters of feminine charm, 93, 126

CHARON (**kā**-ron. Kharon): ferryman of the dead, 87

CHEIRON (**kī**-ron): "hand," the wise Centaur, 153

CHIMAIRA (ki-**mēr**-a): "she-goat," offspring of Typhoeus and Echidna, with a lion's body, snake's tail, and goat's head protruding from the back, killed by Bellerophon, 133

CHIOS (**kē**-os): Greek island near Asia Minor, often claimed as Homer's birthplace, 82, 118, 120, 125, 148–50, 155

CHRISTIANS, 168

CHRONOS (**kron**-os): "time," a Neoplatonic category, 11

CHRYSES (**krī**-sēz): father of Chryseïs, a priest of Apollo whom Agamemnon insulted, 165

CILICIA (si-**lish**-a): region in southeastern Asia Minor, 216

CIMMERIANS (si-**mer**-i-anz): live across the river Ocean, 186

CIRCE (**sir**-sē. Kirke): daughter of Helius, enchantress who entertained Odysseus for a year on her island, 189

COCYTUS (kō-**sīt**-us. Kokytos): "wailing," river in underworld, 216

CORCYRA (cor-**sīr**-a. Kerkyra): modern Corfu, an island off the northwest coast of Greece, identified with Phaeacia in the *Odyssey,* 155

CORINTH (**kor**-inth. Korinth): city on isthmus between central Greece and the Peloponnesos, 33, 94, 128, 129, 131, 149, 151, 152, 160

COSMOGONY: story of the "creation of the ordered world," 8, 11

CRETE: largest island in the Aegean, birthplace of Zeus, 8, 12, 17–23, 27, 29, 35, 62, 97, 99, 120, 122, 136, 138, 141, 147, 160, 163, 164, 170, 174, 176, 182, 187

CRIMEA (krī-**mē**-a): peninsula on the north coast of the Black Sea, 181

CUPID (= Greek Eros): "desire," spirit of sexual attraction, 91, 98

CYBELÊ (**sib**-i-lê. Kybele): great mother goddess of Phrygia, loved Attis, 23, 170, 179, 186, 246

CYCLADES (**sik**-la-dēz): "circle islands," around Delos in the Aegean Sea, 147, 157, 163, 182, 224

CYCLOPES (sī-**klōp**-ēz, sing., Cyclops. Kyklopes, Kyklops): "round-eyes," one-eyed smiths who forged Zeus's thunderbolt and other weapons, 142, 173, 175, 176, 177, 241

CYLLENÊ (si-**lēn**-ê. Kyllenê): mountain in Arcadia, where Hermes was born, 160, 191, 195, 198, 200, 204, 214, 216

CYPRUS: large island in eastern Mediterranean, home of Aphrodite, 5, 93, 94, 96, 99, 107, 108, 110, 148, 216, 226, 237

CYTHERA (**sith**-e-ra. Kythera): island south of the Peloponnesos, sometimes said to be the birthplace of Aphrodite, 90, 94

DACTYLIC HEXAMETER: the meter of Homer, six feet per line, 2, 3

DAIDALOS (**dēd**-a-lus): Athenian craftsman who built a hollow cow for Pasiphaë, the labyrinth, and wings for himself and his son Ikaros to escape from it, 148, 163, 164

DANAÄNS (**dān**-a anz): descendants of Danaös, one of Homer's name for the Greeks, 45

DANAË (**dān**-a-ē): daughter of Akrisios, mother of Perseus, whom Zeus desired, 19, 29

DANAÏDS (**dān**-a-idz): daughters of Danaüs, who killed their husbands, the sons of Aegyptus, on the wedding night, 40

DARDANOS (**dar**-da-nus): son of Zeus, early king of Troy, after whom the Trojans were called Dardanians, 103, 104

DAWN: goddess of the early morning, same as the Latin Aurora or the Greek Eos, 104, 105, 183, 186, 199, 204, 242, 245

DELOS (**dē**-los): "clear," tiny island in the center of the Cyclades, where Apollo and Artemis were born, 7, 29, 117–25, 140, 142, 146–49, 157–67, 170–81

DELPHI (**del**-fī): sanctuary of Apollo at foot of Mount Parnassus, where Apollo slew Python, 117, 118, 125, 129–32, 140–42, 145, 147, 152, 156, 157, 165, 172, 181, 186, 199, 231, 236, 238

DEMETER (de-**mēt**-er): daughter of Cronus and Rhea, mother of Persephonê, goddess of the grain harvest (= Roman Ceres), 2, 5, 6, 7, 12, 14, 29, 32, 52–58, 60–88, 146, 189, 237

DEMODOKOS: oral singer at the court of the Phaeacians in the *Odyssey,* 6, 89

DEMOPHOÖN (dem-**of**-o-on): son of Celeus and Metanira, nursed by Demeter, 5, 53, 66, 67

DEUKALION (dū-**kāl**-i-on): son of Minos, father of Idomeneus, king of Crete, 82

DIANA: goddess of the hunt, Roman equivalent of Greek Artemis, 119

DIKÊ (**dē**-kā): justice, personified as a daughter of Zeus (Dikê), 247

DIODORUS OF SICILY (first century BC): Greek historian, 6, 223

DIOMEDES (dī-ō-**mēd**-ēz): son of Tydeus (who fought in the Seven Against Thebes), a principal Greek warrior at Troy, 35, 38, 40

DIONÊ (dī-**ōn**-ē): feminine form of "Zeus," a consort of Zeus at Dodona, mother of Aphrodite , 114, 121

DITHYRAMB (**dith**-i-ram): a choral song, especially in honor of Dionysus, 223

DODONA (do-**dōn**-a): site of oracular shrine of Zeus in northwestern Greece, 80, 161

DORIANS: a division of the Greek people, 145

DORIC ORDER: in Greek architecture, 38, 75

DOULICHION: one of the Ionian islands, 135

DYAUS PITAR (dē-**yows pi**-tar): Indo-European sky god, 17

ECHINADES (e-kin-**a**-dēz): "sea-urchins," small islands at the mouth of the Acheloös River in southwestern mainland Greece, 155

ECHO: nymph rejected by Narkissos and pursued by Pan, who became only a voice, 220

EILEITHYIA (ē-lē-**thī**-ya): "she who makes one come," goddess of childbirth, 21, 30, 53, 84, 122, 154, 159, 170, 240

EKSTASIS: "standing outside," in the cult of Dionysus, 222

ELEUSIS: site of the mysteries to Demeter and Persephonê, west of Athens, 7, 52–67, 69, 70, 74–79, 84, 85, 88

ELIS: a territory in the northwest Peloponnesos, 135

ELYSIUM (e-**liz**-i-um. Elysion): the Elysian Fields, a paradisiacal land, 53

ENYALIOS: a name for Ares, 240

ENYO: a minor goddess of war, 160

EOS (**ē**-os): the dawn goddess (= Roman Aurora), 104, 183, 242, 245

EPHIALTES (ef-i-**al**-tēz): a giant who stormed heaven, one of the Aloads, 175, 187

EPHYRA (**e**-fir-a): another name for Corinth, 149

EPIC: a long poem on a heroic topic, 5, 8, 167, 241, 242

ERECHTHEUS (e-**rek**-thūs): an early king of Athens, 50, 183

ERICHTHONIOS (er-ik-**thōn**-i-os): "he of earth," an early king of Athens, confused with Erechtheus, 49, 50

EROS (**er**-os): "desire," sprung from Chaos, or the child of Ares and Aphrodite (= Roman Cupid), 91, 98, 109

ERYMANTHOS: mountain range in northwest Peloponnesos, abode of Artemis and wild boars, 21

ETHIOPIA: region in Africa, 158

ETHIOPIANS: "burnt-faced," a people who dwell in never-never land in the extreme south, where Poseidon and Zeus sometimes visit, 78,158

ETNA, MOUNT: volcano in eastern Sicily, 19, 175

EUBOIA (yū-**bē**-a): long island east of Attica, site of vigorous Iron Age community where the alphabet seems to have been invented, 6, 75, 120, 127, 146, 148,149,157, 161,162

EURIPIDES (yū-**rip**-i-dēz) (480–406 BC): Athenian playwright, 150, 182, 229

EUROPA (yū-**rōp**-a): daughter of Agenor, brother of Cadmus, seduced by Zeus in the form of a bull, mother to Minos, 19, 29

EUROTAS: the stream that flows through Sparta, where there was a shrine to Artemis, 39, 40

EURYDIKÊ (yū-**rid**-i-kē): beloved of Orpheus, 10

EURYSTHEUS (yu-**ris**-thē-us): cousin and tormentor of Herakles, 180

FATES: "that which is spoken," 43, 156, 174, 245–47

FICINO (fitch-**ēn**-ō): Marsilio (1433–1499), Italian Neoplatonic philosopher, 16

FOLKTALE: traditional tales that are neither myths nor legends, 196

GAEA (**ghī**-a): "earth," sprung from Chaos, consort of Ouranos, mother of the Titans, 11, 19, 35, 121, 130, 148, 150, 175, 241, 245

GANYMEDE (**gan**-i-mēd): son of Tros, beloved of Zeus, cupbearer of the gods, 4, 19, 104, 105

GARGAROS: the highest peak of Mt. Ida near Troy, 27, 30

GEMINI (**jem**-i-nī): the "twins," Castor and Polydeuces, a constellation, 39

GIANTS: "earth-born ones," sprung from the blood of Ouranos that fell on Gaea, enemies of the gods, 38, 45, 47, 48, 229

GOLDEN AGE, 43

GORGON: terrifying head of Medusa, 46, 96

GORTYN: city in south-central Crete, 182

GRACES (Charites): attendants of Aphrodite, imparters of feminine charm, 9, 93, 99, 100, 108, 126, 172

GREAT GODDESS, 100

GREEK ALPHABET: invented c. 825 BC, 4

HADES (**hā**-dēz): "unseen," lord of the underworld, son of Kronos and Rhea, husband of Persephonê, 10, 23, 32, 44, 52–88, 102, 160, 184, 189, 213, 214; see also Pluto

HALIARTOS: a town in Boeotia, 41, 128

HARMONIA (har-**mōn**-i-a): wife of Cadmus, 126, 222

HEBÊ (**hēb**-ē): "youth," married to Herakles on Olympos, 126, 181

HECTOR: greatest of the Trojan warriors, married to Andromachê, killed by Achilles, 189

HELEN: daughter of Zeus and Leda, husband of Menelaus, lover of Paris, 19, 185

HELIKÊ (**hel**-i-kē): a town in the northeast Peloponnesos, 33, 152

HELIOS: sun god, son of Hyperion, 16, 30, 37, 53, 58, 60, 89, 90, 133, 135, 164, 182, 205, 236, 241–47

HELLENISTIC: referring to Greek culture between Alexander's death in 323 BC and the ascendancy of Rome, 1, 9, 14, 146, 147, 151, 158, 249

HELLENISTIC PERIOD, 323–30 BC, 249

HEMERA (**hēm**-er-a): "day," one of the first beings, daughter of Erebos and Nyx, 185

HEPHAISTOS (he-**fēs**-tos): Greek god of smiths, son of Zeus and Hera or Hera alone; husband of Charis in the *Iliad,* of faithless Aphrodite in the *Odyssey,* 4, 24, 30, 37, 49, 89–93, 114–16, 131, 154–56, 175, 176, 197, 223–25

HERAKLES: son of Zeus and Alkmenê, the strongest man who ever lived, 19, 27, 29, 35, 40, 63, 115, 126, 150, 155, 173, 177, 180, 181, 236, 240

HERMES: "he of the stone heap," son of Zeus and Maia, Greek god of travel, tricks, commerce, and thievery, 6, 7, 19, 35, 69, 71–73, 85, 92, 93, 101, 102, 122, 126, 160, 173, 176, 180, 189–222, 236, 239

HERMOS RIVER: in Lydia, rises in Phrygia, flows into the sea near Smyrna, 125, 159

HERODOTUS (her-**od**-o-tus) (c. 484–425 BC): Greek historian, 142, 161, 163

HESIOD (**hēs**-i-od): Greek poet, eighth century BC, composer of *Works and Days* and *Theogony,* 1, 6–10, 19, 23, 24, 42, 75, 94, 108, 154, 192, 207, 240–42, 245, 249, 251

HESPERIDES (hes-**per**-i-dēz): "daughters of the West," who protect a magical tree with golden apples, 78

HESTIA (**hes**-ti-a): daughter of Kronos and Rhea, Greek goddess of the hearth (= Roman Vesta), 83, 84, 97, 238–40

HETAIRA (he-**tī**-ra): "companioness," Greek courtesan, 209

HIEROPHANT (hī-**er**-o-fant): "revealer of the sacred things," priestly office at Eleusis, 55

HIEROS GAMOS: "holy marriage," ritual sexual union to enhance fertility, 94

HOMER: composer of the *Iliad* and the *Odyssey*, late ninth century BC, see also, *aoidos*, Cyclic Poems, Troy, 1, 5–10, 17, 23, 75, 93, 95, 114, 118, 125, 146, 148, 159, 161, 186, 238, 240, 251

HOMERIC HYMNS: c. seventh-fifth centuries BC, oral dictated texts celebrating the gods, 1–9, 14, 95, 146, 191, 208

HORUS: the child of Isis and Osiris, 158, 165

HUMAN SACRIFICE, 17, 170, 181

HYPERBOREANS (hi-per-**bor**-e-anz): "dwellers beyond the north wind," a mythical people who lived there, 78, 160, 161, 226, 231

HYPERION (hi-**per**-ion): "he who travels above," Titan, father of Helius, Selené, and Eos, 37, 58, 61, 241– 245

IAMBÊ (i-**am**-bê): servant of Celeus and Metanira at Eleusis who amused Demeter, 55, 64, 65, 85

IAPETOS (i-**ap**-e-tos): a Titan, father of Prometheus, Epimetheus, and Atlas, 240

IASION (i-**as**-i-on): consort of Demeter, father of Ploutos, 75, 86

IDA (**ī**-da): Mount, (1) on Crete, 17, 20, 23; (2) another mountain near Troy, 17, 27, 28, 30, 39, 99, 120

ILIUM (Ilion): another name for Troy, 104, 107

ILOS (**ī**-los): early king of Troy, son of Tros, grandfather of Priam, 103, 104

IMBROS: island in the northeast Aegean, 120

INANNA (in-**an**-a): Sumerian fertility goddess, 120

INDO-EUROPEANS: a hypothetical ethnic group who spoke proto-Indo-European, 17, 112

IO (**ī**-ō): Argive princess, daughter of the river Inachus, beloved of Zeus, turned into cow, persecuted by Hera, 40, 92, 186, 189, 195

IOLKOS (i-**olk**-us): city in southeastern Thessaly, home of Jason at the head of the Gulf of Pagasae (= modern Volo), 127, 183

IONIA: the west coast of Asia Minor, 82, 170

IONIANS: a division of the Greek people, 124

IONIC ORDER, in Greek architecture, 75

IRIS (**ī**-ris): "rainbow," messenger of Zeus, 69, 122, 146, 150, 155, 158, 159

ISHTAR: Akkadian fertility goddess (= Sumerian Inanna), 93

ISIS (**ī**-sis): Egyptian goddess, wife of Osiris, whom she resurrected, 110, 170

ISTANBUL: formerly Byzantium, then Constantinople, 186

ITALY, 12, 77, 98, 109, 143, 175, 219, 226

ITHAKA: off the northwest coast of Greece, home of Odysseus, one of the Ionian Islands, 135, 155

IXION (ik-**sī**-on): father of Centaurus, tried to rape Hera, bound to a wheel in Tartarus, 29

MYSIA: territory surrounding the Troad, 178

MYSTAI (**mis**-tī): "those with closed eyes," initiates into the mysteries of Eleusis, 55

JANUS (jā-nus): *numen* of gates, bridges, and archways, 250

JASON: son of Aeson, husband of Medea, leader of the Argonauts, 2, 8, 127, 183

HIEROS GAMOS: "holy marriage," ritual sexual union to enhance fertility, 94

HOMER: composer of the *Iliad* and the *Odyssey*, late ninth century BC, see also, *aoidos*, Cyclic Poems, Troy, 1, 5–10, 17, 23, 75, 93, 95, 114, 118, 125, 146, 148, 159, 161, 186, 238, 240, 251

HOMERIC HYMNS: c. seventh-fifth centuries BC, oral dictated texts celebrating the gods, 1–9, 14, 95, 146, 191, 208

HORUS: the child of Isis and Osiris, 158, 165

HUMAN SACRIFICE, 17, 170, 181

HYPERBOREANS (hi-pĕr-**bor**-e-anz): "dwellers beyond the north wind," a mythical people who lived there, 78, 160, 161, 226, 231

HYPERION (hi-**per**-ion): "he who travels above," Titan, father of Helius, Selenê, and Eos, 37, 58, 61, 241- 245

IAMBÊ (i-**am**-bē): servant of Celeus and Metanira at Eleusis who amused Demeter, 55, 64, 65, 85

IAPETOS (i-**ap**-e-tos): a Titan, father of Prometheus, Epimetheus, and Atlas, 240

IASION (i-**as**-i-on): consort of Demeter, father of Ploutos, 75, 86

IDA (**ī**-da): Mount, (1) on Crete, 17, 20, 23; (2) another mountain near Troy, 17, 27, 28, 30, 39, 99, 120

ILIUM (Ilion): another name for Troy, 104, 107

ILOS (**ī**-los): early king of Troy, son of Tros, grandfather of Priam, 103, 104

IMBROS: island in the northeast Aegean, 120

INANNA (in-**an**-a): Sumerian fertility goddess, related to Aphrodite, 93

INDO-EUROPEANS: a hypothetical ethnic group who spoke proto-Indo-European, 17, 112

IO (**ī**-ō): Argive princess, daughter of the river Inachus, beloved of Zeus, turned into cow, persecuted by Hera, 40, 92, 186, 189, 195

IOLKOS (**ī**-**olk**-us): city in southeastern Thessaly, home of Jason at the head of the Gulf of Pagasae (= modern Volo), 127, 183

IONIA: the west coast of Asia Minor, 82, 170

IONIANS: a division of the Greek people, 124

IONIC ORDER, in Greek architecture, 75

IRIS (**ī**-ris): "rainbow," messenger of Zeus, 69, 122, 146, 150, 155, 158, 159

ISHTAR: Akkadian fertility goddess (= Sumerian Inanna), 93

ISIS (**ī**-sis): Egyptian goddess, wife of Osiris, whom she resurrected, 110, 170

ISTANBUL: formerly Byzantium, then Constantinople, 186

ITALY, 12, 77, 98, 109, 143, 175, 219, 226

ITHAKA: off the northwest coast of Greece, home of Odysseus, one of the Ionian Islands, 135, 155

IXION (ik-**sī**-on): father of Centaurus, tried to rape Hera, bound to a wheel in Tartarus, 29

JANUS (**jā**-nus): *numen* of gates, bridges, and archways, 250

JASON: son of Aeson, husband of Medea, leader of the Argonauts, 2, 8, 127, 183

JUDGMENT OF PARIS: when Paris had to judge whom was most beautiful among Hera, Athena, or Aphrodite, 39, 41, 94

JUPITER: Roman counterpart of Greek Zeus, king of the gods, 236

KADMOS (**kad**-mos): "man of the East," founder of Thebes; son of Agenor, brother of Europa, husband of Harmonia, father of Ino and Pentheus, king of Thebes, 43, 44, 126, 222, 228, 231, 234

KALYDON (**kal**-i-don): main city in Aetolia in southwestern mainland Greece, home of Meleager, site of the Kalydonian Boar Hunt, 184, 187

KAMEIROS: one of the three cities on Rhodes, 111

KARPATHOS (kar-**pā**-thos): an island in the southeastern Aegean, 120

KARYSTOS: a city of the Abantes on the southwestern coast of Euboea, 6

KASTOR: "beaver," son of Tyndareos and Leda, brother of Polydeukes, one of the Dioscuri, 39, 40

KNOSSOS (**knos**-sos): principal Bronze Age settlement in Crete, where labyrinthine ruins have been found, 22, 134, 136, 174, 175, 183

KORÊ (**kō**-rē): "girl," another name for Persephonê, 52, 53, 55, 56, 73, 79

KORONEIA: a city in Boeotia, 41

KOS (**kōs**): Greek island near Asia Minor, 78, 120, 146, 155, 156, 224

KRISA: a town near Delphi, 129, 131, 135, 136, 156

KRONOS: child of Ouranos and Gaia, husband of Rhea, overthrown by his son Zeus, who imprisoned him in Tartaros, 4, 11, 14, 19, 20, 23, 24, 25–30, 32, 35, 43, 58, 61, 69, 71–74, 90, 97, 104, 108, 122, 130, 132, 148, 191, 193, 200, 203, 205, 206, 214, 224, 234–43, 250

KYTHERA (**kith**-e-ra): island south of the Peloponnesos, sometimes said to be the birthplace of Aphrodite, 94, 108

LABYRINTH (**lab**-e-rinth): "house of the double-ax," Cretan maze, home of the Minotaur, 164

LADON (**lā**-don): serpent that guarded the tree with the golden apples in the garden of the Hesperides, 21

LAKEDAIMON: the territory around Sparta, 39, 135

LAOMEDON (lā-**om**-e-don): early king of Troy, father of Priam, 104

LEDA (**lē**-da): wife of Tyndareus, mother of Helen, Clytemnestra, Castor, Polydeuces, 19, 158

LEMNOS: island in the northern Aegean, associated with Hephaestus, 90, 120

LESBOS: island in the Aegean, near Troy, 120

LETO (**lē**-tō): mother of Apollo and Artemis, 29, 100, 117–26, 138–41, 146–59, 162–67, 172–78, 180, 187, 199–203, 206, 209, 211, 213, 240

LIBYA: a fertile country in North Africa, 8, 9, 36, 144, 145, 157

LILAIA: a Phocian city north of Mt. Parnassos, 128

LYCIA (**lish**-i-a. Lykia): region in southwest Anatolia, 112, 113, 117, 125, 147, 163

LYDIA: a region in western Anatolia centered on Sardis, 159

LYKAON (li-**kā**-on): a mountain in Arcadia, 17, 20–22

MAIA (**mī**-a): "mid-wife," a daughter of Atlas, mother of Hermes, one of the
    Pleïades, 191–95, 199–203, 206–16, 239

MAKAR: the legendary colonizer of Lesbos, 120

MALEA: the southernmost cape of the Peloponnesos where ships are blown
    off course, 135

MARATHON: plain near Athens where Persians were defeated in 490 BC, 9, 191

MEDEA (me-**dē**-a): witch from Colchis, daughter of Aeëtes, wife of Jason, 183

MEDICI, LORENZO DE' (1449–1492): ruler of Florence, 2

MEDUSA (me-**dūs**-a. Medousa): "[wide]-ruling," one of the three Gorgons, 32

MEGARA (**meg**-a-ra): city between Corinth and Athens, 63

MELPOMENÊ: "singer," Muse of tragedy, 167

MENELAOS (men-e-**lā**-os): king of Sparta, son of Atreus, husband of Helen,
    brother of Agamemnon, 182, 187

MERCURY: Roman god of commerce, equated with Greek Hermes, 191, 236

METIS (**mē**-tis): "mind," swallowed by Zeus when pregnant with Athena, 19,
    35, 130, 241

MICHELANGELO, BUONAROTTI (bu-**ōn**-ar-**ō**-tē) (1475–1564): Italian sculptor
    and painter, 143

MILETOS: a cultural center in Ionia, 120, 125, 165, 184

MIMAS: a mountain on the coast of Ionia opposite Chios, or in Thessaly, 82,
    120, 150, 155

MINOANS: Bronze Age inhabitants of Crete, 164

MINOS (**mī**-nos): Cretan king of Knossos, son of Zeus and Europa, husband
    of Pasiphaë, judge in the underworld, 19, 29, 134, 163, 164, 182

MINOTAUR (**mīn**-o-tar): "bull of Minos," half-man, half-bull offspring of
    Pasiphaë and a bull, 147, 163, 164

MNEMOSYNÊ (nē-**mos**-i-nē): "memory," consort of Zeus, mother of the
    Muses, 118, 167, 207

MUSES: the inspirers of oral song, a personification of the oral tradition, 96,
    116, 118, 138, 171, 191, 217, 242

MYCENAEAN AGE: between c. 1600–1150 BC, 17, 32

MYRRHA: "myrrh tree," daughter of Kinyras, mother by him of Adonis, 110

MYSIA: territory surrounding the Troad, 178

MYSTAI (**mis**-tī): "those with closed eyes," initiates into the mysteries of
    Eleusis, 55

NAXOS: one of the Cycladic islands, 120, 224

NECTAR (nektar): "deathless," drink of the gods, 60, 104, 119, 123, 201

NELEUS (**nē**-lūs): son of Poseidon and Tyro, father of Nestor, founder of royal house of Pylos, 184

NEMESIS (**nem**-e-sis): goddess of retribution, 81, 185

NEREIDS (**nē**-re-idz): "daughters of Nereus," nymphs of the sea, 131, 223

NEREUS (**nē**-rūs): son of Pontos and Gaea, wise Old Man of the Sea, 22, 131

NESTOR: garrulous septuagenarian Greek at Troy, chieftain of Pylos, 200

NIOBÊ (**nī**-o-bē): daughter of Tantalos, wife of Amphion, whose sons and daughters were killed by Artemis and Apollo, 141, 146, 152

NYMPHS: "young women," spirits of nature, 22, 23, 41, 57, 78, 80, 101, 106, 107, 110, 149–53, 159, 164, 173–75, 181, 217–22, 228–33

NYSA (**nī**-sa): mythical land that received the infant Dionysus, 4, 5, 58, 222, 224, 228, 231, 232

OCEANIDS (ō-**sē**-a-nids): "daughters of Ocean," spirits of the sea, children of Oceanus and Tethys, 57, 72, 174–76

ODYSSEY: by Homer, 1–7, 32, 44, 48, 89, 115, 250

OEDIPUS (**ē**-di-pus, or **ed**-i-pus. Oidipous): "swellfoot," son of Laius and Jocasta, married his mother, killed his father, 5, 44, 144

OENEUS (**ē**-nūs): king of Calydon, father of Meleager and Deianira, 184, 187

OKALEA (ō-**kal**-e-a): a town in Boeotia, 128

OLYMPIA: sanctuary of Zeus in the western Peloponnesos, site of the Olympic games, 196, 200

OLYMPIANS: gods who lived on Moiunt Olympos, 11, 19, 23, 48, 58, 173, 197, 240

OLYMPIC GAMES: founded in 776 BC, 177

OLYMPOS: the highest mountain in Greece, between Thessaly and Macedonia, 17, 23, 27–31, 36, 51, 61, 62, 69, 72–75, 92, 98, 110, 115, 122, 125–27, 137, 147, 153, 154, 158, 167, 173, 175, 178–81, 187, 195, 203, 204, 207, 211, 218, 223–26, 230, 234, 236

OMPHALOS: "navel," egg-shaped stone marking Delphi as center of the earth, 54

ONCHESTOS: town in Boeotian with a shrine to Poseidon (Il. 2), 127, 128, 195, 199

ORESTES (or-**es**-tēz): son of Agamemnon and Clytemnestra, who killed his mother and her lover Aegisthus to avenge his father, 181

ORION (ō-**rī**-on): a hunter, lover of Dawn, turned into a constellation, 187

ORPHEUS (**or**-fūs): son of Apollo, musician, tried to bring back his wife Eurydikê from the dead, 2, 10–14, 57, 147, 167, 230, 231

ORPHISM: teaching allegedly from Orpheus about human destiny, 10

ORTYGIA (or-**tij**-ya): "quail island," equated in classical time with Delos, birthplace of Apollo and Artemis, 119, 142, 149, 167

OSIRIS (ō-**sī**-ris): Egyptian god of resurrection, husband of Isis, 224

OSSA: mountain in Thessaly bordering Macedon, piled on Olympos and Pelion Otos and his brother in order to reach heaven, 153, 154, 175, 187

OTOS (**ō**-tos): a giant, 175, 187

OTREUS (**o**-trūs): "rouser," a leader of the Phrygians against the Amazons, 101, 102

OURANOS (**ou**-ra-nos): "sky," consort of Gaia/Earth, castrated by his son Kronos, 11, 14, 23, 35, 114, 121, 148, 241

OVID (43 BC–AD 17): Roman poet, 9, 241

PALLAS (**pal**-as): an epithet for Athena, 36–41, 45- 48, 72, 196

PAN: "increaser," god of woodland, 7, 166, 173, 176, 177, 189–221, 241, 244

PANATHENAIC FESTIVAL (pan-ath-en-**ē**-ic): annual festival to Athena at Athens where the *Iliad* and the *Odyssey* were performed, 47

PANDORA (pan-**dor**-a): "gift of all," or "all-giver," the first woman, who released evils into the world, 240

PAPHOS (**pāf**-os): city in Cyprus, sacred to Aphrodite, 93, 94, 99, 216

PAPYRUS: Egyptian "the thing of the royal house," because its sale was a royal monopoly, origin of our word *paper,* 2, 8, 13, 14, 57, 223

PARIS: son of Priam and Hekabê, lover of Helen, 11, 37, 39, 79, 105, 140, 219

PARNASSOS, MOUNT (par-**nas**-os): behind Delphi, 128, 129, 131, 134, 138, 140, 152, 165, 213

PAROS: one of the Cycladic islands, 9, 75, 120

PARRHASIA (par-**ras**-i-a): district of Arcadia, 21

PARTHENON: "place of the Virgins," temple to Athena on the Acropolis in Athens, 50

PASIPHAË (pa-**sif**-a-ē): "all-shining," daughter of Helius, wife of Minos, mother of the Minotaur, 163, 164

PEDERASTY: "love for boys," 105

PEIRITHOÖS (pē-**rith**-o-os): son of Zeus by Ixion's wife, king of the Lapiths, friend of Theseus, 29

PELASGIANS: "peoples of the sea," an unknown people or peoples who lived in Greece before the Greeks came; loosely, the Greeks, 78, 161

PELEUS (**pē**-lūs): grandson of Zeus, son of Aiakos, husband of Thetis, father of Achilles, 19

PELIAS (**pel**-i-as): son of Poseidon and Tyro, father of Alkestis, killed by a trick of Medea, 183

PELION: coastal mountain on the Magnesian peninsula in southeastern Thessaly near Iolkos, abode of the Centaurs, 120, 127, 153, 175, 187

PELOPS (**pē**-lops): son of Tantalus, father of Atreus and Thyestes, grandfather of Agamemnon and Menelaos, eponymous hero of the Peloponessus, 128

PENEIOS (pe-**nē**-os): a river in Thessaly the rises in the Pindos and enters the Aegean between Ossa and Olympos, 78, 139, 153–15

PERSEUS (**per**-sūs): "destroyer(?)," son of Zeus and Danaë, beheaded Medusa, married Andromeda, founded Mycenae, 29, 32, 35

PHAËTHON (**fā**-e-thon): "shining," son of Helius, struck down from his father's chariot, 241

PHALLUS: the penis as a religious emblem, 190, 231

PHANES (**fan**-ēz): "he who appears," Orphic primordial being, 11, 12

PHERAI: a city in Thessaly, 186, 187

PHIDIAS (c. 480–430 BC): sculptor who worked on the Parthenon, 50, 235

PHILIP II (382–336 BC): father of Alexander the Great, 56

PHOENICIA: the coast of the Eastern Mediterranean, modern Lebanon, 29, 224

PHOENICIANS: "red-men," from the dye that stained their hands, a Semitic seafaring people living on the coast of the northern Levant, 148

PHOINIX (**foi**-niks): eponym of the Phoenicians, 29

PHRYGIA (**frij**-a): region in Asia Minor, home of fertility religions, 23, 101, 141, 170, 181, 186

PHRYGIANS: inhabitants of Phrygia, 101, 102

PHTHIA (**thī**-a): region in southern Thessaly, home of Achilles, 153

PIERIA (pi-**er**-i-a): "fat," region in Thessaly near Mount Olympus, home of the Muses, where the gods land when coming down from Olympos, 127, 147, 167, 195, 199

PINDAR (c. 522–423 BC): Greek poet, 6, 142, 144, 146

PLATO (428–348 BC): Greek philosopher, 10, 12, 15, 31, 43, 48, 112, 114, 168, 251

PLOTINUS (plo-**tīn**-us) (AD 204–270): Greek Neoplatonic philosopher, 15

POLYPHEMOS (pol-i-**fēm**-os): "much famed," the Cyclops blinded by Odysseus, 32, 175

PRIAM (**prī**-am): king of Troy, son of Laomedon, husband of Hekabê, father of Hector and Paris, 98, 101, 104, 189

PROCLUS: Neoplatonic philosopher and poet (AD 412–485), 1–7, 15, 16, 48, 111–14, 167, 235, 246, 250

PROITOS (**prē**-tos): king of Tiryns, whose wife attempted to seduce Bellerophon, 185

PROKRIS (**pro**-kris): daughter of Erechtheus, king of Athens, 183

PROMETHEUS (prō-**mēth**-ūs): "forethinker," a Titan, maker and benefactor of humankind, 35, 240

PROPHECY, 35, 38, 44, 95, 117, 130, 138, 152, 156, 212

PSYCHÊ (p-**suk**-ā, plural *psychai,* p-**suk**-ī; **si**-kē): "breath, soul," the ghost that survives the death of the body, 12, 16

PTOLEMIES: Macedonian/Greek dynasty who ruled Egypt from 334–30 BC, 9, 156, 157, 162, 186

PTOLEMY II (**to**-le-mē) (285–246 BC): son of Alexander's general, founded the Mouseion in Alexandria, 8, 20, 24, 141, 146, 147, 156, 157

PYLOS (**pī**-los): Bronze Age settlement in the southwest Peloponnesos, kingdom of Nestor where important archaeological remains have been found, 134–36, 200, 204, 206

PYRRHA (**pir**-a): wife of Deukalion, daughter of Epimetheus, 82

PYTHIA (**pith**-e-a): the prophetess at Delphi, 131, 133, 134, 152, 156

PYTHO: name for Delphi, 125, 133, 134, 137, 141, 145, 186, 199, 238

PYTHON: "rotting," the snake that Apollo killed at Delphi, hence the priestess was called the Pythia, 117, 118, 132, 143, 152, 165

RED-FIGURE: a style in Greek pottery decoration, 11, 18, 46, 73, 77, 105, 123, 172, 210

RHEA (**rē**-a. Rheia): a Titaness, wife of Kronos, 11, 14, 19, 21, 22, 27, 31, 32, 60, 61, 73, 74, 97, 121, 238, 249, 250

RHODES (rōdz): Aegean island near southwestern tip of Asia Minor, 111, 148, 241

RHODOPÊ (rod-**ōp**-ē): mountain in Thrace, sacred to Dionysus, 72

SACRIFICE: "making separate," 55, 69, 83, 86, 87, 94, 114, 128, 130, 137, 164, 170, 187, 231

SAGA: another word for legend, 10

SALAMIS (**sal**-a-mis): island near the port of Athens, site of Persian naval defeat in 480 BC, 59, 108

SAMOS (**sā**-mos): "hill," island in the east Aegean, 120, 149, 184, 224

SAMOTHRACE: island in the north Aegean, 120

SAPPHO (sixth century BC): Greek poet, 94, 95

SARDIS: capital of Lydia, 159, 186

SATYRS (**sā**-ters): half-man, half-horse followers of Dionysos, 106

SCYTHIA (**sith**-i-a): territory north of the Black Sea, 181, 186

SELENÊ (se-**lēn**-ē): goddess of the moon, 187, 236, 241–25

SELINUS: powerful Greek city in southwest Sicily, 28

SEMELÊ (**sem**-e-lē): daughter of Kadmos and Harmonia, beloved by Zeus, mother to Dionysos, destroyed by lightning, 12, 29, 49, 126, 222–24

SEMITES: "descendants of Shem," a son of Noah, peoples of the Near East including Assyrians, Babylonians, Hebrews, Phoenicians, 110, 148

SICILY, 19, 28, 80, 154, 175

SIKANIA: a name for Sicily or part of Sicily, 175

SIMOEIS (**sim**-o-ēs): a river in the Troad, 39

SINTIANS: early inhabitants of the island of Lemnos who took care of Hephaistos when he was thrown from heaven, 90

SIRENS: creatures who through the beauty of their song lured sailors to their deaths, 10

SKYROS (**skir**-os): island west of Euboea, 120

SOCRATES (469–399 BC): Athenian philosopher, executed by the state for impiety and corrupting the young, 49

SOUL, 10, 12, 15, 16, 31, 48, 51, 110, 112, 114, 167, 168, 189, 214, 235, 237, 245–21

SOUNION: the southernmost cape in Attica, 149

SPARTA: city in the southern Peloponnesos, 40, 144, 170, 181, 182, 188

STOICISM: Greek philosophy that taught submission to natural law, 14, 19, 112, 115

STYX (stiks): "hate," a river in the underworld, 22, 67, 72, 121, 211, 236

SYRACUSE: powerful Greek city in eastern Sicily, 118

SYRIA: the territory surrounding the upper Euphrates, 110

SYRINX (**sir**-inks): "reed," nymph who rejected pan, turned into reeds from which Pan made his pipes, 217

TARTAROS: place for punishment in the underworld, 19, 87, 130, 132, 201, 205, 217

TAURIANS: inhabitants of the modern Crimea, 181, 182

TAYGETOS (tā-**ig**-e-tos): "big," a mountain range between Messenia and Lakedaimon, 182

TEGEA (**tej**-e-a): a city in Arcadia, 150, 184

TELEPHOS: a son of Herakles, 150

TELESTERION (tel-es-**ter**-i-on): hall of initiation at Eleusis, 55, 57, 59

TEMPÊ, VALLEY OF: in Thessaly, 153

TETHYS (**tē**-this): a Titan, mother of the Oceanids, 28, 148, 175

TEUCER (**tū**-ser): first king of Troy, 185

THEBÊ (**thē**-bē): wife of Zethus, who gave her name to Thebes, 151, 152

THEBES (thēbz): principal city in Boeotia, unsuccessfully attacked by seven heroes, 29, 41–44, 126, 127, 141, 151, 152, 195, 224

THEMIS (**them**-is): "what is laid down," "law," a Titan, early consort of Zeus, 20, 100, 121–13, 126, 236

THEODOSIUS (the-o-**dōs**-i-us) (AD 347–395): Roman emperor, 55

THEOGONY (thē-**og**-o-nē): story of the "birth of the gods," title of a poem by Hesiod, 14

THERA (**thē**-ra): southernmost of the Cyclades (modern Santorini), 8, 142, 144, 148

THESEUS (thē-sūs): son of Poseidon and Aethra, killer of the Minotaur, 9, 147, 149, 163, 164

THESSALY: region in Greece south of Mount Olympus, 13, 75–82, 127, 142, 145, 152–14, 161, 170, 175, 183, 186

THETIS (the-tis): a daughter of Nereus, wife of Peleus, mother of Achilles, 19, 131, 140, 141

THRACE: region northeast of Greece, 10, 47, 90, 93, 148, 150, 154, 178, 235

THUCYDIDES (thu-sid-i-dēz) (c. 460–395 BC): Athenian historian, 6, 7, 175

THYRSUS: phallic staff carried by followers of Dionysos, 230

TIMAEUS: dialogue of Plato, 48, 112

TIRYNS (tir-inz): Bronze Age city in Argive plain, associated with Herakles (Il. 2), 180

TITANS (tī-tans): offspring of Ouranos and Gaea, the generation of the gods before the Olympians, 12, 19, 20, 32, 49, 87, 117, 121, 146, 148, 150, 156, 166, 175, 229, 241, 243, 245

TITHONUS (ti-thōn-os): brother of Priam, beloved of Eos (Dawn): given eternal life without eternal youth, turned into a grasshopper, 104, 215

TIU (tū): Norse god of war, 17

TRACHIS (trā-kis): "rough," a city in Thessaly near Thermopylae, scene of Herakles' death, 181

TRAGEDY: "goat-song," a dramatization of legend in festivals at Athens, 167, 223

TRITOGENEIA (trit-o-gen-ē-a): an obscure epithet of Athena, 36, 47, 48

TRITON (trī-ton): son of Poseidon and Amphitritê, a merman, 36, 144

TROAD: the area around Troy, at the entrance to the Dardanelles, 96

TROIZEN (trē-zen), 149

TROJAN WAR, 94, 95

TROS (trōs): eponymous founder of the Trojan race, father of Ilos and Ganymede, 98, 104, 105

TROY: in northwestern Asia Minor, 3, 20, 27, 38, 98–104, 107, 170, 178, 185

TYPHOEUS (tī-fō-ūs): or Typhon, monstrous offspring of Gaea overcome by Zeus, 19, 30, 87, 130, 133, 154

VENUS: Roman equivalent to Greek Aphrodite, 76, 236

VERGIL (70–19 BC): Roman poet, 3, 107

WHITE-GROUND STYLE, in Greek art, 111

WINCKELMANN, JOHANN (1717–1768): German art historian, 143

WORKS AND DAYS: poem by Hesiod, eighth century BC, 1, 6, 192

WRITING, syllabic, 17, 32, 89

ZAGREUS (**zag**-rūs): Orphic name for Dionysos, 12, 229

ZAKYNTHOS: an island off the southwest coast of Greece, 135

ZEPHYR: "west wind," 144

ZETHOS (**zē**-thos): son of Zeus and Antiopê, twin brother of Amphion, co-founder of Thebes, 151

ZODIAC, 179

Founded in 1893,
UNIVERSITY OF CALIFORNIA PRESS
publishes bold, progressive books and journals
on topics in the arts, humanities, social sciences,
and natural sciences—with a focus on social
justice issues—that inspire thought and action
among readers worldwide.

The UC PRESS FOUNDATION
raises funds to uphold the press's vital role
as an independent, nonprofit publisher, and
receives philanthropic support from a wide
range of individuals and institutions—and from
committed readers like you. To learn more, visit
ucpress.edu/supportus.